# Contents

# Foreword for language teachers

The *Easy Learning German Grammar & Practice* is designed to be used with both young and adult learners, as a group revision and practice book to complement your course book during classes, or as a recommended text for self-study and homework/coursework.

The text specifically targets learners from *ab initio* to intermediate or GCSE level, and therefore its structural content and vocabulary have been matched to the relevant specifications up to and including Higher GCSE.

The approach aims to develop knowledge and understanding of grammar and to improve the ability of learners to apply it by:

- defining parts of speech at the start of each major section, with examples in English to clarify concepts
- minimizing the use of grammar terminology and providing clear explanations of terms both within the text and in the **Glossary**
- illustrating all points with examples (and their translations) based on topics and contexts which are relevant to beginner and intermediate course content
- providing exercises which allow learners to practice grammar points

The text helps you develop positive attitudes to grammar learning in your classes by:

- giving clear, easy-to-follow explanations
- highlighting useful **Tips** to deal with common difficulties
- summarizing **Key points** at the end of sections to consolidate learning
- illustrating **Key points** with practice examples

# Introduction for students

Whether you are starting to learn German for the very first time, brushing up on topics you have studied in class, or revising for your GCSE exams, the *Easy Learning German Grammar & Practice* is here to help. This easy-to-use revision and practice guide takes you through all the basics you will need to speak and understand modern, everyday German.

Newcomers can sometimes struggle with the technical terms they come across when they start to explore the grammar of a new language. The *Easy Learning German Grammar & Practice* explains how to get to grips with all the parts of speech you will need to know, using simple language and cutting out jargon.

The text is divided into sections, each dealing with a particular area of grammar. Each section can be studied individually, as numerous cross-references in the text point you to relevant points in other sections of the book for further information.

Every major section begins with an explanation of the area of grammar covered on the following pages. For quick reference, these definitions are also collected together on pages x–xiv in a glossary of essential grammar terms.

---

### What is a verb?

A **verb** is a 'doing' word which describes what someone or something does, what someone or something is, or what happens to them, for example, *be*, *sing*, *live*.

---

Each grammar point in the text is followed by simple examples of real German, complete with English translations, helping you understand the rules. Underlining has been used in examples throughout the text to highlight the grammatical point being explained.

➤ If you are talking about a part of your body, you usually use a word like *my* or *his* in English, but in German you usually use the definite article.

| | |
|---|---|
| **Er hat sich <u>das</u> Bein gebrochen.** | He's broken his leg. |
| **Sie hat sich <u>die</u> Hände schon gewaschen.** | She's already washed her hands. |

In German, as with any foreign language, there are certain pitfalls which have to be avoided. **Tips** and **Information** notes throughout the text are useful reminders of the things that often trip learners up.

---

*Tip*
Use **Sie** in more formal situations for both singular and plural *you*.

---

**Key points** sum up all the important facts about a particular area of grammar, to save you time when you are revising and help you focus on the main grammatical points.

After each Key point you can find a number of exercises to help you practise all the important grammatical points. You can find the answers to each exercise on pages 266-278.

If you think you would like to continue with your German studies to a higher level, check out the **Grammar Extra** sections. These are intended for advanced students who are interested in knowing a little more about the structures they will come across beyond GCSE.

---

*Grammar Extra!*
Some German adjectives are used as feminine nouns. They have feminine adjective endings which change according to the article which comes before them.

| | |
|---|---|
| **eine Deutsche** | a German woman |
| **die Abgeordnete** | the woman MP |

➪ *For more information on **Adjectives used as nouns** and for **Feminine adjective endings**, see pages 50 and 42*

---

Finally, the supplement at the end of the book contains **Verb Tables**, where 11 important German verbs are conjugated in full. Examples show you how to use these verbs in your own work.

We hope that you will enjoy using the *Easy Learning German Grammar & Practice* and find it useful in the course of your studies.

# Glossary of Grammar Terms

**ABSTRACT NOUN** a word used to refer to a quality, idea, feeling or experience, rather than a physical object, for example, *size, reason, happiness*.

**ACCUSATIVE CASE** the form of nouns, adjectives, pronouns and articles used in German to show the direct object of a verb and after certain prepositions. Compare with **direct object**.

**ACTIVE** in an active sentence, the subject of the verb is the person or thing that carries out the action described by the verb.

**ADJECTIVE** a 'describing' word that tells you more about a person or thing, such as their appearance, colour, size or other qualities, for example, *pretty, blue, big*.

**ADVERB** a word usually used with verbs, adjectives or other adverbs that gives more information about when, where, how or in what circumstances something happens, for example, *quickly, happily, now*.

**AGREE (to)** to change word endings according to whether you are referring to masculine, feminine, neuter, singular or plural people and things.

**AGREEMENT** see **agree (to)**.

**APOSTROPHE S** an ending ('s) added to a noun to show who or what someone or something belongs to, for example, *Danielle's dog, the doctor's husband, the book's cover*.

**ARTICLE** a word like *the, a* and *an*, which is used in front of a noun. Compare with **definite article** and **indefinite article**.

**AUXILIARY VERB** a verb such as *be, have* and *do* when used with a main verb to form some tenses and questions.

**BASE FORM** the form of the verb without any endings added to it, for example, *walk, have, be, go*. Compare with **infinitive**.

**CASE** the grammatical function of a noun, adjective, pronoun or article in a sentence.

**CLAUSE** a group of words containing a verb.

**COMPARATIVE** an adjective or adverb with *-er* on the end of it or *more* or *less* in front of it that is used to compare people, things or actions, for example, *slower, less important, more carefully*.

**COMPOUND NOUN** a word for a living being, thing or idea, which is made up of two or more words, for example, *tin-opener, railway station*.

**CONDITIONAL** a verb form used to talk about things that would happen or would be true under certain conditions, for example, *I would help you if I could*. It is also used to say what you would like or need, for example, *Could you give me the bill?*

**CONJUGATE (to)** to give a verb different endings according to whether you are referring to *I, you, they* and so on, and according to whether you are referring to past, present or future, for example, *I have, she had, they will have*.

**CONJUGATION** a group of verbs which have the same endings or change according to the same pattern.

**CONJUNCTION** a word such as *and, because* or *but* that links two words or phrases of a similar type or two parts of a sentence, for example, *Diane and I have been friends for years; I left because I was bored*. Compare with **coordinating conjunction** and **subordinating conjunction**.

**COORDINATING CONJUNCTION** a word such as *and, but* or *however* that links two words, phrases or clauses.

**CONSONANT** a letter of the alphabet which is not a vowel, for example, *b*, *f*, *m*, *s*, *v*. Compare with **vowel**.

**CONSTRUCTION** an arrangement of words together in a phrase or sentence.

**DATIVE CASE** the form of nouns, adjectives, pronouns and articles used in German to show the indirect object of a verb and after certain verbs and prepositions.

**DECLENSION** German nouns change according to their gender, case and number. This is called declension.

**DEFINITE ARTICLE** the word *the*. Compare with **indefinite article**.

**DEMONSTRATIVE ADJECTIVE** one of the words *this*, *that*, *these* and *those* used with a noun to point out a particular person or thing, for example, *this* woman, *that* dog.

**DEMONSTRATIVE PRONOUN** one of the words *this*, *that*, *these* and *those* used instead of a noun to point out people or things, for example, *That* looks fun.

**DIRECT OBJECT** a noun referring to the person or thing affected by the action described by a verb, for example, *She wrote her name*; *I shut the window*. Compare with **indirect object**.

**DIRECT OBJECT PRONOUN** a word such as *me*, *him*, *us* and *them* which is used instead of a noun to stand in for the person or thing directly affected by the action described by the verb. Compare with **indirect object pronoun**.

**ENDING** a form added to a verb stem, for example, **geh —> geht**, and to adjectives, nouns and pronouns depending on whether they refer to masculine, feminine, neuter, singular or plural things or persons.

**FEMININE** one of three classifications for the gender of German nouns which determines the form of articles, pronouns and adjectives used with the noun and to refer to it. The other two classifications are **masculine** and **neuter**.

**FUTURE** a verb tense used to talk about something that will happen or will be true.

**GENDER** whether a noun, article, pronoun or adjective is feminine, masculine or neuter.

**GENITIVE CASE** the form of nouns, adjectives, pronouns and articles used in German to show that something belongs to someone and after certain prepositions and verbs.

**IMPERATIVE** the form of a verb used when giving orders and instructions, for example, *Shut the door!; Sit down!; Don't go!*

**IMPERFECT** one of the verb tenses used to talk about the past, especially in descriptions, and to say what was happening, for example, *It was sunny at the weekend* or what used to happen, for example, *I used to walk to school*. Compare with **perfect**.

**IMPERSONAL VERB** one which does not refer to a real person or thing and where the subject is represented by *it*, for example, *It's going to rain; It's 10 o'clock*.

**INDEFINITE ADJECTIVE** one of a small group of adjectives used to talk about people or things in a general way, without saying exactly who or what they are, for example, *several, all, every*.

**INDEFINITE ARTICLE** the words *a* and *an*. Compare with **definite article**.

**INDEFINITE PRONOUN** a small group of pronouns such as *everything, nobody* and *something*, which are used to refer to people or things in a general way, without saying exactly who or what they are.

**INDIRECT OBJECT** a noun or pronoun typically used in English with verbs that take two objects. For example, in *I gave the carrot to the rabbit, the rabbit* is the indirect object and *carrot* is the direct object. With some German verbs, what is the direct object in English is treated as an indirect object in, for example, **Ich helfe ihr** —> *I'm helping her.* Compare with **direct object**.

**INDIRECT OBJECT PRONOUN** when a verb has two objects (a direct one and an indirect one), the indirect object pronoun is used instead of a noun to show the person or the thing the action is intended to benefit or harm, for example, *me* in *He gave me a book* and *Can you get me a towel?* Compare with **direct object pronoun**.

**INDIRECT SPEECH** the words you use *to* report what someone has said when you aren't using their actual words, for example, *He said that he was going out.*

**INFINITIVE** the form of the verb with *to* in front of it and without any endings added, for example, *to walk, to have, to be, to go.* Compare with **base form**.

**INTERROGATIVE ADJECTIVE** a question word used with a noun to ask *who?, what?* or *which?,* for example, *What instruments do you play?; Which shoes do you like?*

**INTERROGATIVE PRONOUN** one of the words *who, whose, whom, what* and *which* when they are used instead of a noun to ask questions, for example, *What's happening?; Who's coming?*

**MASCULINE** one of three classifications for the gender of German nouns which determines the form of articles, pronouns and adjectives used with the noun and to refer to it. The other two classifications are **feminine** and **neuter**.

**MIXED VERB** a German verb whose stem changes its vowel to form the imperfect tense and the past participle, like strong verbs. Its past participle is formed by adding -*t* to the verb stem, like weak verbs. Compare with **strong verb** and **weak verb**.

**MODAL VERBS** are used to modify or change other verbs to show such things as *ability, permission* or *necessity*. For example, *he can swim, may I come?* and *he ought to go.*

**NEGATIVE** a question or statement which contains a word such as *not, never* or *nothing,* and is used to say that something is not happening or is not true, for example, *I never eat meat; Don't you love me?*

**NEUTER** one of three classifications for the gender of German nouns which determines the form of articles, pronouns and adjectives used with the noun and to refer to it. The other two classifications are **masculine** and **feminine**.

**NOMINATIVE CASE** the basic form of nouns, pronouns, adjectives and articles used in German and the one you find in the dictionary. It is used for the subject of the sentence. Compare with **subject**.

**NOUN** a 'naming' word for a living being, thing or idea, for example, *woman, desk, happiness, Andrew.*

**OBJECT** a noun or pronoun which refers to a person or thing that is affected by the action described by the verb. Compare with **direct object**, **indirect object** and **subject**.

**OBJECT PRONOUN** one of the set of pronouns including *me, him* and *them,* which are used instead of the noun as the object of a verb or preposition. Compare with **subject pronoun**.

**ORDINAL NUMBER** a number used to indicate where something comes in an order or sequence, for example, *first, fifth, sixteenth.*

**PART OF SPEECH** one of the categories to which all words are assigned and which describe their forms and how they are used in sentences, for example, *noun, verb, adjective, preposition, pronoun.*

**PASSIVE** a form of the verb that is used when the subject of the verb is the person or thing that is affected by the action, for example, *we were told*.

**PAST PARTICIPLE** a verb form, for example, *watched, swum*, which is used with an auxiliary verb to form perfect and pluperfect tenses and passives. Some past participles are also used as adjectives, for example, *a broken watch*.

**PERFECT** one of the verb tenses used to talk about the past, especially about actions that took place and were completed in the past. Compare with **imperfect**.

**PERSONAL PRONOUN** one of the group of words including *I, you* and *they* which are used to refer to yourself, the people you are talking to, or the people or things you are talking about.

**PLUPERFECT** one of the verb tenses used to describe something that <u>had</u> happened or had been true at a point in the past, for example, *I <u>had forgotten</u> to finish my homework*.

**PLURAL** the form of a word which is used to refer to more than one person or thing. Compare with **singular**.

**POSSESSIVE ADJECTIVE** one of the words *my, your, his, her, its, our* or *their*, used with a noun to show that one person or thing belongs to another.

**POSSESSIVE PRONOUN** one of the words *mine, yours, hers, his, ours* or *theirs*, used instead of a noun to show that one person or thing belongs to another.

**PREPOSITION** a word such as *at, for, with, into* or *from*, which is usually followed by a noun, pronoun or, in English, a word ending in *-ing*. Prepositions show how people and things relate to the rest of the sentence, for example, *She's <u>at</u> home; a tool <u>for</u> cutting grass; It's <u>from</u> David*.

**PRESENT** a verb form used to talk about what is true at the moment, what happens regularly, and what is happening now, for example, *I'm a student; I <u>travel</u> to college by train; I'm <u>studying</u> languages*.

**PRESENT PARTICIPLE** a verb form ending in *-ing* which is used in English to form verb tenses, and which may be used as an adjective or a noun, for example, *What are you <u>doing</u>?; the <u>setting</u> sun; <u>Swimming</u> is easy!*

**PRONOUN** a word which you use instead of a noun, when you do not need or want to name someone or something directly, for example, *it, you, none*.

**PROPER NOUN** the name of a person, place, organization or thing. Proper nouns are always written with a capital letter, for example, *Kevin, Glasgow, Europe, London Eye*.

**QUESTION WORD** a word such as *why, where, who, which* or *how* which is used to ask a question.

**REFLEXIVE PRONOUN** a word ending in *-self* or *-selves*, such as *myself* or *themselves*, which refers back to the subject, for example, *He hurt <u>himself</u>; Take care of <u>yourself</u>*.

**REFLEXIVE VERB** a verb where the subject and object are the same, and where the action 'reflects back' on the subject. A reflexive verb is used with a reflexive pronoun such as *myself, yourself, herself*, for example, *I washed myself; He shaved himself*.

**RELATIVE CLAUSE** part of the sentence in which the relative pronoun appears.

**RELATIVE PRONOUN** a word such as *that, who* or *which*, when it is used to link two parts of a sentence together.

**SENTENCE** a group of words which usually has a verb and a subject. In writing, a sentence has a capital letter at the beginning and a full stop, question mark or exclamation mark at the end.

**SINGULAR** the form of a word which is used to refer to one person or thing. Compare with **plural**.

**STEM** the main part of a verb to which endings are added.

**STRONG VERB** a German verb whose stem changes its vowel to form the imperfect tense and the past participle. Its past participle is not formed by adding -t to the verb stem. Also known as irregular verbs. Compare with **weak verb**.

**SUBJECT** the noun or pronoun used to refer to the person which does the action described by the verb, for example, *My cat* doesn't drink milk. Compare with **object**.

**SUBJECT PRONOUN** a word such as *I*, *he*, *she* and *they* which carries out the action described by the verb. Pronouns stand in for nouns when it is clear who is being talked about, for example, *My brother isn't here at the moment. He'll be back in an hour*. Compare with **object pronoun**.

**SUBJUNCTIVE** a verb form used in certain circumstances to express some sort of feeling, or to show doubt about whether something will happen or whether something is true. It is only used occasionally in modern English, for example, *If I were you, I wouldn't bother.; So be it*.

**SUBORDINATE CLAUSE** a clause which begins with a subordinating conjunction such as *because* or *while* and which must be used with a main clause. In German,

the verb always goes to the end of the subordinate clause.

**SUBORDINATING CONJUNCTION** a word such as *when*, *because* or *while* that links the subordinate clause and the main clause in a sentence. Compare with **subordinate clause**.

**SUPERLATIVE** an adjective or adverb with -*est* on the end of it or *most* or *least* in front of it that is used to compare people, things or actions, for example, *thinnest, most quickly, least interesting*.

**SYLLABLE** consonant+vowel units that make up the sounds of a word, for example, ca-the-dral (3 syllables), im-po-ssi-ble (4 syllables).

**TENSE** the form of a verb which shows whether you are referring to the past, present or future.

**VERB** a 'doing' word which describes what someone or something does, what someone or something is, or what happens to them, for example, *be, sing, live*.

**VOWEL** one of the letters *a, e, i, o* or *u*. Compare with **consonant**.

**WEAK VERB** a German verb whose stem does not change its vowel to form the imperfect tense and the past participle. Its past participle is formed by adding –*t* to the verb stem. Also known as regular verbs. Compare with **strong verbs**.

# grammar &
# exercises

# Nouns

---

**What is a noun?**
A **noun** is a 'naming' word for a living being, thing or idea, for example, *woman*, *happiness*, *Andrew*. German nouns change, according to their gender, case and number. This is called declension.

---

## Using nouns

➤ In German, all nouns are either <u>masculine</u>, <u>feminine</u> or <u>neuter</u>. This is called their <u>gender</u>. In English, we call all things – for example, *table, car, book, apple* – 'it', but in German, even words for things have a gender. It is important to know that the gender of German nouns rarely relates to the sex of the person or thing it refers to. For example, in German, the word for 'man' is masculine, but the word for 'girl' is neuter and the word for 'person' is feminine.

| | |
|---|---|
| **<u>der</u> Mann** | man |
| **<u>das</u> Mädchen** | girl |
| **<u>die</u> Person** | person |

---

*Tip*
German nouns are <u>always</u> written with a capital letter.

---

➤ Whenever you are using a noun, you need to know whether it is masculine, feminine or neuter as this affects the form of other words used with it, such as:

- adjectives that describe it

- articles (such as **der** or **ein**) that go before it

- pronouns (such as **er** or **sie**) that replace it

  ⇨ *For more information on **Adjectives**, **Articles** or **Pronouns**, see pages 51, 28 and 89.*

➤ You can find information about gender by looking the word up in a dictionary – in the *Easy Learning German Dictionary*, for example, you will find the <u>definite article</u> (the word for *the*) in front of the word. When you come across a new noun, always learn the word for *the* that goes with it to help you remember its gender.

- **der** before a noun tells you it is <u>masculine</u>

- **die** before a noun tells you it is <u>feminine</u>

- **das** before a noun tells you it is <u>neuter</u>

  ⇨ *For more information on the **Definite article**, see page 28.*

➤ We refer to something as singular when we are talking about just one, and as plural when we are talking about more than one. The singular is the form of the noun you will usually find when you look a noun up in the dictionary. As in English, nouns in German change their form in the plural.

**die Katze** cat → **die Katzen** cats

➤ Adjectives, articles and pronouns are also affected by whether a noun is singular or plural.

> *Tip*
> Remember that you have to use the right word for *the*, *a* and so on according to the gender and case of the German noun.

# Gender

➤ In German a noun can be masculine, feminine or neuter. Gender is quite unpredictable – the best thing is simply to learn each noun with its definite article, that is the word for *the* (**der**, **die** or **das**) which goes with it:

| | |
|---|---|
| **der** Teppich | carpet |
| **die** Zeit | time |
| **das** Bild | picture |

However, there are some clues which can help you work out or remember the gender of a noun, as explained below.

## Masculine nouns

➤ Nouns referring to male people and animals are <u>masculine</u>.

| | |
|---|---|
| **der** Mann | man |
| **der** Löwe | (male) lion |

➤ Seasons, months, days of the week, and points of the compass are <u>masculine</u>.

| | |
|---|---|
| **der** Sommer | summer |
| **der** August | August |
| **der** Freitag | Friday |
| **der** Norden | north |

➤ Most nouns referring to things that perform an action are also <u>masculine</u>.

| | |
|---|---|
| **der** Wecker | alarm clock |
| **der** Computer | computer |

---

*Grammar Extra!*
German nouns taken from other languages and ending in **-ant**, **-ast**, **-ismus**, and **-or** are <u>masculine</u>:

| | |
|---|---|
| **der** Trabant | satellite |
| **der** Ballast | ballast |
| **der** Kapitalismus | capitalism |
| **der** Tresor | safe |

---

➤ Nouns with the following endings are <u>masculine</u>.

| Masculine Ending | Example | Meaning |
|---|---|---|
| -ich | <u>der</u> Tepp<u>ich</u> | carpet |
| -ig | <u>der</u> Ess<u>ig</u> | vinegar |
| -ling | <u>der</u> Früh<u>ling</u> | spring |

**KEY POINTS**
✔ Nouns referring to male people and animals are masculine.
✔ Seasons, months, days of the week, weather and points of the compass are masculine.

## Feminine nouns

➤ Most nouns ending in **-e** are <u>feminine</u>.

| | |
|---|---|
| <u>die</u> **Falte** | crease, wrinkle |
| <u>die</u> **Brücke** | bridge |

🄘 Note that male people or animals ending in **-e** are masculine and nouns beginning with **Ge-** and ending in **-e** are normally neuter.

| | |
|---|---|
| <u>der</u> **Löwe** | the lion |
| <u>das</u> **Getreide** | crop |

➤ Nouns with the following endings are <u>feminine</u>.

| Feminine Ending | Example | Meaning |
|---|---|---|
| **-heit** | <u>die</u> **Schönheit** | beauty |
| **-keit** | <u>die</u> **Sehenswürdigkeit** | sight |
| **-schaft** | <u>die</u> **Gewerkschaft** | trade union |
| **-ung** | <u>die</u> **Zeitung** | newspaper |
| **-ei** | <u>die</u> **Bäckerei** | bakery |

*Grammar Extra!*
German nouns, some taken from other languages and ending in **-anz**, **-enz**, **-ie**, **-ik**, **-ion**, **-tät**, **-ur** are <u>feminine</u>, with some exceptions.

| | | | | |
|---|---|---|---|---|
| **die Distanz** | distance | BUT: | <u>der</u> **Kranz** | wreath |
| **die Konkurrenz** | competition | | | |
| **die Theorie** | theory | BUT: | <u>das</u> **Knie** | knee |
| **die Panik** | panic | BUT: | <u>der</u> **Pazifik** | Pacific |
| **die Union** | union | BUT: | <u>der</u> **Spion** | spy |
| **die Elektrizität** | electricity | | | |
| **die Temperatur** | temperature | BUT: | <u>das</u> **Abitur** | A levels |

➤ Numbers used in counting, for example *one*, *three*, *fifty* are <u>feminine</u>.
   **Er hat <u>eine</u> Drei gekriegt.**    He got a three.

➤ In German, there are sometimes very different words for male and female, just as in English.

| | |
|---|---|
| <u>der</u> **Mann** | man |
| <u>die</u> **Frau** | woman |
| | |
| <u>der</u> **Vater** | father |
| <u>die</u> **Mutter** | mother |
| | |
| <u>der</u> **Bulle** | bull |
| <u>die</u> **Kuh** | cow |

➤ Many masculine German nouns can be made feminine by adding **-in** in the singular and **-innen** in the plural.

| | |
|---|---|
| **der Lehrer** | (male) teacher |
| **die Lehrerin** | (female) teacher |
| **Lehrer und Lehrerinnen** | (male and female) teachers |
| | |
| **der Leser** | (male) reader |
| **die Leserin** | (female) reader |
| **unsere Leser und Leserinnen** | our readers (male and female) |

---

*Grammar Extra!*

Some German adjectives are used as feminine nouns. They have feminine adjective endings which change according to the article which comes before them.

| | |
|---|---|
| **eine Deutsche** | a German woman |
| **die Abgeordnete** | the woman MP |

⇨ *For more information on **Adjectives used as nouns** and for **Feminine adjective endings**, see pages 63 and 53*

---

**KEY POINTS**

✔ Most nouns ending in **-e** are feminine.
✔ Many feminine nouns end in: **-heit**, **-keit**, **-schaft**, **-ung**, **-ei**.
✔ Masculine German words referring to people can be made feminine by adding **-in** in the singular and **-innen** in the plural.
✔ Numbers used in counting are feminine.

## Neuter nouns

➤ Most nouns beginning with **Ge-** are <u>neuter</u>.

| | |
|---|---|
| <u>das</u> **Geschirr** | crockery, dishes |
| <u>das</u> **Geschöpf** | creature |
| <u>das</u> **Getreide** | crop |

➤ Nouns ending in **-lein** or **-chen** are also neuter. These are called the <u>diminutive form</u> and refer to small persons or objects.

| Endings to form the diminutive | Example | Meaning |
|---|---|---|
| -lein | <u>das</u> **Kind<u>lein</u>** | little child |
| -chen | <u>das</u> **Häus<u>chen</u>** | little house |

ⓘ Note that if these words have one of the vowels **a**, **o** or **u**, an umlaut should be added above the vowel. The final **-e** should also be dropped before these endings.

**der Bach → Bäch → das Bächlein**     (small) stream
**die Katze → Kätz → das Kätzchen**     kitten

➤ Fractions are also <u>neuter</u>.
**ein Drittel davon**          a third of it

➤ Nouns which refer to young humans and animals are <u>neuter</u>.

| | |
|---|---|
| <u>das</u> **Baby** | baby |
| <u>das</u> **Kind** | child |
| <u>das</u> **Kalb** | calf |
| <u>das</u> **Lamm** | lamb |

ⓘ Note that the animals themselves can be any gender.

| | |
|---|---|
| <u>der</u> **Hund** | dog |
| <u>die</u> **Schlange** | snake |
| <u>das</u> **Vieh** | cattle |

➤ Infinitives (the 'to' form of verbs) used as nouns are <u>neuter</u>.

| | |
|---|---|
| <u>das</u> **Schwimmen** | swimming |
| <u>das</u> **Spielen** | playing |
| <u>das</u> **Radfahren** | cycling |

⇨ *For more information on* **Infinitives**, *see page* 181.

➤ Most nouns with the following endings are neuter.

| Neuter Ending | Example | Meaning |
|---|---|---|
| -nis | <u>das</u> **Ereig<u>nis</u>** | event |
| -tum | <u>das</u> **Eigen<u>tum</u>** | property |

*Grammar Extra!*

German nouns taken from other languages and ending in **-at**, **-ett**, **-fon**, **-ma**, **-ment**, **-um** are <u>neuter</u>.

| | | | | |
|---|---|---|---|---|
| **das** Reser**vat** | reservation | | | |
| **das** Tabl**ett** | tray | | | |
| **das** Tele**fon** | phone | | | |
| **das** The**ma** | subject, topic | | | |
| **das** Medika**ment** | drug | | | |
| **das** Ultimat**um** | ultimatum | BUT: | **der** Reich**tum** | wealth |
| **das** Studi**um** | studies | | | |

---

## KEY POINTS

✔ Most nouns beginning with **Ge-** are neuter.
✔ The diminutive form of nouns is neuter.
✔ Nouns referring to young humans and animals are neuter.
✔ Infinitives used as nouns are neuter.
✔ Nouns ending in **-nis** or **-tum** are neuter.

# Compound nouns

---
## What is a compound noun?
A **compound noun** is a noun made up of two or more words, for example, *tin-opener* and *railway station*.
---

➤ In German, these words nearly always take their gender from the <u>LAST</u> noun of the compound word.

| | |
|---|---|
| **die Armbanduhr** (**Armband** + **die Uhr**) | wristwatch |
| **der Tomatensalat** (**Tomaten** + **der Salat**) | tomato salad |
| **der Fußballspieler** (**Fußball** + **der Spieler**) | footballer |

---

*Grammar Extra!*
Some German nouns have more than one gender. A few nouns have two genders and sometimes one of them can only be used in certain regions.

| | | |
|---|---|---|
| **der/das Marzipan** | marzipan | (*der Marzipan is used mostly in Austria*) |
| **der/das Keks** | biscuit | (*das Keks is used mostly in Austria*) |
| **der/das Kaugummi** | chewing gum | |

Other nouns have two genders and the meaning of the word changes depending on which gender it has.

| | |
|---|---|
| **der Band** | volume, book |
| **das Band** | ribbon, band, tape; bond |
| | |
| **der See** | lake |
| **die See** | sea |
| | |
| **der Leiter** | leader, manager |
| **die Leiter** | ladder |

---

➤ In German, abbreviations have the same gender as the word they come from.

| | |
|---|---|
| **die BRD** | the Federal Republic of Germany (from **die Bundesrepublik Deutschland**) |
| **die DB** | the German Railways (from **die Deutsche Bahn**) |
| **das ZDF** | German TV channel (from **das Zweite Deutsche Fernsehen**) |

---
### KEY POINTS
✔ Compound nouns are nouns made up of two or more words and usually take their gender from the last part of the compound word.
✔ Some German nouns have more than one gender and this can affect their meaning.
✔ German abbreviations have the same gender as the words they come from.
---

# Test yourself

**1**  **Complete the phrase by adding the feminine form of the noun. Don't forget to include the article.**

**a** der Minister und ..................................

**b** ein König und ..................................

**c** ein Student und ..................................

**d** der Schüler und ..................................

**e** ein Deutscher und ..................................

**f** der Schauspieler und ..................................

**g** ein Angestellter und ..................................

**h** ein Arzt und ..................................

**i** ein Löwe und ..................................

**j** der Besitzer und ..................................

**2**  **Match the two columns.**

**a** der Sonnabend                        eine Jahreszeit

**b** das Mädchen                          ein größerer Ort

**c** die Stadt                                ein Gewicht

**d** der Frühling                         ein Wochentag

**e** das Pfund                         eine weibliche Person

**3**  **Add the correct definite article (*der*, *die* or *das*) to the following nouns.**

**a** ......................... Gesicht

**b** ......................... Krankheit

**c** ......................... Anarchie

**d** ......................... September

**e** ......................... Katze

**f** ......................... Kätzchen

**g** ......................... Italiener

**h** ......................... Finsternis

**i** ......................... Zeitung

**j** ......................... Hase

# Test yourself

**4**   **Form a compound noun, including article, from the two nouns given.**

**a**  das Gummi + der Ball ......................................

**b**  die Hand + die Tasche ....................................

**c**  die Blumen + der Topf .....................................

**d**  die Wand + der Schrank ...................................

**e**  der Kaffee + die Tasse ....................................

**f**  die Karten + das Haus .....................................

**g**  das Papier + die Tüte .....................................

**h**  der Titel + das Bild .....................................

**i**  die Last + der Wagen .....................................

**j**  das Telefon + die Zelle .....................................

# The Cases

➤ In German, there are four grammatical cases – <u>nominative</u>, <u>accusative</u>, <u>genitive</u> and <u>dative</u>. The case you should use depends on the grammatical function of the noun in the sentence.

## The nominative case

➤ The <u>nominative case</u> is the basic form of the noun and is the one you find in the dictionary.

| Case | Masculine | Feminine | Neuter |
|---|---|---|---|
| Nominative | <u>der</u> Wagen | <u>die</u> Dose | <u>das</u> Lied |
| | <u>ein</u> Wagen | <u>eine</u> Dose | <u>ein</u> Lied |

⇨ *For more information on **Articles**, see page 28.*

➤ The <u>nominative case</u> is used for:

- the subject of the sentence, that is the person, animal or thing 'doing' the action
  **Das Mädchen singt.**    <u>The girl</u> is singing.
  **Die Katze schläft.**    <u>The cat</u> is sleeping.

- after the verbs **sein** (meaning *to be*) and **werden** (meaning *to be, to become*)
  **Er ist <u>ein</u> guter Lehrer.**    He is a good teacher.
  **Das wird <u>ein</u> Pullover.**    It's going to be a jumper.

## The accusative case

➤ The article for feminine and neuter nouns in the accusative case has the same form as in the nominative. **Der** for <u>masculine</u> nouns changes to **den** and **ein** to **einen**.

| Case | Masculine | Feminine | Neuter |
|---|---|---|---|
| Nominative | <u>der</u> Wagen | <u>die</u> Dose | <u>das</u> Lied |
| | <u>ein</u> Wagen | <u>eine</u> Dose | <u>ein</u> Lied |
| Accusative | <u>den</u> Wagen | <u>die</u> Dose | <u>das</u> Lied |
| | <u>einen</u> Wagen | <u>eine</u> Dose | <u>ein</u> Lied |

⇨ *For more information on **Articles**, see page 28.*

➤ The <u>accusative case</u> is used:

- to show the <u>direct object</u> of a verb. This is the person, animal or thing affected by the action of the verb.
  He gave me a book. → *'What did he give me?* → a book (=*direct object*)
  Can you get me a towel? → *What can you get me?* → a towel (=*direct object*)
  **Ich sehe <u>den Hund</u>.** → *What do I see?* → **<u>den Hund</u>** (=*direct object*)
  **Er hat <u>ein Lied</u> gesungen.** → *What did he sing?* → **<u>ein Lied</u>** (=*direct object*)

- after certain prepositions (words in English such as *at, for, with, into* or *from*) which are always used with the accusative.

  | | |
  |---|---|
  | **Es ist <u>für</u> seine Freundin.** | It's for his girlfriend. |
  | **Es ist schwierig <u>ohne</u> einen Wagen.** | It's difficult without a car. |
  | **<u>durch</u> das Rauchen wurde ich krank.** | Smoking made me ill. |

⇨ *For more information on **Prepositions followed by the accusative case**, see page 213.*

- after certain prepositions of place when movement is involved:

  | | |
  |---|---|
  | **an** | on, to, at |
  | **auf** | on, in, to, at |
  | **hinter** | behind |
  | **in** | in, into, to |
  | **neben** | next to, beside |
  | **über** | over, across, above |
  | **unter** | under, among |
  | **vor** | in front of, before |
  | **zwischen** | between |

  | | |
  |---|---|
  | **Stell dein Rad <u>neben mein</u> Auto.** | Put your bike next to my car. |
  | **Sie legten ein Brett <u>über das</u> Loch.** | They put a board over the hole. |

🛈 Note that when there is no movement involved after these prepositions, the <u>dative case</u> is used.

| | |
|---|---|
| **Sie geht <u>in die</u> Stadt.** (*accusative*) | She's going into town. |
| **Er war <u>in der</u> Stadt.** (*dative*) | He was in town. |

⇨ *For more information on **Prepositions followed by the accusative or the dative case**, see page 218.*

- in many expressions of time and place which do not have a preposition

  | | |
  |---|---|
  | **Das macht sie <u>jeden</u> Donnerstag.** | She does that every Thursday. |
  | **Die Schule ist <u>einen</u> Kilometer entfernt.** | The school is a kilometre away. |

- in some set expressions

  | | |
  |---|---|
  | **<u>Guten</u> Abend!** | Good evening! |
  | **<u>Vielen</u> Dank!** | Thank you very much! |

## The genitive case

➤ **Der** for masculine nouns and **das** for neuter nouns change to **des**. **Ein** changes to **eines**. The endings of <u>masculine</u> and <u>neuter singular</u> nouns also change in the genitive case.

➤ **-s** is added to masculine and neuter nouns ending in **-en, -el, -er**.

  <u>der</u> Wagen car → <u>des</u> Wagens
  <u>das</u> Rauchen smoking → <u>des</u> Rauchens
  <u>der</u> Esel donkey → <u>des</u> Esels
  <u>der</u> Computer computer → <u>des</u> Computers

| | | | |
|---|---|---|---|
| **Ich mag die Farbe des Wagens.** | | I like the colour of the car. | |
| **Die Größe des Computers ist nicht wichtig.** | | The size of the computer isn't important. | |

➤ **-es** is added to most masculine and neuter nouns of one syllable ending in a consonant.

**der** Freund friend → **des** Freundes
**der** Mann man → **des** Mannes
**der** Sitz seat → **des** Sitzes
**der** Arzt doctor → **des** Arztes
**der** Tisch table → **des** Tisches
**das** Schloss castle → **des** Schlosses

**Die Schwester des Arztes hilft manchmal in der Sprechstunde.** — The doctor's sister helps him in the surgery sometimes.

**Das Museum befindet sich in der Nähe des Schlosses.** — The museum is near the castle.

➤ **Die** changes to **der** and **eine** to **einer** in the genitive. The endings of feminine singular nouns in the genitive case are the same as in the nominative.

**die Ärztin** (female) doctor → **der Ärztin**

| Case | Masculine | Feminine | Neuter |
|---|---|---|---|
| **Nominative** | der Wagen | die Dose | das Lied |
| | ein Wagen | eine Dose | ein Lied |
| **Accusative** | den Wagen | die Dose | das Lied |
| | einen Wagen | eine Dose | ein Lied |
| **Genitive** | des Wagens | der Dose | des Lieds |
| | eines Wagens | einer Dose | eines Lieds |

⇨ *For more information on **Articles**, see page 28.*

➤ The genitive case is used:

● to show that something belongs to someone
**Das Auto der Frau war rot.** — The woman's car was red.
**Der Hund meiner Mutter ist ganz klein.** — My mother's dog is really small.

● after certain prepositions which always take the genitive
**Wegen des schlechten Wetters müssen wir nach Hause gehen.** — We'll have to go home because of the bad weather.
**Trotz ihrer Krankheit geht sie jeden Tag spazieren.** — She goes for a walk every day, despite her illness.

● in some expressions of time
**eines Tages** — one day

## The dative case

➤ **Der** changes to **dem** and **ein** to **einem** in the dative. Singular nouns in the dative have the same form as in the nominative.

| | |
|---|---|
| **dem** Auto | to the car |
| **dem** Mädchen | to the girl |

➤ **Die** changes to **der** and **eine** to **einer** in the dative. Singular nouns in the dative have the same form as in the nominative.

| Case | Masculine | Feminine | Neuter |
|---|---|---|---|
| **Nominative** | <u>der</u> Wagen | <u>die</u> Dose | <u>das</u> Lied |
| | <u>ein</u> Wagen | <u>eine</u> Dose | <u>ein</u> Lied |
| **Accusative** | <u>den</u> Wagen | <u>die</u> Dose | <u>das</u> Lied |
| | <u>einen</u> Wagen | <u>eine</u> Dose | <u>ein</u> Lied |
| **Genitive** | <u>des</u> Wagen<u>s</u> | <u>der</u> Dose | <u>des</u> Lied<u>s</u> |
| | <u>eines</u> Wagen<u>s</u> | <u>einer</u> Dose | <u>eines</u> Lied<u>s</u> |
| **Dative** | <u>dem</u> Wagen | <u>der</u> Dose | <u>dem</u> Lied |
| | <u>einem</u> Wagen | <u>einer</u> Dose | <u>einem</u> Lied |

⇨ *For more information on **Articles**, see page 28.*

➤ **-e** is added to some nouns in certain set phrases.

| | |
|---|---|
| **Wir gehen nach Haus<u>e</u>.** | We're going home. |
| **Er hat sich zu Tod<u>e</u> gearbeitet.** | He worked himself to death. |

---

*Grammar Extra!*
**-e** may also be added to the dative singular of masculine and neuter nouns to make the phrase easier to pronounce.
**zu welchem Zweck<u>e</u>?**    to what purpose?

---

➤ The dative case is used:

- to show the <u>indirect object</u> of a verb – an indirect object answers the question *who to/for?* or *to/for what?*
  He gave the man the book. → *Who did he give the book to?* → the man (= *noun indirect object*)
  **Er gab <u>dem</u> <u>Mann</u> das Buch.**    He gave the man the book.

- after certain verbs
  **Er hilft <u>seiner</u> <u>Mutter</u> im Haushalt.**    He helps his mother with the housework.

⇨ *For more information on **Verbs followed by the dative case**, see page 202.*

- after certain prepositions which always take the dative
  **Nach <u>dem</u> Essen gingen wir spazieren.**    After eating we went for a walk.
  **Er kam mit <u>einer</u> Freundin.**    He came with a friend.

⇨ *For more information on **Prepositions followed by the dative case**, see page 210.*

For further explanation of grammatical terms, please see pages viii-xii.

- after certain prepositions to show position

| | |
|---|---|
| **an** | on, to, at |
| **auf** | on, in, to, at |
| **hinter** | behind |
| **in** | in, into, to |
| **neben** | next to, beside |
| **über** | over, across, above |
| **unter** | under, among |
| **vor** | in front of, before |
| **zwischen** | between |

| | |
|---|---|
| **Ich sitze <u>neben</u> <u>dem</u> Fenster.** | I'm sitting next to the window. |
| **Die Katze lag <u>unter</u> <u>dem</u> Tisch.** | The cat lay under the table. |

[*i*] Note that when there is some movement involved after these prepositions, the <u>accusative case</u> is used.

| | |
|---|---|
| **Er war <u>in der</u> Stadt.** (*dative*) | He was in town. |
| **Sie geht <u>in die</u> Stadt.** (*accusative*) | She's going into town. |

⇨ *For more information on **Prepositions followed by the accusative or the dative case**, see page 218.*

- in certain expressions

| | |
|---|---|
| **<u>Mir</u> ist kalt.** | I'm cold. |

- instead of the possessive adjective (*my, your, his, her, its, our* or *their*) to refer to parts of the body and items of clothing

| | |
|---|---|
| **Ich habe <u>mir die</u> Haare gewaschen.** | I washed my hair. |
| **Zieh <u>dir die</u> Jacke aus.** | Take your jacket off. |

⇨ *For more information on **Possessive adjectives**, see page 47.*

➤ Changes to the definite and indefinite articles **der**, **die** or **das** and **ein**, **eine** or **ein** for each case are summarized in the table below, to help make it easier for you to remember them.

| Case | Masculine Singular | Feminine Singular | Neuter Singular |
|---|---|---|---|
| **Nominative** | der<br>ein | die<br>eine | das<br>ein |
| **Accusative** | den<br>einen | die<br>eine | das<br>ein |
| **Genitive** | des<br>eines | der<br>einer | des<br>eines |
| **Dative** | dem<br>einem | der<br>einer | dem<br>einem |

⇨ *For more information on **Articles**, see page 28.*

**KEY POINTS**

✔ In German, there are four grammatical cases – nominative, accusative, genitive and dative.

✔ The case you use depends on the grammatical function of the noun in the sentence.

✔ The nominative case is used to show the subject of a sentence and after the verbs **sein** and **werden**.

✔ The accusative case is used to show the direct object of a sentence, and after certain prepositions.

✔ The genitive case is used to show that something belongs to somebody, and after certain prepositions.

✔ The dative case is used to show the indirect object of a sentence, and after certain prepositions and verbs.

For further explanation of grammatical terms, please see pages viii-xii.

# Test yourself

**5** **Insert the correct form of the definite article.**

**a** Ich setzte mich neben ........................ Mädchen.

**b** Ich saß neben ........................ Mädchen

**c** Die Augen ........................ Lehrers waren grün.

**d** Er stand auf ........................ Balkon.

**e** ........................ Kind ist 12 Jahre alt.

**f** Die Stimme ........................ Sängerin ist sehr hoch.

**g** Ich mag die Farben ........................ Bildes.

**h** Die Lehrerin lobte ........................ Schülerin.

**i** Sie gab ........................ Freundin das Buch zurück.

**j** Meine Mutter ist nicht da, sie ist in ........................ Stadt gegangen.

**6** **Insert the correct form of the indefinite article.**

**a** Möchten Sie einen Kaffee oder ........................ Tee?

**b** Das Haus ........................ Engländers ist sein Schloss.

**c** Ich hätte gern ........................ Steak mit Pommes frites.

**d** Er öffnete ........................ Flasche Rotwein.

**e** Man sollte ........................ Freund in Not immer helfen.

**f** Ich habe Lust auf ........................ Glas Apfelsaft.

**g** Ich habe mir gestern ........................ Computer gekauft.

**h** Ich bin noch nie mit ........................ Flugzeug geflogen.

**i** Ist das ein Mädchen oder ........................ Junge?

**j** Wenn es regnet, stellen wir uns unter ........................ Baum.

# Test yourself

**7**  **Cross out the cases that do not correspond to the German item.**

**a** der Mann          nominative/accusative/genitive/dative

**b** der Freundin      nominative/accusative/genitive/dative

**c** ein Auto          nominative/accusative/genitive/dative

**d** eine Katze        nominative/accusative/genitive/dative

**e** dem Esel          nominative/accusative/genitive/dative

**f** die Straße        nominative/accusative/genitive/dative

**g** des Kindes        nominative/accusative/genitive/dative

**h** das Buch          nominative/accusative/genitive/dative

**i** einen Hund        nominative/accusative/genitive/dative

**j** einer Frage       nominative/accusative/genitive/dative

**8**  **Translate the following sentences into German.**

**a** I gave the book to my sister. ........................................................................

**b** The man's sister is called Martina. ...............................................................

**c** He stood next to the car. .............................................................................

**d** We went across the bridge. ..........................................................................

**e** Markus sat down on the sofa. .......................................................................

**f** We were flying high above the sea. ...............................................................

**g** He could walk without a stick. ......................................................................

**h** I would like a beer. .....................................................................................

**i** Las Vegas was built in a desert. ....................................................................

**j** Her son has a German passport. ...................................................................

## Forming plurals

➤ In English we usually make nouns plural by adding an -s to the end (*garden* → *gardens*; *house* → *houses*), although we do have some nouns which are <u>irregular</u> and do not follow this pattern (*mouse* → *mice*; *child* → *children*).

➤ In German, there are several different ways of making nouns plural.

➤ The definite article changes in the plural, as shown in the table below.

| Case | Masculine Singular | Feminine Singular | Neuter Singular | All Genders Plural |
|------|--------------------|--------------------|------------------|---------------------|
| Nominative | der | die | das | die |
| Accusative | den | die | das | die |
| Genitive | des | der | des | der |
| Dative | dem | der | dem | den |

⇨ *For more information on **Articles**, see page 28.*

> *Tip*
>
> Nouns in the dative plural <u>ALWAYS</u> end in **-n**, except those nouns which come from other languages. Most of their plural forms end in **-s**. For example:
>
> **Mit <u>den</u> Autos hatte sie ständig Probleme.**   The cars caused her constant problems.

## Feminine plural nouns ending in -n, -en, -nen

➤ Most German <u>feminine nouns</u> form their plural by adding **-n**, **-en** or **-nen** to their singular form.

| Case | Singular | Plural |
|------|----------|--------|
| Nominative | die **Blume** (flower)<br>die **Frau** (woman)<br>die **Lehrerin** (teacher) | die **Blumen**<br>die **Frauen**<br>die **Lehrerinnen** |
| Accusative | die **Blume**<br>die **Frau**<br>die **Lehrerin** | die **Blumen**<br>die **Frauen**<br>die **Lehrerinnen** |
| Genitive | der **Blume**<br>der **Frau**<br>der **Lehrerin** | der **Blumen**<br>der **Frauen**<br>der **Lehrerinnen** |
| Dative | der **Blume**<br>der **Frau**<br>der **Lehrerin** | den **Blumen**<br>den **Frauen**<br>den **Lehrerinnen** |

| | |
|---|---|
| **Die Blumen waren nicht teuer.** | The flowers weren't expensive. |
| **Die Lehrerinnen sind ziemlich jung.** | The (female) teachers are quite young. |
| **Das Leben der Frauen in vielen Ländern ist schwierig.** | In many countries, women's lives are difficult. |
| **Wo gehst du mit den Blumen hin?** | Where are you going with the flowers? |

## Nouns with no ending in the plural

➤ Many nouns have no plural ending – these are mostly <u>masculine</u> or <u>neuter nouns</u> ending in **-en**, **-er** or **-el**.

| Case | Singular | Plural |
|---|---|---|
| **Nominative** | **der Kuchen** (cake) <br> **der Lehrer** (teacher) <br> **der Onkel** (uncle) | **die Kuchen** <br> **die Lehrer** <br> **die Onkel** |
| **Accusative** | **den Kuchen** <br> **den Lehrer** <br> **den Onkel** | **die Kuchen** <br> **die Lehrer** <br> **die Onkel** |
| **Genitive** | **des Kuchens** <br> **des Lehrers** <br> **des Onkels** | **der Kuchen** <br> **der Lehrer** <br> **der Onkel** |
| **Dative** | **dem Kuchen** <br> **dem Lehrer** <br> **dem Onkel** | **den Kuchen** <br> **den Lehre<u>n</u>** <br> **den Onkel<u>n</u>** |

| | |
|---|---|
| **Die Kuchen sehen lecker aus.** | The cakes look delicious. |
| **Die Onkel kommen morgen an.** | The uncles are coming tomorrow. |
| **Das war die Schuld der Lehrer.** | That was the teachers' fault. |
| **Es gibt ein kleines Problem mit den Kuchen.** | There's a slight problem with the cakes. |

➤ Some of these nouns also have an umlaut added to the first vowel **a**, **o** or **u** in the plural.

| Case | Singular | Plural |
|---|---|---|
| **Nominative** | **der Apfel** (apple) <br> **der Garten** (garden) | **die Äpfel** <br> **die Gärten** |
| **Accusative** | **den Apfel** <br> **den Garten** | **die Äpfel** <br> **die Gärten** |
| **Genitive** | **des Apfels** <br> **des Gartens** | **der Äpfel** <br> **der Gärten** |
| **Dative** | **dem Apfel** <br> **dem Garten** | **den Äpfel<u>n</u>** <br> **den Gärten** |

| | |
|---|---|
| **Die Äpfel sind nicht reif genug.** | The apples aren't ripe enough. |
| **Die Gärten waren wunderschön.** | The gardens were beautiful. |
| **Schau mal die Größe der Äpfel an!** | Look at the size of the apples! |
| **Den Äpfeln fehlt ein bisschen Sonne.** | The apples need a bit of sun. |

For further explanation of grammatical terms, please see pages viii–xii.

## Plural nouns ending in ̈-e

➤ Some masculine nouns add an umlaut above the first vowel **a**, **o** or **u** and an **-e** ending to form the plural. A few feminine nouns with **a** in the stem also follow this pattern. Nouns in this group often have one syllable only.

| Case | Singular | Plural |
|---|---|---|
| Nominative | **der Stuhl** (chair)<br>**die Angst** (fear) | **die Stühle**<br>**die Ängste** |
| Accusative | **den Stuhl**<br>**die Angst** | **die Stühle**<br>**die Ängste** |
| Genitive | **des Stuhl(e)s**<br>**der Angst** | **der Stühle**<br>**der Ängste** |
| Dative | **dem Stuhl**<br>**der Angst** | **den Stühlen**<br>**den Ängsten** |

**Die Stühle sind neu.** — The chairs are new.
**Die Regierung muss die Ängste der Bevölkerung ernst nehmen.** — The government has to take the population's fears seriously.
**Die Farbe der Stühle.** — The colour of the chairs.
**Der Tischler macht den Stühlen neue Beine.** — The carpenter is making new legs for the chairs.

## Masculine and neuter plural nouns ending in -e, -er or ̈-er

➤ Masculine or neuter nouns often add **-e** or **-er** to form the plural.

| Case | Singular | Plural |
|---|---|---|
| Nominative | **das Geschenk** (present)<br>**der Tisch** (table)<br>**das Kind** (child) | **die Geschenke**<br>**die Tische**<br>**die Kinder** |
| Accusative | **das Geschenk**<br>**den Tisch**<br>**das Kind** | **die Geschenke**<br>**die Tische**<br>**die Kinder** |
| Genitive | **des Geschenks**<br>**des Tisches**<br>**des Kindes** | **der Geschenke**<br>**der Tische**<br>**der Kinder** |
| Dative | **dem Geschenk**<br>**dem Tisch**<br>**dem Kind** | **den Geschenken**<br>**den Tischen**<br>**den Kindern** |

**Die Geschenke sind auf dem Tisch.** — The presents are on the table.
**Ich muss die Kinder abholen.** — I have to pick up the children.
**Die Auswahl der Tische im Laden war groß.** — The shop had a large selection of tables.
**Sie geht mit den Kindern spazieren.** — She's going for a walk with the children.

➤ Some <u>masculine</u> and <u>neuter nouns</u> add an umlaut above the first vowel **a**, **o** or **u** and an **-er** ending in the plural.

| Case | Singular | Plural |
|------|----------|--------|
| Nominative | das Dach (roof)<br>der Mann (man) | die Dächer<br>die Männer |
| Accusative | das Dach<br>den Mann | die Dächer<br>die Männer |
| Genitive | des Dach(e)s<br>des Mannes | der Dächer<br>der Männer |
| Dative | dem Dach<br>dem Mann | den Dächern<br>den Männern |

| | |
|---|---|
| **Die Dächer werden repariert.** | The roofs are being repaired. |
| **Man hatte die Männer völlig vergessen.** | The men had been completely forgotten. |
| **Was ist die Rolle der Männer in unserer Gesellschaft?** | What is the role of men in our society? |
| **Die Frauen sollten den Männern nicht immer recht geben.** | Women should not always agree with men. |

## Some unusual plurals

➤ There is another group of German nouns which don't follow any of the rules for forming plurals – you just have to remember them! Here are some of the most common ones. As you will see, many of them are words from other languages, and it is common for such words to form their plural by adding **-s**.

| Singular | Meaning | Plural |
|----------|---------|--------|
| **das Auto** | car | **die Autos** |
| **das Hotel** | hotel | **die Hotels** |
| **das Restaurant** | restaurant | **die Restaurants** |
| **das Baby** | baby | **die Babys** |
| **das Thema** | theme, topic, subject | **die Themen** |
| **das Drama** | drama | **die Dramen** |
| **das Risiko** | risk | **die Risiken** |
| **der Park** | park | **die Parks** |
| **der Chef** | boss, chief, head | **die Chefs** |
| **die Firma** | firm | **die Firmen** |

| | |
|---|---|
| **Die Hotels in der Stadt sind ziemlich teuer.** | The hotels in town are quite expensive. |
| **Die Risiken sind sehr hoch.** | The risks are very high. |
| **Die Kinder finden die Babys ganz niedlich.** | The children think the babies are really cute. |
| **Was hältst du von den Preisen der Autos?** | What do you think of the prices of the cars? |
| **Das ist die Stadt mit den vielen Parks.** | That's the town with all the parks. |

For further explanation of grammatical terms, please see pages viii–xii.

## Plural versus singular

➤ Some nouns are always plural in English, but singular in German.

| | |
|---|---|
| **eine Brille** | glasses, spectacles |
| **eine Schere** | scissors |
| **eine Hose** | trousers |

➤ These nouns are only used in the plural in German to mean more than one pair.

| | |
|---|---|
| **zwei Hosen** | two pairs of trousers |

## Nouns of measurement and quantity

➤ These nouns, used to describe the quantity or size of something, usually remain singular in German, even if preceded by a plural number.

| | |
|---|---|
| **Möchten Sie zwei <u>Stück</u>?** | Would you like two? |
| **Ich wiege fünfzig <u>Kilo</u>.** | I weigh fifty kilos. |

➤ The substance which they measure follows in the same case as the noun of quantity, and <u>NOT</u> in the genitive case as in English.

| | |
|---|---|
| **Sie hat drei Tassen <u>Kaffee</u> getrunken.** | She drank three cups of coffee. |
| **Er wollte zwei Kilo <u>Kartoffeln</u>.** | He wanted two kilos of potatoes. |
| **Drei Glas <u>Weißwein</u>, bitte!** | Three glasses of white wine, please. |

---

### KEY POINTS

✔ Most German feminine nouns form their plural by adding **-n**, **-en** or **-nen** to their singular form.

✔ Many nouns have no plural ending – these are mostly masculine or neuter singular nouns ending in **-en**, **-er** or **-el**. Some of these nouns also have an umlaut added to the vowel in the plural.

✔ Some masculine nouns add an umlaut above the first vowel **a**, **o** or **u** and an **-e** ending to form the plural. A few feminine nouns with **a** in the stem also follow this pattern.

✔ Masculine and neuter nouns often add **-e** or **-er** in the plural, and can sometimes add an umlaut above the first vowel **a**, **o** or **u**.

✔ There are some unusual plural nouns in German which don't follow any pattern.

✔ Some nouns are always plural in English, but singular in German.

✔ Nouns of measurement and quantity usually remain singular even if preceded by a plural number.

✔ The substance which they measure follows in the same case as the noun of quantity.

# Test yourself

**9** After each number below, write the plural form of the equivalent German noun. The first one has been done for you.

**a** zwei ....... *Freunde* ....... [female friend]

**b** fünf ............................ [wasp]

**c** drei ............................ [hotel]

**d** zehn ............................ [number]

**e** vier ............................ [present]

**f** tausend ............................ [metre]

**g** zwölf ............................ [month]

**h** vier ............................ [season]

**i** hundert ............................ [year]

**j** elf ............................ [card]

**10** Write 1 in the gap if the noun is singular, and 2 if it is plural.

**a** ..................... Fenster          **f** ..................... Rhinozeros

**b** ..................... Gespenster       **g** ..................... Kontaktlinse

**c** ..................... Feder            **h** ..................... Garten

**d** ..................... Eltern           **i** ..................... Decken

**e** ..................... Kinos            **j** ..................... Becken

**11** Write the plural form in the gap, adding an umlaut.

**a** die Maus; die .....................

**b** das Buch; die .....................

**c** das Dach; die .....................

**d** der Frosch; die .....................

**e** das Glas; die .....................

**f** der Hafen; die .....................

**g** der Koch; die .....................

**h** der Kuss; die .....................

**i** der Traum; die .....................

**j** das Wort; die .....................

# Weak nouns

➤ As we have seen, German nouns may change, according to their <u>gender</u>, <u>case</u> and <u>number</u>. This is called <u>declension</u>.

➤ Some masculine nouns have a <u>weak declension</u> – this means that they end in **-en** or, if the word ends in a vowel, in **-n**, in every case <u>EXCEPT</u> in the nominative singular case.

➤ Weak masculine nouns follow the pattern shown.

| Case | Singular | Plural |
|------|----------|--------|
| **Nominative** | **der Junge** | **die Jungen** |
| **Accusative** | **den Jungen** | **die Jungen** |
| **Genitive** | **des Jungen** | **der Jungen** |
| **Dative** | **dem Jungen** | **den Jungen** |

➤ Weak masculine nouns include:

- those ending in **-og(e)** referring to men
  **der Psychologe**                    the psychologist

  **Der Psychologe half ihm in**        The psychologist helped him
  **seiner Krise.**                       through his crisis.

- those ending in **-aph** (or **-af**) or **-oph**
  **der Paragraf**                      the paragraph
  **der Philosoph**                     the philosopher

  **Der Paragraf umfasste 350 Wörter.** The paragraph was 350 words long.

- those ending in **-ant**
  **der Elefant**                       the elephant
  **der Diamant**                       the diamond

  **Der Diamant war sehr viel Geld wert.** The diamond was worth a lot of money.

- those ending in **-t** referring to men
  **der Astronaut**                     the astronaut
  **der Komponist**                     the composer
  **der Architekt**                     the architect

  **Um Astronaut zu werden, muss**      You have to train for years to become
  **man jahrelang trainieren.**          an astronaut.

- some other common masculine nouns
  **der Chirurg**                       surgeon
  **der Franzose**                      Frenchman
  **der Kollege**                       colleague
  **der Mensch**                        human being
  **der Ochse**                         ox
  **der Spatz**                         sparrow

**Der junge Franzose wollte
  Schottland besuchen.**
The young French guy wanted to visit
  Scotland.
**Ich habe den Franzosen seit
  einer Woche nicht mehr gesehen.**
I haven't seen the French guy for a week.

---

*Grammar Extra!*

The noun **der Name** follows the same pattern as **der Junge**, except in the genitive singular, where it adds **-ns** instead of just **-n**. **Der Buchstabe** (meaning *letter (of the alphabet)*), **der Funke** (meaning *spark*) and **der Gedanke** (meaning *thought*) also follow this pattern.

| Case | Singular | Plural |
|------|----------|--------|
| Nominative | der Name | die Namen |
| Accusative | den Namen | die Namen |
| Genitive | des Namens | der Namen |
| Dative | dem Namen | den Namen |

**Das hängt von der Wichtigkeit
  des Namens ab.**
That depends on how important
  the name is.

---

# Proper nouns

➤ In German, names of people and places only change in the <u>genitive singular</u> when they add **-s**, unless they are preceded by the definite article or a demonstrative adjective (in English, *this, that, these* and *those*).

| | |
|---|---|
| **Annas Buch** | Anna's book |
| **Klaras Mantel** | Klara's coat |
| **die Werke Goethes** | Goethe's works |
| BUT | |
| **der Untergang <u>der</u> Titanic** | the sinking of <u>the</u> Titanic |

⇨ *For more information on **Articles** and **demonstrative adjectives**, see pages 28 and 37.*

---

*Grammar Extra!*
Where proper names end in **-s**, **-sch**, **-ss**, **-ß**, **-x**, **-z**, or **-tz**, adding an extra **-s** for the genitive makes them very difficult to pronounce. This is best avoided by using **von** + the dative case.

| | |
|---|---|
| **das Buch von Hans** | Hans's book |
| **die Werke von Marx** | the works of Marx |
| **die Freundin von Klaus** | Klaus's girlfriend |

---

➤ **Herr** (meaning *Mr*) is always declined when it is part of a proper name.

| | |
|---|---|
| **an Herr<u>n</u> Schmidt** | to Mr Schmidt |
| **Sehr geehrte Herr<u>en</u>** | Dear Sirs |

➤ Surnames usually form their plurals by adding **-s**, unless they end in **-s**, **-sch**, **-ss**, **-ß**, **-x**, **-z**, or **-tz**, in which case they add **-ens**. They are often preceded by the definite article.

| | |
|---|---|
| **Die Schmidt<u>s</u> haben uns zum Abendessen eingeladen.** | The Schmidts have invited us to dinner. |
| **Die Schultz<u>ens</u> waren nicht zu Hause.** | The Schultzes weren't at home. |

⇨ *For more information on **Articles**, see page 28.*

# Articles

---

**What is an article?**
In English, an **article** is one of the words *the*, *a* and *an* which is used
in front of a noun.

---

## Different types of articles

➤ There are two types of article.

- the <u>definite</u> article: *the* in English. This is used to identify a particular thing or person.

  I'm going to <u>the</u> supermarket.
  That's <u>the</u> woman I was talking to.

- the <u>indefinite</u> article: *a* or *an* in English, *some* or *any* (or no word at all) in the plural. This is used to refer to something unspecific, or something that you do not really know about.

  Is there <u>a</u> supermarket near here?
  I need <u>a</u> day off.

## The definite article

➤ In English the definite article *the* always keeps the same form.
  *the* book
  *the* books
  with *the* books

➤ In German, however, the definite article has many forms. All German nouns are either
<u>masculine</u>, <u>feminine</u> or <u>neuter</u> and, just as in English, they can be either <u>singular</u> or <u>plural</u>.
The word you choose for *the* depends on whether the noun it is used with is masculine,
feminine or neuter, singular or plural AND it also depends on the case of the noun. This may
sound complicated, but it is not too difficult.

| | |
|---|---|
| <u>Die</u> **Frau ging spazieren.** | The woman went for a walk. |
| <u>Der</u> **Mann ist geschieden.** | The man is divorced. |
| **Sie fährt mit <u>dem</u> Auto in die Stadt.** | She travels into town by car. |
| <u>Die</u> **Farbe <u>der</u> Jacke gefällt mir nicht.** | I don't like the colour of the jacket. |
| **Ich muss <u>die</u> Kinder abholen.** | I have to pick up the children. |
| **Das will ich mit <u>den</u> Behörden besprechen.** | I want to discuss that with the authorities. |

⇨ *For more information on* **Nouns**, *see page 1.*

---

➤ The definite article changes for <u>masculine</u>, <u>feminine</u> and <u>neuter</u> singular nouns.

|  | Definite Article +Singular Noun | Meaning |
|---|---|---|
| Masculine | <u>der</u> Mann | the man |
| Feminine | <u>die</u> Frau | the woman |
| Neuter | <u>das</u> Mädchen | the girl |

➤ The <u>plural</u> forms of the definite article are the same for all genders.

|  | Definite Article + Plural Noun | Meaning |
|---|---|---|
| Masculine | <u>die</u> Männer | the men |
| Feminine | <u>die</u> Frauen | the women |
| Neuter | <u>die</u> Mädchen | the girls |

> *Tip*
> It is a good idea to learn the <u>article</u> or the <u>gender</u> with the noun when you come across a word for the first time, so that you know whether it is masculine, feminine or neuter. A good dictionary will also give you this information.

➤ The definite article also changes according to the case of the noun in the sentence – nominative, accusative, genitive or dative.

⇨ *For more information on **Cases**, see page 11.*

➤ The forms of the definite article in each case are as follows:

| Case | Masculine Singular | Feminine Singular | Neuter Singular | All Genders Plural |
|---|---|---|---|---|
| Nominative | der | die | das | die |
| Accusative | den | die | das | die |
| Genitive | des | der | des | der |
| Dative | dem | der | dem | den |

| | |
|---|---|
| **<u>Der</u> Mann ging ins Haus.** | The man went into the house. |
| **<u>Die</u> Frau geht jeden Abend schwimmen.** | The woman goes swimming every night. |
| **Sie wollen <u>das</u> Mädchen adoptieren.** | They want to adopt the girl. |
| **<u>Die</u> zwei Frauen nebenan wollen ihr Haus renovieren.** | The two women next door want to renovate their house. |
| **<u>Der</u> Mann mit <u>der</u> reichen Frau.** | The man with the rich wife. |
| **<u>Die</u> Mädchen gehen morgen ins Kino.** | The girls are going to the cinema tomorrow. |
| **Ich will nicht nur mit <u>den</u> Männern arbeiten.** | I don't just want to work with the men. |

## KEY POINTS

✔ The definite article changes for masculine, feminine and neuter singular nouns.

✔ The plural forms of the definite article are the same for all genders.

✔ The form of the definite article also changes depending on the case of the noun in the sentence.

# Test yourself

**12** **Translate the following phrases into German.**

**a** the house and the roof ........................................................................................

**b** the pupil and the teacher (*both male*) ................................................................

**c** the pupil and the teacher (*both female*)

........................................................................................................................

**d** the month and the year ......................................................................................

**e** the German (*woman*) and the Englishman

........................................................................................................................

**f** the book and the page ........................................................................................

**g** the computer and the mouse ..............................................................................

**h** the telephone and the receiver ..........................................................................

**i** the opera and the singer (*male*) ........................................................................

**j** the window and the frame ..................................................................................

**13** **Add the correct form of the definite article.**

**a** ........................ Krankenhaus

**b** ........................ Herbst

**c** ........................ Körbe

**d** ........................ Baby

**e** ........................ Radio

**f** ........................ Sprecherin

**g** ........................ Maschine

**h** ........................ Dorf

**i** ........................ Schwimmbäder

**j** ........................ Fest

## Using the definite article

➤ The definite article in German (**der**, **die** or **das**) is used in more or less the same way as we use *the* in English, but it is also used in German in a few places where you might not expect it.

➤ The definite article is used with words like *prices*, *life* and *time* that describe qualities, ideas or experiences (called <u>abstract nouns</u>) rather than something that you can touch with your hand. Usually, *the* is missed out in English with this type of word.

| | |
|---|---|
| <u>Die</u> **Preise sind wirklich hoch.** | Prices are really high. |
| <u>Das</u> **Leben ist schön.** | Life is wonderful. |
| <u>Die</u> **Zeit vergeht schnell.** | Time passes quickly. |

*ⓘ* Note that these nouns are sometimes used <u>WITHOUT</u> the article.

| | |
|---|---|
| **Es braucht <u>Mut</u>.** | It needs (some) courage. |
| **Gibt es dort <u>Leben</u>?** | Is there (any) life there? |

➤ You also use the definite article with the genitive case to show that something belongs to someone.

**die Jacke <u>der</u> Frau**                   the woman's jacket

*ⓘ* Note that you do not usually use the definite article with the genitive case if the noun is a proper name or is being used as a proper name. A proper name is the name of a person, place, organization or thing.

| | |
|---|---|
| **Jans Auto** | Jan's car |
| **Muttis Auto** | Mummy's car |

Occasionally, the definite article IS used with proper names:

- to make the sex of the person or the case clearer
  **Er hat es <u>dem</u> Kekilli gegeben.**     He gave it to Kekilli.

- where an adjective is used before the proper name
  **Die <u>alte</u> Frau Schnorr ist**     Old Frau Schnorr has died.
  **gestorben.**

- in certain informal situations or to emphasize something
  **Ich habe heute <u>den</u> Kevin**     I saw Kevin today.
  **gesehen.**

➤ In German, you have to use the definite article in front of <u>masculine</u> and <u>feminine</u> countries and districts, but you don't need it for neuter ones.

| | |
|---|---|
| **Die Schweiz ist auch schön.** | Switzerland is also beautiful. |
| **Deutschland ist sehr schön.** | Germany is very beautiful. |

---

*Grammar Extra!*
You also use the definite article when geographical names are preceded by an adjective.

**<u>das</u> heutige Deutschland**                   today's Germany

---

➤ The definite article is used with names of seasons.

**Der Winter kommt bald.**　　　　　Soon it will be winter.

➤ You often use the definite article with meals.

**Im Hotel wird <u>das</u> Abendessen**　　Dinner is served from eight o'clock
　**ab acht Uhr serviert.**　　　　　　in the hotel.

[i] Note that there are certain expressions with meals when you don't use the definite article.

**Um acht Uhr ist Frühstück.**　　　Breakfast is at eight o'clock.

➤ You also use the definite article with the names of roads.

**Sie wohnt jetzt in <u>der</u> Geisener**　　She lives in Geisener Road now.
　**Straße.**

➤ The definite article is used with months of the year, except after the prepositions **seit**, **nach** and **vor**.

**<u>Der</u> Dezember war ziemlich kalt.**　The December was quite cold.
**Wir sind seit September hier.**　　We have been here since September.

⇨ *For more information on **Prepositions**, see page 210.*

➤ If you're talking about prices and want to say *each*, *per* or *a*, you use the definite article.

**Die kosten fünf Euro <u>das</u> Pfund.**　They cost five euros a pound.
**Ich habe sechs Euro <u>das</u> Stück**　　I paid six euros each.
　**bezahlt.**

➤ In certain common expressions the definite article is used.

**in <u>die</u> Stadt fahren**　　　　　to go into town
**mit <u>der</u> Post**　　　　　　　　by post
**mit <u>dem</u> Zug/Bus/Auto**　　　　by train/bus/car

---

*Grammar Extra!*
In German, the definite article can be used instead of <u>a demonstrative adjective</u>.
**Du willst <u>das</u> Buch lesen!**　　　You want to read <u>that</u> book!

⇨ *For more information on **demonstrative adjectives**, see page 37.*

---

➤ In German, the definite article is left out in certain set expressions.

**von Beruf**　　　　　　　　　　by profession
**Nachrichten hören**　　　　　　to listen to the news

## Shortened forms of the definite article

➤ After certain prepositions, the definite article can be shortened, though it is best to avoid using some of these forms in writing.

● **für das → fürs**
　**Es ist <u>fürs</u> Baby.**　　　　　　It's for the baby.

- vor dem → vorm
  **Es liegt vorm Haus.**           It's lying in front of the house.

- um das → ums
  **Es geht ums Geld.**           It's a question of money.

➤ The following shortened forms can be used in writing.

- an dem → am
  **Am 1. Mai fahren wir in die Ferien.**     We go on holiday on the 1st of May.

- in dem → im
  **Das Buch liegt im Haus.**           The book's in the house.

- zu dem → zum
  **Ich muss zum Bahnhof gehen.**         I have to go to the station.

- zu der → zur
  **Sie geht jeden Tag zur Schule.**        She goes to school every day.

⇨ *For more information on **Shortened forms of prepositions**, see page 229.*

---

### KEY POINTS

✔ The definite article is used in German with:
  - abstract nouns
  - the genitive case to show possession
  - proper names, in certain exceptional cases
  - masculine and feminine countries and districts
  - names of seasons and with months of the year, except after the prepositions **seit**, **nach** and **vor**
  - names of roads
  - meals and prices
  - certain set expressions

✔ When combined with certain prepositions, the definite article can be shortened.

---

**14** **Complete these phrases with the correct <u>genitive</u> form of the definite article.**

   **a** das Auto ......................... Mutter

   **b** die Jacke ......................... Kindes

   **c** die Blätter ......................... Bäume

   **d** das Kind ......................... Lehrerin

   **e** die Seiten ......................... Bücher

   **f** die Tastatur ......................... Computers

   **g** der Hörer ......................... Telefons

   **h** die Dächer ......................... Häuser

   **i** das Fell ......................... Katze

   **j** der Untergang......................... Schiffes

**15** **Complete these sentences with the correct form of the definite article.**

   **a** Ich gebe mit meiner Freundin in ......................... Stadt.

   **b** ......................... Sommer war sehr heiß.

   **c** Meine Schwester fährt mit ......................... Bus zur Aibeit.

   **d** ......................... Slovakei ist sehr schön.

   **e** ......................... Kälte ist vorüber.

   **f** Das Paket kam mit ......................... Post.

   **g** Meine Familie wohnt in ......................... Tullastraße.

   **h** ......................... Leben ist zu kurz.

   **i** ......................... Frühling ist eine schöne Jahreszeit.

   **j** Ich gebe ......................... Kellner ein Trinkgeld.

# Test yourself

16 **Complete the following sentences with a preposition + shortened form of the definite article. The first one has been done for you.**

**a** Wir gehen ...........*ins*........... Kino. **[in das]**

**b** Wir laufen ............................... Haus. **[um das]**

**c** Das Schiff fährt ............................... Meer. **[über das]**

**d** ............................... Haus steht ein Baum. **[Hinter dem]**

**e** Die Kinder schwimmen ............................... See. **[in dem]**

**f** Sie kommt immer zu spät ............................... Unterricht. **[zu dem]**

**g** Er hat ............................... 1. April Geburtstag. **[an dem]**

**h** Sonntags geht sie immer ............................... Kirche. **[zu der]**

**i** Mein Bruder hat ein Haus ............................... Meer. **[an dem]**

**j** Er stieg mit der Leiter ............................... Haus. **[auf das]**

## Words declined like the definite article

➤ These words follow the same patterns as the definite article:

| | Nominative | Accusative | Genitive | Dative |
|---|---|---|---|---|
| **Plural only** | alle | alle | aller | allen |
| **Singular** | beides | beides | beides | beiden |
| **Plural** | beide | beide | beider | beiden |
| **Singular** | dieser, diese, dieses | diesen, diese, dieses | dieses/diesen, dieser, dieses/diesen | diesem, dieser, diesem |
| **Plural** | diese | diese | dieser | diesen |
| **Singular** | einiger, einige, einiges | einigen, einige, einiges | einiges/einigen, einiger, einiges/einigen | einigem, einiger, einigem |
| **Plural** | einige | einige | einiger | einigen |
| **Singular** | jeder, jede, jedes | jeden, jede, jedes | jedes/jeden, jeder, jedes/jeden | jedem, jeder, jedem |
| **Plural** | jede | jede | jeder | jeden |
| **Singular** | jener, jene, jenes | jenen, jene, jenes | jenes/jenen, jener, jenes/jenen | jenem, jener, jenem |
| **Plural** | jene | jene | jener | jenen |
| **Singular** | mancher, manche, manches | manchen, manche, manches | manches/manchen, mancher, manches/manchen | manchem, mancher, manchem |
| **Plural** | manche | manche | mancher | manchen |
| **Singular** | solcher, solche, solches | solchen, solche, solches | solches/solchen, solcher, solches/solchen | solchem, solcher, solchem |
| **Plural** | solche | solche | solcher | solchen |
| **Singular** | welcher, welche, welches | welchen, welche, welches | welches/welchen, welcher, welches/welchen | welchem, welcher, welchem |
| **Plural** | welche | welche | welcher | welchen |

ⓘ Note that **dieser** or **jener** are used to translate the English demonstrative adjectives *this*, *that*, *these* and *those*.

- alle, aller, allen (*plural* only)                all, all of them
  **Wir haben <u>alle</u> gesehen.**               We saw all of them.
  **Die Eltern fuhren mit <u>allen</u>**            The parents went off with all their children.
  **Kindern weg.**

- beide (*plural* only)                             both
  **Ich habe <u>beide</u> Bücher gelesen.**         I've read both books

- dieser, diese, dieses                             this, this one, these
  **<u>Dieser</u> junge Mann ist begabt.**          This young man is talented.
  **<u>Dieses</u> alte Haus ist wirklich schön.**   This old house is really beautiful.

- einiger, einige, einiges                          some, a few, a little
  **<u>Einige</u> von uns gingen spazieren.**       Some of us went for a walk.
  **Wir haben <u>einiges</u> gesehen.**             We saw quite a lot of things.

- jeder, jede, jedes                                each, each one, every
  **<u>Jeder</u> Schüler bekommt ein Zeugnis.**     Every pupil receives a report.
  **Sie kommt <u>jedes</u> Mal zu spät.**           She arrives late every time.

- jener, jene, jenes                                that, that one, those
  **<u>Jener</u> Junge hatte seine Brieftasche**    That boy had lost his wallet.
  **verloren.**

- mancher, manche, manches                          many a, some
  **<u>Mancher</u> Mann bleibt gern mit den**       Some men like staying at home with
  **Kindern zu Hause.**                               the children.
  **<u>Manches</u> Auto fährt schneller als**       Some cars can go faster than 220 km/h.
  **220 km/h.**

- solcher, solche, solches                          such, such a
  **Ein <u>solches</u> Mountainbike hätte ich**     I'd really like to have a mountain bike like
  **auch gern.**                                      that too.

- welcher, welche, welches                          which, which one
  **<u>Welche</u> Frau hat die Stelle bekommen?**   Which woman got the job?

---

*Grammar Extra!*
**sämtliche** and **irgendwelcher** also follow the same pattern as the definite
article:

- **sämtliche**                                     all, entire (*usually plural*)
  **Sie besitzt Tolkiens <u>sämtliche</u> Werke.**  She owns the complete works
                                                      of Tolkien.

- **irgendwelcher, -e, -es**                        some or other
  **Sind noch <u>irgendwelche</u> Reste da?**       Are there any leftovers?

---

➤ The words listed above can be used as:

- articles
  **Dieser Mann kommt aus Südamerika.**     This man comes from South America.
  **Sie geht jeden Tag ins Büro.**     She goes to the office every day.

- pronouns – a pronoun is a word you use instead of a noun, when you do not need or want to name someone or something directly, for example, *it*, *you*, *none*.
  **Willst du diesen?**     Do you want this one?
  **Man kann ja nicht alles wissen.**     You can't know everything.
  **Es gibt manche, die keinen**     There are some people who don't like
    **Alkohol mögen.**     alcohol.

⇨ *For more information on **Pronouns**, see page 89.*

---

*Grammar Extra!*
**einiger** and **irgendwelcher** end in **-en** in the genitive before masculine or neuter nouns ending in **-s**.
**Er musste wegziehen wegen**     He had to move away because of
  **irgendwelchen Geredes.**     some gossip.

**jeder**, **welcher**, **mancher** and **solcher** can also do this or can have the usual **-es** ending.
**Das Kind solcher Eltern wird**     The child of such parents will have
  **Probleme haben.**     problems.
**Trotz jeden Versuchs scheiterten**     Despite all attempts, the negotiations
  **die Verhandlungen.**     failed.

---

➤ **solcher**, **beide** and **sämtliche** can be used after another article or possessive adjective (in English, one of the words *my*, *your*, *his*, *her*, *its*, *our* or *their*).
  **Ein solches Rad habe ich früher**     I used to have a bike like that too.
    **auch gehabt.**
  **Diese beiden Männer haben es**     Both of these men have seen it.
    **gesehen.**

➤ Although **beide** generally has plural forms only, there is one singular form, **beides**. While **beide** is more common and can refer to both people and things, **beides** refers only to things. **Beide** is used for two examples of the same thing or person, while **beides** is used for two different examples.
  **Es gab zwei Bleistifte und er hat**     There were two pencils and he took both.
    **beide genommen.**
  BUT
  **Es gab einen Bleistift und ein Bild**     There was one pencil and one picture and
    **und er hat beides genommen.**     he took both.

ⓘ Note that **beides** is singular in German, whereas *both* is plural in English.

  **Beides ist richtig.**     Both are correct.

➤ **dies** often replaces the nominative and accusative **dieses** and **diese** when it is used as a pronoun.

| | |
|---|---|
| **Hast du <u>dies</u> schon gelesen?** | Have you already read this? |
| **<u>Dies</u> sind meine neuen Sachen.** | These are my new things. |

⇨ *For more information on **Pronouns**, see page 89.*

➤ **alle** also has a fixed form, **all**, which is used together with other articles or possessive pronouns.

| | |
|---|---|
| **<u>All</u> sein Mut war verschwunden.** | All his courage had disappeared. |
| **Was machst du mit <u>all</u> diesem Geld?** | What are you doing with all this money? |

➤ **ganz** can be used to replace both **alle** and **all** and is declined like an adjective.

| | |
|---|---|
| **Sie ist mit dem ganzen Geld verschwunden.** | She disappeared with all the money. |

⇨ *For more information on **Adjectives**, see page 51.*

➤ **ganz** must be used:

- in time phrases

| | |
|---|---|
| **Es hat den <u>ganzen</u> Tag geschneit.** | It snowed all day. |

- when talking about geography

| | |
|---|---|
| **Im <u>ganzen</u> Land gab es keinen besseren Wein.** | There wasn't a better wine in the whole country. |

- with nouns referring to a collection of people or animals (*collective* nouns)

| | |
|---|---|
| **Die <u>ganze</u> Gesellschaft war auf der Versammlung vertreten.** | The entire company was represented at the meeting. |

---

*Grammar Extra!*
**derjenige/diejenige/dasjenige** (*the one, those*) is declined in the same way as the definite article **der** + a weak adjective.

⇨ *For more information on **Weak adjectives**, see page 53.*

| Case | Masculine | Feminine | Neuter |
|---|---|---|---|
| **Nominative** | <u>der</u>jenige Mann | <u>die</u>jenige Frau | <u>das</u>jenige Kind |
| **Accusative** | <u>den</u>jenigen Mann | <u>die</u>jenige Frau | <u>das</u>jenige Kind |
| **Genitive** | <u>des</u>jenigen Mann(e)s | <u>der</u>jenigen Frau | <u>des</u>jenigen Kind(e)s |
| **Dative** | <u>dem</u>jenigen Mann | <u>der</u>jenigen Frau | <u>dem</u>jenigen Kind |

**derselbe/dieselbe/dasselbe** (*the same, the same one*) is declined in the same way as **derjenige**. However, after prepositions, the shortened forms of the definite article are used for the appropriate parts of **derselbe**.

| | |
|---|---|
| **zur selben (=zu derselben) Zeit** | at the same time |
| **im selben (=in demselben) Zimmer** | in the same room |

⇨ *For more information on **Shortened forms of prepositions**, see page 229.*

---

For further explanation of grammatical terms, please see pages viii-xii.

**KEY POINTS**

✔ There is a group of words which are declined like the definite article **der**.

✔ These words can be used as articles or pronouns.

✔ **solcher**, **beide** and **sämtliche** can be used after another article or possessive adjective.

✔ **beide** generally has plural forms only, but there is one singular form, **beides**.

✔ When it is used as a pronoun **dies** often replaces the nominative and accusative **dieses** and **diese**.

✔ **alle** also has a fixed form, **all**.

✔ **ganz** must be used instead of **alle** in certain situations.

# Test yourself

**17** **Complete the following phrases with the correct form of** *beide*.

**a** ......................... Brüder

**b** die ......................... Autos

**c** ......................... ist falsch.

**d** der Preis ......................... Computer

**e** diese ......................... Frauen

**f** ......................... Mädchen

**g** Hast du es ......................... gesagt?

**h** ......................... haben recht.

**i** ......................... Fahrräder

**j** die Bärte ......................... Männer

**18** **Translate the following sentences into German.**

**a** All parents love their children. ..................................................................

**b** This child is very clever. ..................................................................

**c** Some vases are round. ..................................................................

**d** I have seen both films. ..................................................................

**e** There are some people who don't write letters.

........................................................................................................

**f** Which book are you reading? ..................................................................

**g** This woman comes from Ireland. ..................................................................

**h** The entire house was empty. ..................................................................

**i** He knows everything. ..................................................................

**j** This is my sister. ..................................................................

**19** **Match the two columns according to gender and case.**

| **a** einige | Kindern |
| **b** mancher | Frau |
| **c** welches | Mütter |
| **d** dieselbe | Mann |
| **e** allen | Haus |

## The indefinite article

➤ In English we have the indefinite article *a*, which changes to *an* in front of a word that starts with a vowel. In the plural we say either *some*, *any* or nothing at all.

➤ In German the word you choose for *a* depends on whether the noun it is used with is masculine, feminine or neuter, singular or plural AND it also depends on the case of the noun.

| | |
|---|---|
| **Da ist <u>ein</u> Auto.** | There's a car. |
| **Sie hat <u>eine</u> Wohnung.** | She has a flat. |
| **Er gab es <u>einem</u> Kind.** | He gave it to a child. |

➤ The indefinite article has no plural forms.

| | |
|---|---|
| **Computer sind in letzter Zeit teurer geworden.** | Computers have become more expensive recently. |

➤ The indefinite article is formed as follows.

| Case | Masculine | Feminine | Neuter |
|---|---|---|---|
| **Nominative** | ein | eine | ein |
| **Accusative** | einen | eine | ein |
| **Genitive** | eines | einer | eines |
| **Dative** | einem | einer | einem |

## Using the indefinite article

➤ The indefinite article is used very much as in English.

| | |
|---|---|
| **Da ist <u>ein</u> Bus.** | There's <u>a</u> bus. |
| **Sie hat <u>eine</u> neue Jacke.** | She has <u>a</u> new jacket. |
| **Sie gab es <u>einer</u> alten Dame.** | She gave it to <u>an</u> old lady. |

➤ In certain situations, you do not use the indefinite article:

- when talking about the job someone does
  | | |
  |---|---|
  | **Sie ist Ärztin.** | She's a doctor. |

- when talking about someone's nationality or religion
  | | |
  |---|---|
  | **Sie ist Deutsche.** | She's (a) German. |
  | **Er ist Moslem.** | He's (a) Muslim. |

  ⓘ Note that the indefinite article IS used when an adjective comes before the noun.

  | | |
  |---|---|
  | **Sie ist <u>eine</u> sehr begabte Journalistin.** | She's a very talented journalist. |

- in certain fixed expressions
  | | |
  |---|---|
  | **Es ist Geschmacksache.** | It's a question of taste. |
  | **Tatsache ist ...** | It's a fact ... |

- after **als** (meaning *as a*)
  **Als Lehrerin verdiene ich nicht gut.**     I don't earn very much as a teacher.
  **Als Großmutter darf ich meine**            As a grandmother, I'm allowed to spoil my
  **Enkel verwöhnen.**                         grandchildren.

## The indefinite article in negative sentences

➤ In English we use words like *not* and *never* to indicate that something is not happening or is not true. The sentences that these words are used in are called <u>negative</u> sentences.
  I <u>don't</u> know him.
  I <u>never</u> do my homework on time.

➤ In German, you use a separate negative form of the indefinite article, which is formed exactly like **ein** in the singular, and also has plural forms. It means *no/not a/not one/not any*.

| Case | Masculine Singular | Feminine Singular | Neuter Singular | All Genders Plural |
|---|---|---|---|---|
| **Nominative** | kein | keine | kein | keine |
| **Accusative** | keinen | keine | kein | keine |
| **Genitive** | keines | keiner | keines | keiner |
| **Dative** | keinem | keiner | keinem | keinen |

**Er hatte <u>keine</u> Geschwister.**     He had no brothers or sisters.
**Ich sehe <u>keinen</u> Unterschied.**    I don't see any difference.
**Das ist <u>keine</u> richtige Antwort.** That's not a correct answer.
**<u>Kein</u> Mensch hat es gesehen.**     Not one person has seen it.

*Tip*
This negative form of the indefinite article is even used when the *positive* form of the phrase has no article.
**Er hatte Angst davor.**          He was afraid of it.
**Er hatte <u>keine</u> Angst davor.**     He wasn't afraid of it.

*Grammar Extra!*
The negative form of the indefinite article is also used in many informal expressions.
**Sie hatte <u>kein</u> Geld mehr.**           All her money was gone.
**Es waren <u>keine</u> drei Monate**          It was less than three months later
  **vergangen, als ...**                        that ...
**Es hat mich <u>keine</u> zehn Euro gekostet.** It cost me less than ten euros.

If you want to emphasize the **ein** in the sentence, **nicht ein** can be used instead of **kein**.
**<u>Nicht ein</u> Kind hat es singen können.**   Not *one* child could sing it.

⇨ *For more information on **Negatives**, see page 246.*

**KEY POINTS**

✔ The indefinite article is used in German
  - to translate the English *a* and *any* in the singular
  - in negative sentences in its separate negative form, **kein**, to translate *no*

✔ The indefinite article in German is NOT used when:
  - talking about someone's job, nationality or religion, unless an adjective is used before the noun
  - in certain set expressions or after **als** meaning *as a*

# Test yourself

**20 Complete the phrase with _ein_ or _eine_ as required.**

a ..................... Baum

b ..................... Wohnung

c ..................... guter Wein

d ..................... Jacke

e ..................... Jackett

f ..................... rote Blume

g ..................... Matratze

h ..................... Vorhang

i ..................... Freundin

j ..................... Maus

**21 Translate the following sentences into German.**

a That's a fact. ......................................................................

b I have bought a car. ............................................................

c I have a new car. .................................................................

d He's an old man. .................................................................

e She's a friend of mine. .........................................................

f There's a tree in front of the house. ......................................

g Have you got a smartphone? ................................................

h We have to ask a doctor. ......................................................

i Do you have a girlfriend? ......................................................

j She's a very beautiful girl. .....................................................

**22 Complete the following phrases with the correct form of _kein_.**

a Es ist ..................... Benzin im Tank.

b Ich habe wirklich ..................... Zeit.

c Das macht alles ..................... Sinn.

d Ich habe ..................... Geld zum Einkaufen.

e Das Auto hat ..................... 2000 Euro gekostet.

f Kann mir denn ..................... helfen?

g Das ist gar ..................... schlechte Idee.

h ..................... Kind wurde bei dem Unfall verletzt.

i ..................... der Kinder ist in der Schule.

j Ich kann ..................... Mathematik.

# Words declined like the indefinite article

➤ The following words are <u>possessive adjectives</u>, one of the words *my, your,* [...]
*their* used with a noun to show that one person or thing belongs to anothe[...]
same pattern as the indefinite articles **ein** and **kein**.

| | |
|---|---|
| **mein** | my |
| **dein** | your (*singular familiar*) |
| **sein** | his/its |
| **ihr** | her/its |
| **unser** | our |
| **euer** | your (*plural familiar*) |
| **ihr** | their |
| **Ihr** | your (*polite singular and plural*) |

➤ Possessive adjectives are formed in the following way.

| | Nominative | Accusative | Genitive | Dative |
|---|---|---|---|---|
| **Singular** | mein, meine, mein | meinen, meine, mein | meines, meiner, meines | meinem, meiner, meinem |
| **Plural** | meine | meine | meiner | meinen |
| **Singular** | dein, deine, dein | deinen, deine, dein | deines, deiner, deines | deinem, deiner, deinem |
| **Plural** | deine | deine | deiner | deinen |
| **Singular** | sein, seine, sein | seinen, seine, sein | seines, seiner, seines | seinem, seiner, seinem |
| **Plural** | seine | seine | seiner | seinen |
| **Singular** | ihr, ihre, ihr | ihren, ihre, ihr | ihres, ihrer, ihres | ihrem, ihrer, ihrem |
| **Plural** | ihre | ihre | ihrer | ihren |
| **Singular** | unser, unsere, unser | unseren, unsere, unser | unseres, unserer, unseres | unserem, unserer, unserem |
| **Plural** | unsere | unsere | unserer | unseren |
| **Singular** | euer, eu(e)re, eu(e)res | eu(e)ren, eu(e)re, eu(e)res | eu(e)res, eu(e)rer, eu(e)res | eu(e)rem, eu(e)rer, eu(e)rem |
| **Plural** | eu(e)re | eu(e)re | eu(e)rer | eu(e)ren |
| **Singular** | ihr, ihre, ihr | ihren, ihre, ihr | ihres, ihrer, ihres | ihrem, ihrer, ihrem |
| **Plural** | ihre | ihre | ihrer | ihren |
| **Singular** | Ihr, Ihre, Ihr | Ihren, Ihre, Ihr | Ihres, Ihrer, Ihres | Ihrem, Ihrer, Ihrem |
| **Plural** | Ihre | Ihre | Ihrer | Ihren |

| | |
|---|---|
| **Mein kleiner Bruder will auch mitkommen.** | My little brother wants to come too. |
| **Wo steht dein altes Auto?** | Where is your old car? |
| **Er spielt Fußball mit seiner Tante.** | He is playing football with his aunt. |
| **Was ist mit ihrem Computer los?** | What is wrong with her computer? |
| **Ihre Kinder sind wirklich verwöhnt.** | Their children are really spoiled. |
| **Wie geht es Ihrer Schwester?** | How is your sister? |
| **Ich will meine Kinder regelmäßig sehen.** | I want to see my children regularly. |

---

*Grammar Extra!*

Possessive adjectives are often followed by other adjectives in German sentences. These adjectives then have the same endings as the indefinite article.

| | |
|---|---|
| **Er liebt sein altes Auto.** | He loves his old car. |
| **Sie hat ihren neuen Computer verkauft.** | She sold her new computer. |
| **Wo ist deine rote Jacke?** | Where is your red jacket? |

**irgendein** (meaning *some ... or other*) and its plural form **irgendwelche** also take these endings.

| | |
|---|---|
| **Er ist irgendein bekannter Schauspieler.** | He's some famous actor or other. |
| **Sie ist nur irgendeine alte Frau.** | She's just some old woman or other. |
| **Sie hat irgendein neues Buch gekauft.** | She bought some new book or other. |
| **Ich muss irgendwelche blöden Touristen herumführen.** | I have to show some stupid tourists or other round. |

---

> **KEY POINTS**
> ✔ Possessive adjectives, one of the words *my, your, his, her, its, our* or *their*, are declined like the indefinite articles **ein** and **kein**.

For further explanation of grammatical terms, please see pages viii-xii.

**23 Cross out the nouns that cannot go with the form of the definite or indefinite article.**

| | | |
|---|---|---|
| **a** | des | Mannes/Männer/Radios/Haus |
| **b** | die | Frau/Gläser/Telefone/Arbeit |
| **c** | eine | Telefon/Engländerin/Blumen/Deutsche |
| **d** | der | Frau/Mann/Mannes/Telefon |
| **e** | einem | Tag/Kerze/Decken/Papier |
| **f** | dem | Zug/Lampe/Kind/Stift |
| **g** | ein | Mädchen/Hammer/Kugelschreiber/Bücherei |
| **h** | das | Hamster/Ei/Katze/Schaf |
| **i** | den | Nachbarn/Kinder/Frauen/Filme |
| **j** | einen | Brille/Mantel/Auto/Papier |

**24 Translate the following sentences into German.**

**a** How is your brother? ......................................................................................

**b** What colour is his car? ...................................................................................

**c** She lives with her parents. .............................................................................

**d** Rita is my fiancée. .........................................................................................

**e** We should pay our bill. ..................................................................................

**f** This is not our table. .....................................................................................

**g** Eva and Karin, have you done your homework?

................................................................................................................

**h** I don't want to lose my children. ....................................................................

**i** Where is your green anorak? ..........................................................................

**j** They told him their names. .............................................................................

# Test yourself

**25** **Complete the following sentences with the correct form of the possessive adjective.**

**a** Er fährt mit ................................ Auto. **[mein]**

**b** Ist das ................................ Bruder? **[euer]**

**c** Kann ich mal ................................ Pass sehen? **[Ihr]**

**d** Wir feiern Weihnachten mit ................................ Familie. **[unser]**

**e** Ist das ................................ kleine Schwester? **[dein]**

**f** Er ist mit ................................ Klasse in die Schweiz gefahren. **[sein]**

**g** Das haben wir ................................ Sohn noch nicht gesagt. **[unser]**

**h** Ist das die Handtasche ................................ Frau? **[Ihr]**

**i** Habt ihr ................................ Fahrräder dabei? **[euer]**

**j** Grüße bitte ................................ Onkel von mir. **[dein]**

# Adjectives

---

### What is an adjective?

An **adjective** is a 'describing' word that tells you more about a person
or thing, such as their appearance, colour, size or other qualities, for example,
*pretty*, *blue*, *big*.

---

## Using adjectives

➤ Adjectives are words like *clever*, *expensive* and *silly* that tell you more about a noun (a living being, thing or idea). They can also tell you more about a pronoun, such as *he* or *they*. Adjectives are sometimes called 'describing words'. They can be used right next to a noun they are describing, or can be separated from the noun by a verb like *be*, *look*, *feel* and so on.

> a <u>clever</u> girl
> an <u>expensive</u> coat
> a <u>silly</u> idea
> He's just being <u>silly</u>.

⇨ *For more information on **Nouns** and **Pronouns**, see pages 1 and 89.*

➤ In English, the only time an adjective changes its form is when you are making a comparison.

> She's <u>cleverer</u> than her brother.
> That's the <u>silliest</u> idea I ever heard!

➤ In German, however, adjectives usually <u>agree</u> with what they are describing. This means that their endings change depending on whether the person or thing you are referring to is masculine, feminine or neuter, and singular or plural. It also depends on the case of the person or thing you are describing and whether it is preceded by the definite or indefinite article.

> **Das neu<u>e</u> Buch ist da.**    The new book has arrived.
> **Ich wollte es der alt<u>en</u> Frau geben.** I wanted to give it to the old woman.
> **Sie erzählte mir eine langweilig<u>e</u>** She told me a boring story.
>  **Geschichte.**
> **Die deutsch<u>en</u> Traditionen**   German traditions

⇨ *For more information on **Cases** and **Articles**, see pages 11 and 28.*

➤ As in English, German adjectives come <u>BEFORE</u> the noun they describe, but <u>AFTER</u> the verb in the sentence. The only time the adjective does not agree with the word it describes is when it comes <u>AFTER</u> the verb.

> **eine <u>schwarze</u> Katze**  a <u>black</u> cat
> **Das Buch ist <u>neu</u>.**   The book is <u>new</u>.

---

### KEY POINTS

✔ Most German adjectives change their form according to the case
of the noun they are describing and whether the noun is masculine,
feminine or neuter, singular or plural.

✔ In German, the only time the adjective does not agree with the word
it describes is when it comes <u>AFTER</u> the verb.

# Test yourself

**26** **Fill the gap with the correct form of the adjective *deutsch*.**

    **a** ein ........................ Mann

    **b** ein ........................ Buch

    **c** eine ........................ Geschichte

    **d** ein ........................ Kind

    **e** ein ........................ Film

    **f** eine ........................ Tradition

    **g** eine ........................ Zeitung

    **h** ein ........................ Flugzeug

    **i** ein ........................ Junge

    **j** ein ........................ Auto

**27** **Translate the following phrases into German.**

    **a** an old book .........................................................................................

    **b** the new school ....................................................................................

    **c** an English boy .....................................................................................

    **d** a big tree ..............................................................................................

    **e** a long story ..........................................................................................

    **f** the white cat ........................................................................................

    **g** a heavy stone ......................................................................................

    **h** a good picture .....................................................................................

    **i** the clever girl .......................................................................................

    **j** a bad idea .............................................................................................

**28** **Match the two columns to complete the sentences.**

    **a** Ich sehe ein                 Glas Wein.

    **b** Er ist ein                     würzige Suppe.

    **c** Ich trinke ein              schönes Auto.

    **d** Ich kaufe eine            großer Mann.

    **e** Sie bestellt eine         neue Gitarre.

# Making adjectives agree

## The basic rules

➤ In dictionaries, only the basic form of German adjectives is shown. You need to know how to change it to make it agree with the noun or pronoun the adjective describes.

➤ To make an adjective agree with the noun or pronoun it describes, you simply add one of three sets of different endings, as described in the next few pages.

## The Weak Declension

➤ The endings used after the definite articles **der**, **die** and **das** and other words declined like them are shown below.

| Case | Masculine Singular | Feminine Singular | Neuter Singular | All Genders Plural |
|------|--------------------|--------------------|-----------------|---------------------|
| Nominative | -e | -e | -e | -en |
| Accusative | -en | -e | -e | -en |
| Genitive | -en | -en | -en | -en |
| Dative | -en | -en | -en | -en |

➤ The following table shows you how these different endings are added to the adjective **alt**, meaning *old*, when it is used with the definite article.

| Case | Masculine Singular | Feminine Singular | Neuter Singular |
|------|--------------------|--------------------|-----------------|
| Nominative | der alte Mann | die alte Frau | das alte Haus |
| Accusative | den alten Mann | die alte Frau | das alte Haus |
| Genitive | des alten Mann(e)s | der alten Frau | des alten Hauses |
| Dative | dem alten Mann | der alten Frau | dem alten Haus |

Nominative:
  **Der alte Mann wohnt nebenan.**　　　The old man lives next door.
Accusative:
  **Ich habe die alte Frau in der**　　　I saw the old woman in the library.
  **Bibliothek gesehen.**
Genitive:
  **Die Besitzerin des alten Hauses**　　　The owner of the old house is very rich.
  **ist ganz reich.**
Dative:
  **Er hilft dem alten Mann beim**　　　He helps the old man to do his shopping.
  **Einkaufen.**

➤ These are the plural endings of adjectives when they have a weak declension.

| Plural | All Genders |
|---|---|
| Nominative | die alt<u>en</u> Männer/Frauen/Häuser |
| Accusative | die alt<u>en</u> Männer/Frauen/Häuser |
| Genitive | der alt<u>en</u> Männer/Frauen/Häuser |
| Dative | den alt<u>en</u> Männern/Frauen/Häusern |

## The Mixed Declension

➤ The endings used after **ein**, **kein**, **irgendein** and the possessive adjectives are shown below.

🛈 Note that this declension differs from the weak declension only in the three forms underlined below.

| Case | Masculine Singular | Feminine Singular | Neuter Singular | All Genders Plural |
|---|---|---|---|---|
| Nominative | -<u>er</u> | -e | -<u>es</u> | -en |
| Accusative | -en | -e | -<u>es</u> | -en |
| Genitive | -en | -en | -en | -en |
| Dative | -en | -en | -en | -en |

▷ For more information on **Possessive adjectives**, see page 47.

➤ The following table shows you how these different endings are added to the adjective **lang**, meaning *long*.

| Case | Masculine Singular | Feminine Singular | Neuter Singular |
|---|---|---|---|
| Nominative | ein lang<u>er</u> Weg | eine lang<u>e</u> Reise | ein lang<u>es</u> Spiel |
| Accusative | einen lang<u>en</u> Weg | eine lang<u>e</u> Reise | ein lang<u>es</u> Spiel |
| Genitive | eines lang<u>en</u> Weg(e)s | einer lang<u>en</u> Reise | eines lang<u>en</u> Spiel(e)s |
| Dative | einem lang<u>en</u> Weg | einer lang<u>en</u> Reise | einem lang<u>en</u> Spiel |

Nominative:
**Eine lang<u>e</u> Reise muss geplant werden.** You have to plan a long trip.
Accusative:
**Ich habe einen lang<u>en</u> Weg nach Hause.** It takes me a long time to get home.
Genitive:
**Die vielen Nachteile einer lang<u>en</u> Reise ...** The many disadvantages of a long journey ...

For further explanation of grammatical terms, please see pages viii-xii.

Dative:

**Bei einem langen Spiel kann man sich langweilen.**   You can get bored with a long game.

➤ These are the plural endings of adjectives when they have a mixed declension.

| Plural | All Genders |
|---|---|
| **Nominative** | ihre lang**en** Wege/Reisen/Spiele |
| **Accusative** | ihre lang**en** Wege/Reisen/Spiele |
| **Genitive** | ihrer lang**en** Wege/Reisen/Spiele |
| **Dative** | ihren lang**en** Wege**n**/Reisen/Spiele**n** |

## The Strong Declension

➤ The endings used when there is no article before the noun are shown below.

| Case | Masculine Singular | Feminine Singular | Neuter Singular | All Genders Plural |
|---|---|---|---|---|
| **Nominative** | -er | -e | -es | -e |
| **Accusative** | -en | -e | -es | -e |
| **Genitive** | -en | -er | -en | -er |
| **Dative** | -em | -er | -em | -en |

➤ The following table shows you how these different endings are added to the adjective **gut**, meaning *good*.

| Case | Masculine Singular | Feminine Singular | Neuter Singular |
|---|---|---|---|
| **Nominative** | gut**er** Käse | gut**e** Marmelade | gut**es** Bier |
| **Accusative** | gut**en** Käse | gut**e** Marmelade | gut**es** Bier |
| **Genitive** | gut**en** Käses | gut**er** Marmelade | gut**en** Bier(e)s |
| **Dative** | gut**em** Käse | gut**er** Marmelade | gut**em** Bier |

Nominative:

**Gut**es **Bier ist sehr wichtig auf einer Party.**   Good beer is very important at a party.

Accusative:

**Wo finde ich gut**en **Käse?**   Where will I get good cheese?

Genitive:

**Das ist ein Zeichen gut**er **Marmelade.**   That is a sign of good jam.

Dative:

**Zu gut**em **Käse braucht man auch Oliven.**   You need olives to go with good cheese.

➤ These are the plural endings of adjectives when they have a strong declension.

ℹ Note that the plural form of **Käse** is normally **Käsesorten**.

| Plural | All Genders |
|---|---|
| **Nominative** | gut<u>e</u> Käsesorten/Marmeladen/Biere |
| **Accusative** | gut<u>e</u> Käsesorten/Marmeladen/Biere |
| **Genitive** | gut<u>er</u> Käsesorten/Marmeladen/Biere |
| **Dative** | gut<u>en</u> Käsesorten/Marmeladen/Bieren |

ℹ Note that these endings allow the adjective to do the work of the missing article by showing the case of the noun and whether it is singular or plural, masculine, feminine or neuter.

➤ The article is omitted more often in German than in English, especially where you have *preposition + adjective + noun* combinations.

| | |
|---|---|
| **Nach kurz<u>er</u> Fahrt kamen wir in Glasgow an.** | After a short journey we arrived in Glasgow. |
| **Mit gleich<u>em</u> Gehalt wie du würde ich mir einen Urlaub leisten können.** | I'd be able to afford a holiday on the same salary as you. |

➤ These strong declension endings are also used after any of the following words when the noun they refer to is not preceded by an article.

| Word | Meaning |
|---|---|
| **ein bisschen** | a little, a bit of |
| **ein wenig** | a little |
| **ein paar** | a few, a couple |
| **weniger** | fewer, less |
| **einige** (*plural forms only*) | some |
| **etwas** | some, any (*singular*) |
| **mehr** | more |
| **lauter** | nothing but, sheer, pure |
| **solch** | such |
| **was für** | what, what kind of |
| **viel** | much, many, a lot of |
| **welch ...!** | what ...! what a ...! |
| **manch** | many a |
| **wenig** | little, few, not much |
| **zwei, drei** *etc* | two, three *etc* |

| | |
|---|---|
| **Morgen hätte ich ein wenig freie Zeit für dich.** | I could spare you some time tomorrow. |
| **Sie hat mir ein paar gute Tipps gegeben.** | She gave me a few good tips. |
| **Er isst weniger frisches Obst als ich.** | He eats less fresh fruit than me. |
| **Heutzutage wollen mehr junge Frauen Ingenieurin werden.** | Nowadays, more young women want to be engineers. |
| **Solche leckere Schokolade habe ich schon lange nicht mehr gegessen.** | I haven't had such good chocolate for a long time. |
| **Wir haben viel kostbare Zeit verschwendet.** | We have wasted a lot of valuable time. |
| **Welch herrliches Wetter!** | What wonderful weather! |

➤ With **wenig** and numbers from **zwei** onwards, adjectives behave as follows:

- Strong, when there is no article:

| | |
|---|---|
| **Es gab damals nur wenig frisches Obst.** | There was little fresh fruit at that time. |
| **Zwei kleine Jungen kamen die Straße entlang.** | Two small boys came along the street. |

- Weak, when the definite article comes first:

| | |
|---|---|
| **Das wenige frische Obst, das es damals gab, war teuer.** | The little fresh fruit that was available then, was expensive. |
| **Die zwei kleinen Jungen, die die Straße entlangkamen.** | The two small boys who came along the street. |

- Mixed, when a possessive adjective comes first:

| | |
|---|---|
| **Meine zwei kleinen Jungen sind manchmal frech.** | My two small sons are cheeky sometimes. |

➤ These strong declension endings also need to be used after possessives where no other word shows the case of the following noun and whether it's masculine, feminine or neuter, singular or plural.

| | |
|---|---|
| **Sebastians altes Buch lag auf dem Tisch.** | Sebastian's old book was lying on the table. |
| **Mutters neuer Computer sieht toll aus.** | Mum's new computer looks great. |

*Tip*

When these various endings are added to adjectives, you have to watch out for some spelling changes.

When endings are added to the adjective **hoch**, meaning *high*, the simple form changes to **hoh**.

| | |
|---|---|
| **Das Gebäude ist hoch.** | The building is high. |
| **Das ist ein hohes Gebäude.** | That is a high building. |

Adjectives ending in **-el** lose the **-e** when endings are added.

| | |
|---|---|
| **Das Zimmer ist dunkel.** | The room is dark. |
| **Man sieht nichts in dem dunklen Zimmer.** | You can't see anything in the dark room. |

Adjectives ending in **-er** often lose the **-e** when endings are added.

| | |
|---|---|
| **Das Auto war teuer.** | The car was expensive. |
| **Sie kaufte ein teures Auto.** | She bought an expensive car. |

### KEY POINTS

✔ To make an adjective agree with the noun it is describing, you simply add one of three sets of endings: weak, mixed or strong.

✔ Strong endings are also used after particular words when not preceded by an article, for example, **ein bisschen**, **ein paar**, **wenig**, and after possessive adjectives.

# Test yourself

**29** **Complete the following sentences with the correct form of the adjective.**

   **a** Mein Bruder ist ein ............................... Mann. **[alt]**

   **b** Es ist eine ............................... Reise bis nach Köln. **[lang]**

   **c** Frank ist ein ............................... Freund von mir. **[gut]**

   **d** Die ............................... Frau ging einkaufen. **[jung]**

   **e** Eine ............................... Ernährung ist wichtig. **[gesund]**

   **f** Wir haben einen ............................... Urlaub gehabt. **[schön]**

   **g** Frau Müller ist eine ............................... Witwe. **[reich]**

   **h** Ich lese gerade ein sehr ............................... Buch. **[dick]**

   **i** Ich gab dem ............................... Mann etwas Geld. **[arm]**

   **j** Der Geschmack eines ............................... Weins ist einzigartig. **[gut]**

**30** **Translate the following sentences into German.**

   **a** I saw two small boys. ................................................................................

   **b** They are on a long journey. ................................................................................

   **c** I have bought good cheese. ................................................................................

   **d** The young woman lives next door. ................................................................................

   **e** I help my neighbour (*female*) to do her shopping. ................................................................................

   **f** That's a beautiful picture! ................................................................................

   **g** We are flying in a big plane. ................................................................................

   **h** I went into a big shop. ................................................................................

   **i** Did you see the tall man? ................................................................................

   **j** We are drinking a French wine. ................................................................................

# Test yourself

**31** **Fill the gap with the correct form of the adjective using strong declension endings. The first one has been done for you.**

**a** Wir wünschen uns ein bisschen ..........*schönes*.......... Wetter im Urlaub. **[schön]**

**b** Jens und Ralph sind zwei ............................. Kinder. **[glücklich]**

**c** Junge Leute haben heute weniger ............................. Zeit. **[frei]**

**d** Was für ............................. Farben! **[herrlich]**

**e** Weniger ............................. Essen ist gesünder. **[kalorienreich]**

**f** Wir aßen lauter ............................. Bonbons. **[bunt]**

**g** Der Krieg dauerte dreißig ............................. Jahre. **[lang]**

**h** Wir sollten mehr ............................. Früchte essen. **[frisch]**

**i** Hast du etwas ............................. Wasser? **[kalt]**

**j** Wir tranken ein bisschen ............................. Apfelsaft. **[süß]**

## Participles as adjectives

➤ In English, the present participle is a verb form ending in -*ing*, which may be used as an adjective or a noun. In German, you simply add **-d** to the infinitive of the verb to form the present participle, which may then be used as an adjective with all the usual endings.

| | |
|---|---|
| **Auf dem Tisch stand ein Foto von einem <u>lachenden</u> Kind.** | There was a photo of a laughing child on the table. |

⟨*i*⟩ Note that the present participles of **sein** and **haben** cannot be used like this.

➤ The past participle of a verb can also be used as an adjective.

| | |
|---|---|
| **Meine Mutter hat meine <u>verlorenen</u> Sachen gefunden.** | My mother found my lost things. |

⟹ *For more information on **Past participles**, see page 153.*

## Adjectives preceded by the dative case

➤ With many adjectives you use the dative case, for example:

- ähnlich
  **Er ist seinem Vater sehr ähnlich.**

  similar to
  He's very like his father.

- bekannt
  **Sie kommt mir bekannt vor.**

  familiar to
  She seems familiar to me.

- dankbar
  **Ich bin dir sehr dankbar.**

  grateful to
  I'm very grateful to you.

- fremd
  **Das ist mir fremd.**

  strange, alien to
  That's alien to me.

- gleich
  **Es ist mir gleich.**

  all the same to/like
  It's all the same to me.

- leicht
  **Du machst es dir wirklich zu leicht.**

  easy for
  You really make things too easy for yourself.

- nah(e)
  **Unser Haus ist nahe der Universität.**

  close to
  Our house is near the university.

- peinlich
  **Das war ihr aber peinlich.**

  embarrassing for
  She was really embarrassed.

- unbekannt
  **Das war mir unbekannt.**

  unknown to
  I didn't know that.

---

**KEY POINTS**

✔ In German, both present and past participles can also be used as adjectives.
✔ With many German adjectives you use the dative case.

# Test yourself

**32**  **Cross out the adjectives that do not go with the noun.**

**a** ein … Haus        altes/hohe/schönes/weißes

**b** eine … Frau        schöne/englischer/deutsche/gute

**c** das … Wetter        schönes/sonnige/guter/gute

**d** auf der … Straße        großer/langen/breiten/schöne

**e** meine … Familie        große/junge/deutsche/reichen

**f** die … Mädchen        attraktive/hübschen/reichen/lachenden

**g** mein … Arm        linker/rechte/lange/kurze

**h** das … Auto        rote/neues/schnelle/teure

**i** viele … Frauen        reichen/schönen/alte/jungen

**j** zwei … Gebäude        hoch/weiße/hohe/alter

**33**  **Insert the form in the dative case to precede the adjective. The first one has been done for you.**

**a** Ich war ............*ihm*............ sehr dankbar. **[er]**

**b** Das ist ............................. nicht bekannt. **[wir]**

**c** Ist ............................. das ganz egal? **[Sie]**

**d** Das ist ............................. wirklich unangenehm. **[ich]**

**e** Das Museum ist nahe ............................. . **[der Park]**

**f** Dieses Wort war ............................. fremd. **[sie]**

**g** Ihr macht es ............................. nicht einfach. **[ihr]**

**h** Dieser Politiker ist ............................. unbekannt. **[ich]**

**i** Du solltest ............................. das gut überlegen. **[du]**

**j** Er sieht ............................. sehr ähnlich. **[dieser Mann]**

**34**  **Match the two columns.**

**a** eine verschlossene        Geldbörse

**b** ein lachender        Studentin

**c** eine verlorene        Essen

**d** eine gut ausgebildete        Clown

**e** ein gut gesalzenes        Tür

# Adjectives used as nouns

➤ All adjectives in German, and participles used as adjectives, can also be used as nouns. These are often called <u>adjectival nouns</u>.

➤ Adjectives and participles used as nouns have:

- a capital letter like other nouns

| | |
|---|---|
| **Der neue Angestellte ist früh angekommen.** | The new employee arrived early. |

- weak, strong or mixed endings, depending on which article, if any, comes before them

| | |
|---|---|
| **Sie ist die neue Angestellte.** | She is the new employee. |
| **Das Gute daran ist, dass ich mehr verdiene.** | The good thing about it is that I'm earning more. |
| **Es bleibt beim Alten.** | Things remain as they were. |

---

**KEY POINTS**

✔ Adjectives in German, and participles used as adjectives, can also be used as nouns. These are often called <u>adjectival nouns</u>.

✔ <u>Adjectival nouns</u> begin with a capital letter and take the same endings as normal adjectives.

# Test yourself

**35** **Complete the sentences with a noun formed from the adjective given. The first one has been done for you.**

**a** Sie ist eine ........ *Bekannte* ........ von mir. **[bekannt]**

**b** Er ist ein .................................... bei der Firma "Ökolex". **[angestellt]**

**c** Das .................................... ist, dass wir gewonnen haben. **[gut]**

**d** Bei dem Unfall gab es 35 .................................... . **[tot]**

**e** Ich war der ...................................., der es gesehen hat. **[erste]**

**f** Die .................................... wurden ins Krankenhaus gebracht. **[verletzt]**

**g** Der .................................... kann schon gut sprechen. **[dreijährig]**

**h** Sonntags gehe ich meine .................................... besuchen. **[verwandt]**

**i** Mein .................................... heißt Silvio. **[verlobt]**

**j** Das Verbrechen wurde von einem .................................... verübt. **[unbekannt]**

**36** **Match the noun to an appropriate adjective.**

| | |
|---|---|
| **a** eine … Prüfung | wichtiges |
| **b** ein … Fußballspiel | spannende |
| **c** ein … Stein | entscheidender |
| **d** eine … Geschichte | schwerer |
| **e** ein … Gedanke | schwierige |

# Some other points about adjectives

## Adjectives describing nationality

➤ These are not spelt with a capital letter in German except in public or official names.

| | |
|---|---|
| **Die deutsche Sprache ist schön.** | The German language is beautiful. |
| **Das französische Volk war entsetzt.** | The people of France were horrified. |
| BUT: | |
| **Die Deutsche Bahn hat Erfolg.** | The German railways are successful. |

➤ However, when these adjectives are used as nouns to refer to a language, a capital letter is used.

| | |
|---|---|
| **Sie sprechen kein Englisch.** | They don't speak English. |

➤ In German, for expressions like *he is English/he is German etc* a noun or adjectival noun is used instead of an adjective.

| | |
|---|---|
| **Er ist Deutscher.** | He is German. |
| **Sie ist Deutsche.** | She is German. |

## Adjectives taken from place names

➤ These are formed by adding **-er** to names of towns. They never change by adding endings to show case.

| | |
|---|---|
| **Kölner, Frankfurter, Berliner** *etc* | from Cologne, Frankfurt, Berlin *etc* |
| **Der Kölner Dom ist wirklich beeindruckend.** | Cologne cathedral is really impressive. |
| **Ich möchte ein Frankfurter Würstchen.** | I'd like a frankfurter sausage. |

➤ Adjectives from **die Schweiz**, meaning Switzerland, and some other regions can also be formed in this way.

| | |
|---|---|
| **Schweizer Käse mag ich gern.** | I really like Swiss cheese. |

➤ Adjectives like these can be used as nouns denoting the inhabitants of a town, in which case they take the same endings as normal nouns.

| | |
|---|---|
| **Die Sprache des Kölners heißt Kölsch.** | People from Cologne speak Kölsch. |
| **Die Entscheidung wurde von den Frankfurtern begrüsst.** | People from Frankfurt welcomed the decision. |

[i] Note that the feminine form of such nouns is formed by adding **-in** in the singular and **-innen** in the plural.

| | |
|---|---|
| **Christine, die Londonerin war, wollte nach Glasgow ziehen.** | Christine, who was from London, wanted to move to Glasgow. |

---

**KEY POINTS**

✔ Adjectives describing nationality are not spelt with a capital letter in German except in public or official names, BUT when they are used as nouns to refer to a language, they do have a capital letter.

✔ Adjectives taken from place names are formed by adding **-er** to the name of the town and never change by adding endings to show case.

✔ They can also be used as nouns denoting the inhabitants of a place.

# Test yourself

**37** **Complete the following sentences to indicate the person's nationality or place of residence.**

    **a** Er ist aus England; er ist ......................................... .

    **b** Sie kommt aus der Schweiz; sie ist ...................................... .

    **c** Er wohnt in Stuttgart; er ist ...................................... .

    **d** Er ist in Italien geboren; er ist ...................................... .

    **e** Sie lebt in Hamburg; sie ist ...................................... .

    **f** Er kommt aus Amerika; er ist ...................................... .

    **g** Sie stammt aus Deutschland; sie ist ...................................... .

    **h** Er kommt aus Japan; er ist ...................................... .

    **i** Sie wohnt in Berlin; sie ist ...................................... .

    **j** Er ist in Leipzig geboren; er ist ...................................... .

**38** **Match the two columns.**

    **a** Frankfurter              Dom

    **b** Kölner                    Würstchen

    **c** Schweizer             Schnitzel

    **d** Münchner            Käse

    **e** Wiener                   Oktoberfest

# Comparatives of adjectives

---

### What is a comparative adjective?
A **comparative adjective** in English is one with *-er* added to it or *more* or *less* in front of it, that is used to compare people or things, for example, *slower, more beautiful*.

---

➤ In German, to say that something is *easier, more expensive* and so on, you add **-er** to the simple form of most adjectives.

> **einfach → einfach<u>er</u>**
> **Das war viel einfacher für dich.**      That was much easier for you.

*ⓘ* Note that adjectives whose simple form ends in **-en** or **-er** may drop the final **-e** to form the comparative, as in **teurer**.

> **teuer → teurer**
> **Diese Jacke ist teu<u>rer</u>.**      This jacket is more expensive.

➤ To introduce the person or thing you are making the comparison with, use **als** (meaning *than*).

> **Er ist kleiner <u>als</u> seine Schwester.**      He is smaller than his sister.
> **Diese Frage ist einfacher <u>als</u> die**      This question is easier than the first one.
>    **erste.**

➤ To say that something or someone is *as ... as* something or someone else, you use **so ... wie** or **genauso ... wie**, if you want to make it more emphatic. To say *not as ... as*, you use **nicht so ... wie**.

> **Sie ist <u>so</u> gut <u>wie</u> ihr Bruder.**      She is as good as her brother.
> **Er war <u>genauso</u> glücklich <u>wie</u> ich.**      He was just as happy as I was.
> **Sie ist <u>nicht so</u> alt <u>wie</u> du.**      She is not as old as you.

➤ Here are some examples of commonly used adjectives which have a vowel change in the comparative form:

| Adjective | Meaning | Comparative | Meaning |
|---|---|---|---|
| **alt** | old | **älter** | older |
| **stark** | strong | **stärker** | stronger |
| **schwach** | weak | **schwächer** | weaker |
| **scharf** | sharp | **schärfer** | sharper |
| **lang** | long | **länger** | longer |
| **kurz** | short | **kürzer** | shorter |
| **warm** | warm | **wärmer** | warmer |
| **kalt** | cold | **kälter** | colder |
| **hart** | hard | **härter** | harder |
| **groß** | big | **größer** | bigger |

➤ Adjectives whose simple form ends in **-el** lose the **-e** before adding the comparative ending **-er**.

| | |
|---|---|
| **eitel → eitler** | vain → vainer |
| **Er ist eitl<u>er</u> als ich.** | He is vainer than me. |
| **dunkel → dunkler** | dark → darker |
| **Deine Haare sind dunkl<u>er</u> als ihre.** | Your hair is darker than hers. |

➤ When used before the noun, comparative forms of adjectives take the same weak, strong or mixed endings as their simple forms.

| | |
|---|---|
| **Die jünger<u>e</u> Schwester ist größer als die ältere.** | The younger sister is bigger than the older one. |
| **Mein jünger<u>er</u> Bruder geht jetzt zur Schule.** | My younger brother goes to school now. |

⇨ *For more information on **Making adjectives agree**, see pages 53-58.*

---

### Grammar Extra!
➤ With a few adjectives, comparative forms may also be used to translate the idea of -*ish* or *rather*.

| Comparative | Meaning |
|---|---|
| älter | elderly |
| dünner | thinnish |
| dicker | fattish |
| größer | largish |
| jünger | youngish |
| kleiner | smallish |
| kürzer | shortish |
| neuer | newish |

| | |
|---|---|
| **Eine ältere Frau kam die Straße entlang.** | An elderly woman was coming along the street. |
| **Er war von jüngerem Aussehen.** | He was of youngish appearance. |

---

### KEY POINTS
✔ In German, to form the comparative you add **-er** to the simple form of most adjectives.
✔ To compare people or things in German, you use **so ... wie**, **genauso ... wie**, if you want to make it more emphatic, or **nicht so ... wie**.
✔ *Than* in comparatives corresponds to **als**.
✔ There is a change in the vowel in many of the simple forms of German adjectives when forming their comparatives.
✔ Adjectives whose simple form ends in **-el**, such as **dunkel**, lose the **-e** before adding the comparative ending **-er**.

# Test yourself

**39** **Translate the following sentences into German.**

**a** My brother is younger than me. ...............................................................

**b** He's my younger brother. .................................................................

**c** I'm smaller than my sister. .................................................................

**d** I'm just as old as you are. .................................................................

**e** My jacket is more expensive than yours.

   .................................................................................................

**f** It was easier for me. .................................................................

**g** I'm stronger than you. .................................................................

**h** Your house is bigger than mine. .................................................................

**i** This question is much easier. .................................................................

**j** You're not as old as me. .................................................................

**40** **Complete these sentences with the comparative form of the adjective.**

**a** Ich bin klein, aber du bist ............................... .

**b** Unser Haus ist alt, aber eures ist ............................... .

**c** Eure Straße ist dunkel, aber unsere ist ............................... .

**d** Die Schere ist scharf, aber das Messer ist ............................... .

**e** Ein Fernseher ist teuer, aber ein Computer ist ............................... .

**f** Mein Bruder ist glücklich, aber meine Schwester ist ............................... .

**g** Das Schlafzimmer ist warm, aber das Wohnzimmer ist ............................... .

**h** Gisela ist dünn, aber Liane ist ............................... .

**i** Holz ist hart, aber Stahl ist ............................... .

**j** Hier ist es kalt, aber in Russland ist es ............................... .

# Test yourself

**41** **Fill the gap using either** *als* **or** *wie*.

**a** Mathias ist älter ......................... Max.

**b** Sie ist genauso groß ......................... du.

**c** Sie singt so gut ......................... ihr Bruder.

**d** Sie singt besser ......................... ihr Bruder.

**e** Er ist viel stärker ......................... ich.

**f** Mein Computer ist nicht viel teurer ......................... deiner.

**g** Sie ist so intelligent ......................... ihre Schwester.

**h** Er ist fünf Jahre älter ......................... ich.

**i** Heute kommt die Post später ......................... gestern.

**j** Heute ist das Wetter nicht so schön ......................... letzte Woche.

# Superlatives of adjectives

---

### What is a superlative adjective?
A **superlative adjective** in English is one with -est on the end of it or most
or least in front of it, that is used to compare people or things, for example,
thinnest, most beautiful.

---

➤ In German, to say that something or someone is *easiest, youngest, most expensive* and so on,
you add **-st** to the simple form of the adjective. As with comparative forms, the vowel in the
simple form can change. Superlative forms are generally used with the definite article and
take the same weak endings as their simple forms.

| | |
|---|---|
| **Deine Hausaufgaben waren die einfach<u>sten</u>.** | Your homework was easiest. |
| **Sie ist die Jüng<u>ste</u> in der Familie.** | She is the youngest in the family. |
| **Ich wollte die teuer<u>ste</u> Jacke im Laden kaufen.** | I wanted to buy the most expensive jacket in the shop. |

➤ Adjectives ending in **-t**, **-tz**, **-z**, **-sch**, **-ss** or **-ß** form the superlative by adding **-est** instead of
**-st**.

| | |
|---|---|
| **der/die/das schlechteste** | the worst |
| **Das war der schlecht<u>este</u> Film seit Jahren.** | That was the worst film in years. |
| **der/die/das schmerzhafteste** | the most painful |
| **Das war ihre schmerzhaft<u>este</u> Verletzung.** | That was her most painful injury. |
| **der/die/das süßeste** | the sweetest |
| **Ich möchte den süß<u>esten</u> Nachtisch.** | I would like the sweetest dessert. |
| **der/die/das stolzeste** | the proudest |
| **Sie war die stolz<u>este</u> Mutter in der Gegend.** | She was the proudest mother in the area. |
| **der/die/das frischeste** | the freshest |
| **Für dieses Rezept braucht man das frisch<u>este</u> Obst.** | You need the freshest fruit for this recipe. |

➤ Adjectives ending in **-eu** and **-au** also add **-est** to form the superlative.

| | |
|---|---|
| **der/die/das neueste** | the newest, the latest |
| **Ich brauche die neu<u>este</u> Ausgabe des Wörterbuchs.** | I need the latest edition of the dictionary. |
| **der/die/das schlaueste** | the cleverest |
| **Sie ist die schlau<u>este</u> Schülerin in der Klasse.** | She is the cleverest student in the class. |

➤ The English superlative most, meaning *very*, can be expressed in German by any of the following words.

| Superlative | Meaning |
|---|---|
| äußerst | extremely |
| sehr | very |
| besonders | especially |
| außerordentlich | exceptionally |
| höchst | extremely (*not used with words of one syllable*) |
| furchtbar | terribly (*used only in conversation*) |
| richtig | really/most (*used only in conversation*) |

**Sie ist ein äußerst begabter Mensch.**     She is a most gifted person.
**Das Essen war besonders schlecht.**     The food was really dreadful.
**Der Wein war furchtbar teuer.**     The wine was terribly expensive.
**Das sieht richtig komisch aus.**     That looks really funny.

> *Tip*
> Just as English has some irregular comparative and superlative forms –
> *better* instead of '*more good*', and *worst* instead of '*most bad*' – German also has
> a few irregular forms.

| Adjective | Meaning | Comparative | Meaning | Superlative | Meaning |
|---|---|---|---|---|---|
| gut | good | besser | better | der beste | the best |
| hoch | high | höher | higher | der höchste | the highest |
| viel | much/a lot | mehr | more | der meiste | the most |
| nah | near | näher | nearer | der nächste | the nearest |

**Ich habe eine bessere Idee.**     I have a better idea.
**Wo liegt der nächste Bahnhof?**     Where is the nearest station?

---

### KEY POINTS

✔ Most German superlatives are formed by adding **-st** to the simple form of the adjective.
✔ Adjectives ending in **-t, -tz, -z, -sch, -ss, -ß, -eu** or **-au** form the superlative by adding **-est** instead of **-st**.
✔ **Gut**, **hoch**, **viel** and **nah** have irregular comparative and superlative forms: **gut/besser/der beste, hoch/höher/der höchste, viel/mehr/ der meiste, nah/näher/der nächste**.

---

# Test yourself

**42**  **Translate the following phrases into German.**

**a** the highest mountain ...................................................................................

**b** the most expensive car ...............................................................................

**c** the smallest town ........................................................................................

**d** the biggest shop ..........................................................................................

**e** the sweetest drink .......................................................................................

**f** the most intelligent boy .............................................................................

**g** the worst newspaper ...................................................................................

**h** the most interesting question ...................................................................

**i** the youngest student ..................................................................................

**j** the latest news .............................................................................................

**43**  **Complete the sentences with the correct article and form of the superlative adjective.**

**a** Sie ist ............................. Mädchen in unserer Klasse. **[jung]**

**b** Er hat ............................. Appetit. **[viel]**

**c** Clara ist die Sängerin mit ............................. Stimme. **[hoch]**

**d** Martina ist ............................. Schülerin. **[schlecht]**

**e** Er ist ............................. Boxer der Welt. **[stark]**

**f** Wir dürfen nicht ............................. Fehler machen. **[klein]**

**g** Dies ist ............................. Haus der Stadt. **[groß]**

**h** Er ist ............................. Sänger Deutschlands. **[erfolgreich]**

**i** Von unserem Balkon hat man ............................. Aussicht. **[herrlich]**

**j** Sie ist ............................. Läuferin über 100 Meter. **[schnell]**

**44**  **Match the two columns.**

| | |
|---|---|
| **a** hoch | mehr; meiste |
| **b** gut | näher; nächste |
| **c** viel | lieber; liebste |
| **d** nah | höher; höchste |
| **e** gern | besser; beste |

# Adverbs

## How adverbs are used

➤ In general, adverbs are used together with:

- verbs (*act <u>quickly</u>, speak <u>strangely</u>, smile <u>cheerfully</u>*)

- adjectives (<u>*rather*</u> *ill, <u>a lot</u> better, <u>deeply</u> sorry*)

- other adverbs (<u>*really*</u> *fast, <u>too</u> quickly, <u>very</u> well*)

➤ Adverbs can also relate to the whole sentence; they often tell you what the speaker is thinking or feeling.
<u>Fortunately</u> , Jan had already left.
<u>Actually</u>, I don't think I'll come.

## How adverbs are formed

### The basic rules

➤ Many English adverbs end in *-ly*, which is added to the end of the adjective
(*quick* → *quickly*; *sad* → *sadly*; *frequent* → *frequently*).

➤ In contrast, most German adverbs used to comment on verbs are simply adjectives used as adverbs. And the good news is that unlike adjectives, they do not change by adding different endings.
**Habe ich das <u>richtig</u> gehört?**     Did I hear that correctly?
**Er war <u>schick</u> angezogen.**     He was stylishly dressed.

➤ A small number of German adverbs which do not directly comment on the verb are formed by adding **-weise** or **-sweise** to a noun.

| Noun | Meaning | Adverb | Meaning |
|------|---------|--------|---------|
| **das Beispiel** | example | **beispielsweise** | for example |
| **die Beziehung** | relation, connection | **beziehungsweise** | or/or rather/ that is to say |
| **der Schritt** | step | **schrittweise** | step by step |
| **die Zeit** | time | **zeitweise** | at times |
| **der Zwang** | compulsion | **zwangsweise** | compulsorily |

For further explanation of grammatical terms, please see pages viii-xii.

*Grammar Extra!*
Some German adverbs are also formed by adding **-erweise** to an uninflected adjective.
These adverbs are mainly used by the person speaking to express an opinion.

| Adjective | Meaning | Adverb | Meaning |
|---|---|---|---|
| erstaunlich | astonishing | erstaunlicherweise | astonishingly enough |
| glücklich | happy, fortunate | glücklicherweise | fortunately |
| komisch | strange, funny | komischerweise | strangely enough |

➤ There is another important group of adverbs which are NOT formed from adjectives or nouns, for example, words like **unten**, **oben** and **leider**.

| **Das beste Buch lag <u>unten</u> auf dem Stapel.** | The best book was at the bottom of the pile. |
|---|---|
| **Die Schlafzimmer sind <u>oben</u>.** | The bedrooms are upstairs. |
| **Ich kann <u>leider</u> nicht kommen.** | Unfortunately I can't come. |

➤ Adverbs of time fit into this category and the following are some common ones.

| Adverb of time | Meaning |
|---|---|
| endlich | finally |
| heute | today |
| immer | always |
| morgen | tomorrow |
| morgens | in the mornings |
| sofort | at once |

| **Sie kann erst <u>morgen</u> kommen.** | She can't come till tomorrow. |
|---|---|
| **Priska hat <u>immer</u> Hunger.** | Priska is always hungry. |
| **Ja, ich mache das <u>sofort</u>.** | Yes, I'll do it at once. |

➤ Adverbs often express the idea of 'to what extent', for example, words in English like *extremely* and *especially*. These are sometimes called adverbs of degree. Some common adverbs of this type in German are:

| Adverb of degree | Meaning |
|---|---|
| äußerst | extremely |
| besonders | especially |
| beträchtlich | considerably |
| fast | almost |
| kaum | hardly, scarcely |
| ziemlich | fairly |

| Es hat mir nicht <u>besonders</u> gefallen. | I didn't particularly like it. |
| Ich bin <u>fast</u> fertig. | I'm almost finished. |
| Er war <u>ziemlich</u> sauer. | He was quite angry. |

## Adverbs of place

➤ Adverbs of place are words such as *where?*, *there*, *up*, *nowhere*. German adverbs of place behave very differently from their English counterparts.

- where there is no movement involved and the adverb is simply referring to a location, you use the form of the adverb you find in the dictionary.

| <u>Wo</u> ist sie? | Where is she? |
| Sie sind nicht <u>da</u>. | They're not there. |
| <u>Hier</u> darf man nicht parken. | You can't park here. |

- to show some movement AWAY from the person speaking, you use the adverb **hin**.

| Oliver und Andrea geben heute eine Party. Gehen wir <u>hin</u>? | Oliver and Andrea are having a party today. Shall we go? |

In German, **hin** is often added to another adverb to create what are called compound adverbs, which show there is some movement involved. In English, we would just use adverbs in this case.

| Compound adverb | Meaning |
| --- | --- |
| dahin | (to) there |
| dorthin | there |
| hierhin | here |
| irgendwohin | (to) somewhere or other |
| überallhin | everywhere |
| wohin? | where (to)? |

| <u>Wohin</u> fährst du? | Where are you going? |
| Sie liefen <u>überallhin</u>. | They ran everywhere. |

- to show some movement TOWARDS the person speaking, you use the adverb **her**. As with **hin**, this is often added to another adverb.

| Compound adverb | Meaning |
| --- | --- |
| daher | from there |
| hierher | here |
| irgendwoher | from somewhere or other |
| überallher | from all over |
| woher? | where from? |

| <u>Woher</u> kommst du? | Where do you come from? |
| <u>Woher</u> hast du das? | Where did you get that from? |
| Das habe ich <u>irgendwoher</u> gekriegt. | I got that from somewhere or other. |

For further explanation of grammatical terms, please see pages viii-xii.

**KEY POINTS**

✔ Many German adverbs are simply adjectives used as adverbs, but they are not declined, unlike adjectives.

✔ In German, some adverbs are formed by adding **-weise** or **-sweise** to a noun.

✔ Compound adverbs formed by adding **hin** or **her** are often used to show movement away from or towards the person speaking (or writing).

# Test yourself

**45** **Fill the gap with an adverb ending in -weise made from the noun or adjective shown. The first one has been done for you.**

**a** Er hat das Rennen ..*erstaunlicherweise*.. gewonnen. **[erstaunlich]**

**b** Deutschland hat viele Berge, ........................................... die Zugspitze. **[Beispiel]**

**c** Ihre Leistungen haben sich ........................................... verbessert. **[Schritt]**

**d** Er kaufte sich ........................................... einen Laptop. **[klug]**

**e** Es gab ........................................... keine Unfälle. **[glücklich]**

**f** Wir mussten ........................................... eine andere Wohnung mieten. **[Zeit]**

**g** Petra trank ........................................... Limonade. **[Liter]**

**h** Sie hat mir ........................................... mit den Hausaufgaben geholfen. **[nett]**

**i** Er wollte das Geld ........................................... wieder zurückhaben. **[verständlich]**

**j** Ich habe mich ........................................... geirrt. **[möglich]**

**46** **Translate the following sentences into German.**

**a** My room is downstairs. ...........................................................................

**b** Unfortunately we lost the match.

...........................................................................

**c** Please do it at once. ...........................................................................

**d** It's almost 3 o'clock. ...........................................................................

**e** I'll go shopping tomorrow. ...........................................................................

**f** I was there too. ...........................................................................

**g** I really don't think that's a good idea.

...........................................................................

**h** Did I understand you correctly?

...........................................................................

**i** Please do your homework quickly.

...........................................................................

**j** Unfortunately I couldn't hear what he said.

...........................................................................

# Test yourself

**47** **Fill the gap using** *hin* **(for movement away) or** *her* **(for movement towards). The first one has been done for you.**

**a** Heute Abend ist eine Party - da gehen wir .........*hin*.........!

**b** Wo kommst du denn ......................... ?

**c** Komm ......................... zu mir!

**d** Wenn du willst, geh doch ......................... zu ihr!

**e** Wir buchten die Reise ......................... und zurück.

**f** Die Menschen kamen von überall ......................... .

**g** Berlin? Da fliege ich morgen ......................... .

**h** Wo hast du das ganze Geld ......................... ?

**i** Wo willst du ......................... ?

**j** Wir fuhren bis zum Wald ......................... .

# Comparatives and superlatives of adverbs

## Comparative adverbs

> **What is a comparative adverb?**
> A **comparative adverb** is one which, in English, has -er on the end of it
> or *more* or *less* in front of it, for example, *earlier, later, sooner,*
> *more/less frequently.*

➤ Adverbs can be used to make comparisons in German, just as they can in English. The comparative of adverbs is formed in exactly the same way as that of adjectives, that is by adding **-er** to the basic form. **Als** is used for *than*.

| | |
|---|---|
| **Sie läuft schneller als ihr Bruder.** | She runs faster than her brother. |
| **Ich sehe ihn seltener als früher.** | I see him less often than before. |

➤ To make *as ... as* or *not as ... as* comparisons with adverbs, you use the same phrases as with adjectives.

- **so ... wie**  as ... as
  **Er läuft so schnell wie sein Bruder.**   He runs as fast as his brother.

- **nicht so ... wie**  not as ... as
  **Sie kann nicht so gut schwimmen**   She can't swim as well as you.
  **wie du.**

➤ The idea of *more and more ...* is expressed in German by using **immer** and the comparative form.

| | |
|---|---|
| **Die Männer sprachen immer lauter.** | The men were talking louder and louder. |

➤ *the more ... the more ...* is expressed in German by **je ... desto ...** or **je ... umso ...**

| | |
|---|---|
| **Je eher, desto besser.** | The sooner the better. |
| **Je schneller sie fährt, umso mehr Angst habe ich!** | The faster she drives, the more frightened I am! |

⇨ *For more information on **Comparatives of adjectives**, see page 67.*

## Superlative adverbs

> **What is a superlative adverb?**
> A **superlative adverb** is one which, in English, has -est on the end of it or *most* or
> *least* in front of it, for example, *soonest, fastest, most/least frequently.*

➤ The superlative of adverbs in German is formed in the following way and, unlike adjectives, is not declined:

**am** + *adverb* + **-sten**

| | |
|---|---|
| **Wer von ihnen arbeitet am schnellsten?** | Which of them works fastest? |
| **Er hat es am langsamsten gemacht.** | He did it slowest. |

For further explanation of grammatical terms, please see pages viii-xii.

➤ Adverbs ending in **-d, -t, -tz, -z, -sch, -ss,** or **-ß** form the superlative by adding **-esten**. This makes pronunciation easier.

| | |
|---|---|
| **Das Erdbeereis war bei den Kindern am beliebt<u>esten</u>.** | The strawberry ice cream was the most popular one with the kids. |
| **Am heiß<u>esten</u> war es in Südspanien.** | It was hottest in southern Spain. |

⇨ *For more information on **Superlatives of adjectives**, see page 71.*

[*i*] Note that some superlative adverbs are used to show the extent of a quality rather than a comparison. The following adverbs are used in this way:

| Adverb | Meaning |
|---|---|
| **bestens** | very well |
| **höchstens** | at the most/at best |
| **meistens** | mostly/most often |
| **spätestens** | at the latest |
| **wenigstens** | at least |

| | |
|---|---|
| **Die Geschäfte gehen <u>bestens</u>.** | Business is going very well. |
| **Er kommt <u>meistens</u> zu spät an.** | He usually arrives late. |
| **<u>Wenigstens</u> bekomme ich mehr Geld dafür.** | At least I'm getting more money for it. |

## Adverbs with irregular comparatives and superlatives

➤ A few German adverbs have irregular comparative and superlative forms.

| Adverb | Meaning | Comparative | Meaning | Superlative | Meaning |
|---|---|---|---|---|---|
| **gern** | well | **lieber** | better | **am liebsten** | best |
| **bald** | soon | **eher** | sooner | **am ehesten** | soonest |
| **viel** | much, a lot | **mehr** | more | **am meisten** | most |

| | |
|---|---|
| **<u>Am liebsten</u> lese ich Kriminalromane.** | I like detective stories best. |
| **Sie hat <u>am meisten</u> gewonnen.** | She won the most. |

---

### KEY POINTS

✔ Comparatives of adverbs are formed in the same way as comparatives of adjectives, adding **-er** to the basic form.

✔ To compare people or things, you use **so ... wie**, **ebenso ... wie** or **nicht so ... wie**.

✔ *Than* in comparatives of adverbs corresponds to **als**.

✔ Superlatives of adverbs are formed by using the formula **am** + *adverb* + **-sten/-esten**.

✔ Unlike adjectives, adverbs do not change their form to agree with the verb, adjective or other adverb they relate to.

# Test yourself

**48** **Fill the gap with a comparative adverb.**

**a** Ich kann dich nicht hören. Du musst ......................... sprechen. **[laut]**

**b** Er ist sehr sportlich. Er geht ......................... ins Fitnessstudio als ich. **[oft]**

**c** Wir müssen ......................... gehen oder wir kommen zu spät! **[schnell]**

**d** Sie sind reich. Sie verdienen ......................... als ich. **[mehr]**

**e** Du bist zu dick. Du solltest ......................... essen. **[wenig]**

**f** In Italien scheint immer die Sonne. Dort ist es ......................... als hier. **[warm]**

**g** Du hättest fast einen Unfall gehabt. Du musst auf der Straße .........................
aufpassen! **[gut]**

**h** Ich stehe nicht gern früh auf. In den Ferien kann ich ......................... schlafen. **[lang]**

**i** Wenn du über den Zaun willst, musst du ......................... springen. **[hoch]**

**j** Der Bildschirm ist viel zu hell. Du solltest ihn ......................... einstellen. **[dunkel]**

**49** **Match the sentences that go together.**

**a** Sie hat teuer eingekauft.    Sie liebt gutes Essen.

**b** Sie ist sehr fit.    Sie trinkt gerne Bier.

**c** Sie isst zu viel.    Sie hat wenig Geld.

**d** Sie geht abends in die Kneipe.    Sie hat viel bezahlen müssen.

**e** Sie ist arm.    Sie treibt viel Sport.

**50** **Fill the gap with the appropriate superlative adverb, using *am*. The first one has been done for you**

**a** Er arbeitet von allen Schülern *am fleißigsten*. **[fleißig]**

**b** Im Fernsehen sieht sie ......................... Krimis. **[gern]**

**c** Peter ist ......................... gelaufen. **[schnell]**

**d** Von allen meinen Freunden sehe ich Thomas ......................... . **[selten]**

**e** Alle sagten ihre Meinung, aber er sprach ......................... **[laut]**

**f** Claudia hat die Aufgabe ......................... gelöst. **[gut]**

**g** Max wird ......................... 18 Jahre alt werden. **[bald]**

**h** Meine Mutter sieht in unserer Familie ......................... fern. **[viel]**

**i** Himbeereis verkauft sich von allen Sorten ......................... **[schlecht]**

**j** Im Fernsehen liebe ich Talkshows ......................... **[wenig]**

# Word order with adverbs

➤ In English, adverbs can come in different places in a sentence.
  I'm <u>never</u> coming back.
  See you <u>soon</u>!
  <u>Suddenly</u> the phone rang.
  I'd <u>really</u> like to come.

➤ This is also true of adverbs in German, but as a general rule they are placed close to the word to which they refer.

- Adverbs of <u>time</u> often come first in the sentence, but this is not fixed.
  **<u>Morgen</u> gehen wir ins Theater** OR      We're going to the theatre tomorrow.
  **Wir gehen <u>morgen</u> ins Theater.**

- Adverbs of <u>place</u> can be put at the beginning of a sentence to provide emphasis.
  **<u>Dort</u> haben sie Fußball gespielt** OR     They played football there.
  **Sie haben <u>dort</u> Fußball gespielt**

- Adverbs of <u>manner</u> are adverbs which comment on verbs. These are likely to come <u>after</u> the verb to which they refer, but in tenses which are made up of **haben** or **sein** + the past participle of the main verb, they come immediately <u>before</u> the past participle.
  **Sie spielen <u>gut</u>.**             They play well.
  **Sie haben heute <u>gut</u> gespielt.**     They played well today.
  **Du benimmst dich immer <u>schlecht</u>.**   You always behave badly.
  **Du hast dich <u>schlecht</u> benommen.**   You have behaved badly.

⇨ *For more information on* **Forming the past participle**, *see page 154.*

➤ Where there is more than one adverb in a sentence, it's useful to remember the following rule: 'time, manner, place'
  **Wir haben <u>gestern</u> <u>gut</u> <u>dorthin</u>**     We found our way there all right yesterday.
     **gefunden.**
  **gestern** = adverb of time
  **gut** = adverb of manner
  **dorthin** = adverb of place

➤ Where there is a pronoun object (a word like *her*, *it*, *me* or *them*) in a sentence, it comes before all adverbs.
  **Sie haben <u>es gestern sehr billig</u>**     They bought it very cheaply yesterday.
     **gekauft**.
  **es** = pronoun object
  **gestern** = adverb of time
  **billig** = adverb of manner

⇨ *For more information on* **Using direct object pronouns**, *see page 94.*

---

**KEY POINTS**

✔ In German, the position of adverbs in a sentence is not fixed, but they generally come close to the words they refer to.
✔ Where there is more than one adverb in a sentence, it is useful to remember the rule: time, manner, place.
✔ Where there is a pronoun object in a sentence, it comes before all adverbs.

# Test yourself

**51** **Translate the following sentences into German.**

**a** I bought it cheaply. ......................................................................................

**b** Shall we go to the cinema today? ...................................................................

**c** You behaved well yesterday. .........................................................................

**d** She earns a lot of money. .............................................................................

**e** It took quite a long time. ..............................................................................

**f** There's not enough milk in the fridge.

......................................................................................................................

**g** She buys too many shoes. .............................................................................

**h** It rains a lot in Scotland. ..............................................................................

**i** There's not a lot to see here. ........................................................................

**j** They played football yesterday. ....................................................................

**52** **Make a sentence with the elements provided, putting the adverb in the correct place. The first one has been done for you.**

**a** billig/gestern/wir/eingekauft/haben
   *Wir haben gestern billig eingekauft.* ..........................................................

**b** heute/Fußball/wollen/spielen/wir ..............................................................

**c** alle/haben/gegessen/gut/wir ......................................................................

**d** du/gegangen/dorthin/warum/bist

......................................................................................................................

**e** möchte/gehen/ich/nach Hause/gern

......................................................................................................................

**f** euch/am meisten/wer/verdient/von

......................................................................................................................

**g** langsam/zu/kam/er/mich/auf ......................................................................

**h** benehmen/du/schlecht/musst/dich/so

......................................................................................................................

**i** schwimmt/als/Schwester/ihre/sie/schneller

......................................................................................................................

**j** spät/er/zu/meistens/kommt .........................................................................

**53 Cross out the adverbs that are unlikely to fit in the gap.**

| | | |
|---|---|---|
| **a** | Sie haben ... gespielt. | gut/am höchsten/leider/gestern |
| **b** | Das ist ... passiert. | leider/gestern/langsamer/dorthin |
| **c** | Er hat ... Durst. | gestern/immer/ständig/schnell |
| **d** | Du kommst ... zu spät. | gewöhnlich/meistens/oft/bald |
| **e** | Sie fährt ... Fahrrad. | am liebsten/gestern/heute/meistens |
| **f** | Es geht mir ... . | besser/schneller/äußerst/schlecht |
| **g** | Ich war ... zornig. | schrittweise/ständig/ziemlich/äußerst |
| **h** | Die Ware ist ... teuer. | heute/sehr/besonders/fast |
| **i** | Wir sind ... gekommen. | hierher/irgendwoher/schnell/spätestens |
| **j** | Sie arbeitet ... . | am besten/am schnellsten/am höchsten/am meisten |

# Emphasizers

> **What is an emphasizer?**
> An **emphasizer** is a type of word commonly used in both German and English, especially in the spoken language, to emphasize or change the meaning of a sentence.

➤ The following words are the most common emphasizers.

- **aber** is used to add emphasis to a statement

  **Das ist <u>aber</u> schön!**      Oh, that's pretty!

  **Diese Jacke ist <u>aber</u> teuer!**      This jacket is really expensive!

- **denn** is also used as a conjunction, but here it is used as an adverb to emphasize the meaning.

  **Was ist <u>denn</u> hier los?**      What's going on here then?

  **Wo <u>denn</u>?**      Where?

> *Tip*
> You can't always translate emphasizers directly, especially **denn** and **aber**.

⇨ *For more information on **Conjunctions**, see page 233.*

- **doch** is used in one of three ways

  As a positive reply to a negative statement or question:

  **Hat es dir nicht gefallen? – <u>Doch</u>!**      Didn't you like it? – Oh yes, I did!

  To strengthen an imperative, that is the form of a verb used when giving instructions:

  **Lass ihn <u>doch</u>!**      Just leave him.

  To make a question out of a statement:

  **Das schaffst du <u>doch</u>?**      You'll manage it, won't you?

⇨ *For more information on **Imperatives**, see page 143.*

- **mal** can be used in one of two ways

  With imperatives:

  **Komm <u>mal</u> her!**      Come here!

  **Moment <u>mal</u>, bitte!**      Just a minute!

  In informal language:

  **<u>Mal</u> sehen.**      We'll see.

  **Hören Sie <u>mal</u> ...**      Look here now ...

  **Er soll es nur <u>mal</u> versuchen!**      Just let him try it!

- **ja** can also be used in one of two ways
  To strengthen a statement:

| | |
|---|---|
| **Er sieht ja wie seine Mutter aus.** | He looks like his mother. |
| **Das kann ja sein.** | That may well be. |

  In informal language:

| | |
|---|---|
| **Ja und?** | So what?/What then? |
| **Das ist ja lächerlich.** | That's ridiculous. |
| **Das ist es ja.** | That's just it. |

- **schon** also has more than one use
  It is used informally with an imperative:

| | |
|---|---|
| **Mach schon!** | Get on with it! |

  It is also used in other informal statements:

| | |
|---|---|
| **Da kommt sie schon wieder!** | Here she comes again! |
| **Schon gut. Ich habe verstanden.** | Okay, I get the message. |

---

**KEY POINTS**

✔ There are lots of little adverbs used in both English and German to emphasize the meaning of a sentence in some way.

✔ The most common of these are **aber**, **denn**, **doch**, **mal**, **ja** and **schon**.

**54** **Form a sentence using the elements below. The first one has been done for you.**

**a** aber/ist/billig/das   *Das ist aber billig!*

**b** her/doch/mal/komm

**c** ja/ist/das/gerade/es

**d** verstanden/schon/ich/dich/habe

**e** wirklich/ist/ärgerlich/das

**f** war/da/was/denn/los

**g** kann/gut/das/sein/schon

**h** weiß/auch/ich/nicht/es/ja

**i** mir/Sie/hören/doch/zu/mal

**j** reden/ihn/doch/lass

**55** **Match the two columns to indicate the correct translation of the word *doch*.**

**a** Du hast ihn nicht gesehen? – Doch!      Yes, I do.

**b** Du bist mir nicht böse? – Doch!      Yes, I have.

**c** Du magst kein Kaugummi? – Doch!      Yes, I was.

**d** Du hast nicht abgenommen? – Doch!      Yes, I did.

**e** Du warst nicht in der Schule? – Doch!      Yes, I am.

# Pronouns

## What is a pronoun?
A **pronoun** is a word you use instead of a noun, when you do not need or want to name someone or something directly, for example, *it*, *you*, *none*.

➤ There are several different types of pronoun:

- personal pronouns such as *I*, *you*, *he*, *her* and *they*, which are used to refer to yourself, the person you are talking to, or other people and things. They can be either subject pronouns (*I*, *you*, *he* and so on) or object pronouns (*him*, *her*, *them* and so on).

- possessive pronouns like *mine* and *yours*, which show who someone or something belongs to.

- indefinite pronouns like *someone* or *nothing*, which refer to people or things in a general way without saying exactly who or what they are.

- relative pronouns like *who*, *which* or *that*, which link two parts of a sentence together.

- demonstrative pronouns like *this* or *those*, which point things or people out.

- reflexive pronouns – a type of object pronoun that forms part of German reflexive verbs like **sich setzen** (meaning *to sit down*) or **sich waschen** (meaning *to wash*).

  ⇨ *For more information on **Reflexive verbs**, see page 138.*

- the pronouns **wer?** (meaning *who?*) and **was?** (meaning *what?*) and their different forms, which are used to ask questions.

➤ Pronouns often stand in for a noun to save repeating it.
  I finished my homework and gave <u>it</u> to my teacher.
  Do you remember Jack? I saw <u>him</u> at the weekend.

➤ Word order with personal pronouns is usually different in German and English.

# Personal pronouns: subject

---

### What is a subject pronoun?

A **subject pronoun** is a word such as *I*, *he*, *she* and *they*. It refers to the person or thing which performs the action expressed by the verb. Pronouns stand in for nouns when it is clear who is being talked about, for example: *My brother isn't here at the moment. He'll be back in an hour.*

---

## Using subject pronouns

➤ Here are the German subject pronouns or personal pronouns in the nominative case:

| Subject Pronoun (Nominative Case) | Meaning |
|---|---|
| ich | I |
| du | you (*familiar*) |
| er | he/it |
| sie | she/it |
| es | it/he/she |
| man | one |
| wir | we |
| ihr | you (*plural*) |
| sie | they |
| Sie | you (*polite*) |

| | |
|---|---|
| **Ich fahre nächste Woche nach Italien.** | I'm going to Italy next week. |
| **Wir wohnen in Frankfurt.** | We live in Frankfurt. |

⇨ *For more information on the **Nominative case**, see page 11.*

## du, ihr or Sie?

➤ In English we have only <u>one</u> way of saying *you*. In German, there are <u>three</u> words: **du**, **ihr** and **Sie**. The word you use depends on:

- whether you are talking to one person or more than one person

- whether you are talking to a friend or family member, or someone else

➤ Use the familiar **du** if talking to one person <u>you know well</u>, such as a friend, someone younger than you or a relative

    **Kommst <u>du</u> mit ins Kino?**      Are you coming to the cinema?

➤ Use the formal or polite **Sie** if talking to one person <u>you do not know so well</u>, such as your teacher, your boss or a stranger.

    **Was haben <u>Sie</u> gesagt?**      What did you say?

---

For further explanation of grammatical terms, please see pages viii-xii.

➤ Use the familiar **ihr** if talking to <u>more than one person you know well</u> or relatives.
   **Also, was wollt <u>ihr</u> heute Abend essen?**   So, what do you want to eat tonight?

➤ Use **Sie** if talking to <u>more than one person you do not know so well</u>.
   **Wo fahren <u>Sie</u> hin?**           Where are you going to?

| | |
|---|---|
| **<u>Ich</u> gebe dir das Buch zurück, wenn <u>ich</u> es zu Ende gelesen habe.** | I'll give you the book back when I've finished reading it. |
| **<u>Du</u> kannst mich morgen besuchen, wenn <u>du</u> Zeit hast.** | You can come and visit me tomorrow, if you have time. |
| **Wir wären Ihnen sehr dankbar, wenn <u>Sie</u> uns telefonisch benachrichtigen würden.** | We'd be very grateful if you could phone and let us know. |

## er/sie/es

➤ In English we generally refer to things (such as *table, book, car*) only as *it*. In German, **er** (meaning *he*), **sie** (meaning *she*) and **es** (meaning *it*) are used to talk about a thing, as well as about a person or an animal. You use **er** for <u>masculine nouns</u>, **sie** for <u>feminine nouns</u> and **es** for <u>neuter nouns</u>.

| | | |
|---|---|---|
| **<u>Der</u> Tisch ist groß**. | → | **<u>Er</u> ist groß**. |
| The table is large. | → | It is large. |
| **<u>Die</u> Jacke ist blau**. | → | **<u>Sie</u> ist blau**. |
| The jacket is blue. | → | It is blue. |
| **<u>Das</u> Kind stand auf**. | → | **<u>Es</u> stand auf**. |
| The child stood up. | → | He/she stood up. |

ⓘ Note that English speakers often make the mistake of calling all objects *es*.

➤ The subject pronoun **sie** (meaning *they*) is used in the plural to talk about things, as well as people or animals. Use **sie** for <u>masculine</u>, <u>feminine</u> and <u>neuter nouns</u>.

| | |
|---|---|
| **„Wo sind Michael und Sebastian?" –** | "Where are Michael and Sebastian?" – |
| **„<u>Sie</u> sind im Garten."** | "They're in the garden." |
| **„Hast du die Karten gekauft?" –** | "Did you buy the tickets?" – |
| **„Nein, <u>sie</u> waren ausverkauft."** | "No, they were sold out." |

## man

➤ This is often used in German in the same way as we use *you* in English to mean people in general.

| | |
|---|---|
| **Wie schreibt <u>man</u> das?** | How do you spell that? |
| **<u>Man</u> kann nie wissen.** | You never know. |

➤ **Man** can also mean *they* used in a vague way.

| | |
|---|---|
| **<u>Man</u> sagt, dass das Wetter immer** **schlecht ist.** | They say the weather is always bad. |

---

*Tip*

**Man** is often used to avoid a passive construction in German.

| | |
|---|---|
| **<u>Man</u> hat das schon oft im** **Fernsehen gezeigt.** | It's already been shown a lot on TV. |

⇨ *For more information on the* **Passive**, *see page 205.*

The form of the verb you use with **man** is the same as the **er/sie/es** form.

⇨ *For more information on* **Verbs**, *see page 122.*

---

**KEY POINTS**

✔ The German subject pronouns are: **ich**, **du**, **er**, **sie**, **es**, **Sie** and **man** in the singular, and **wir**, **ihr**, **sie** and **Sie** in the plural.

✔ To say *you* in German, use **du** if you are talking to one person you know well or to a child; use **ihr** if you are talking to more than one person you know well and use **Sie** if you are talking to one or more people you do not know well.

✔ **Er/sie/es** (masculine/feminine/neuter singular) and **sie** (masculine or feminine or neuter plural) are used to refer to things, as well as to people or animals.

✔ **Man** can mean *you*, *they* or people in general. It is often used instead of a passive construction.

---

# Test yourself

**56** **Translate the following sentences into German.**

**a** He speaks German. ..........................................................................................

**b** She eats a lot. ..............................................................................................

**c** Does he have any sisters? ...............................................................................

**d** We have a cat. .............................................................................................

**e** I can't swim. ...............................................................................................

**f** She has black hair. .......................................................................................

**g** How old is she? ...........................................................................................

**h** I live in Birmingham. ....................................................................................

**i** How do you say that? (use **man**) .....................................................................

**j** They are married. .........................................................................................

**57** **Match the noun to the pronoun that would replace it.**

| | | |
|---|---|---|
| **a** der Zug | ihr |
| **b** das Buch | sie |
| **c** meine Klassenkameraden | wir |
| **d** mein Vater und ich | er |
| **e** Max und du | es |

**58** **Fill the gap with _er, sie, es_ (singular) or _sie_ (plural).**

**a** Ich lese gerade ein Buch, ........................ ist sehr interessant.

**b** Wo ist dein Bruder? – ........................ ist in der Schule.

**c** Habt ihr eure Bücher mitgebracht? – Nein, wir haben ........................ vergessen.

**d** Euer Haus gefällt mir, ........................ ist sehr schön.

**e** Ich möchte diese Jacke, aber ........................ ist sehr teuer.

**f** Ich habe eine Katze, ........................ ist 8 Jahre alt.

**g** Wo ist Ihr Pass? – ........................ ist in meiner Tasche.

**h** Das ist Frau Schmidt, ........................ ist Krankenschwester.

**i** Wo sind Peter und Leo? – ........................ sind ins Kino gegangen.

**j** Das ist eine schöne Hose. – Ich habe ........................ in Paris gekauft.

# Personal pronouns: direct object

> **What is a direct object pronoun?**
> A **direct object pronoun** is a word such as *me*, *him*, *us* and *them* which is used instead of the noun to stand in for the person or thing most directly affected by the action expressed by the verb.

## Using direct object pronouns

➤ Direct object pronouns stand in for nouns when it is clear who or what is being talked about, and save having to repeat the noun.

> I've lost my glasses. Have you seen <u>them</u>?
> "Have you met Jo?"– "Yes, I really like <u>her</u>!"

➤ Here are the German direct object pronouns in the accusative case:

| Direct Object Pronoun (Accusative Case) | Meaning |
|---|---|
| mich | me |
| dich | you (*familiar*) |
| ihn | him/it |
| sie | her/it |
| es | it/him/her |
| einen | one |
| uns | us |
| euch | you (*plural*) |
| sie | them |
| Sie | you (*polite*) |

| | |
|---|---|
| **Ich lade <u>dich</u> zum Essen ein.** | I'll invite you for a meal. |
| **Sie hat <u>ihn</u> letztes Jahr kennengelernt.** | She met him last year. |

## Word order with direct object pronouns

➤ In tenses consisting of one verb part only, for example the present and the simple past, the direct object pronoun usually comes directly <u>AFTER</u> the verb.

> **Sie bringen <u>ihn</u> nach Hause.**          They'll take him home.

➤ In tenses such as the perfect that are formed with **haben** or **sein** and the past participle, the direct object pronoun comes <u>AFTER</u> the part of the verb that comes from **haben** or **sein** and <u>BEFORE</u> the past participle.

> **Er hat <u>mich</u> durchs Fenster gesehen.**     He saw me through the window.

➤ When a modal verb like **wollen** (meaning to *want*) or **können** (meaning *to be able to*, *can*) is followed by another verb in the infinitive (the to form of the verb), the direct object pronoun comes directly <u>AFTER</u> the modal verb.

    **Wir wollen <u>Sie</u> nicht mehr sehen.**       We don't want to see you anymore.

⇨ *For more information on **Modal verbs**, see page 184.*

---

### KEY POINTS

✔ The German direct object pronouns are: **mich**, **dich**, **ihn**, **sie**, **es**, **Sie** and **einen** in the singular, and **uns**, **euch**, **sie** and **Sie** in the plural.

✔ The direct object pronoun usually comes directly after the verb, but in tenses like the perfect it comes after the part of the verb that comes from **haben** or **sein** and before the past participle.

✔ When a modal verb such as **wollen** is followed by the infinitive of another verb, the direct object pronoun comes directly after the modal verb.

# Test yourself

**59 Cross out the names and things the object pronoun could not refer to.**

**a dich**      meinen Freund/Peter/den Direktor/meine Schwester

**b sie**      meine Eltern/das Publikum/Peter und Inge/die Engländer

**c ihn**      Peter/meine Katze/mein Buch/meinen Bruder

**d euch**      die Lehrer/den Lehrer/meine Kinder/meine Eltern

**e es**      meine Katze/mein Buch/das Klavier/mein Haus

**f uns**      meine Klassenkameraden/dich und mich/euch und sie/meine Familie

**g Sie**      Herrn Becker/Frau Schmidt/meine Mutter/meinen Bruder

**h einen**      alle Menschen/den Stuhl/die Leute/Peter

**i sie**      Frau Schmidt/Marie/meinen Hund/meine Katze

**j Sie**      das Publikum/Frau Müller und Herrn Schulz/meine Eltern/unsere Gäste

**60 Replace the highlighted words with an object pronoun.**

**a** Siehst du **Frau Schmidt**? ..................................................................................

**b** Wir haben **Peter und Inge** besucht. ..................................................................

**c** Möchten Sie **diesen Wein** probieren? ................................................................

**d** Du musst **dein Zimmer** aufräumen! ...................................................................

**e** Hast du **deinen Bruder** eingeladen? ...................................................................

**f** Du solltest mehr auf **deine Eltern** hören. ............................................................

**g** Hast du **meine Schlüssel** irgendwo gesehen? .......................................................

**h** Bitte rufen Sie **Petra und mich** morgen an. .........................................................

**i** Hast du **diese CD** gekauft? ..............................................................................

**j** Du musst **dein Auto** öfter waschen. ...................................................................

# Test yourself

**61**  **Translate the following sentences into German.**

**a** Can you see her? ...................................................................................

**b** Do you like this teacher? – No, I hate him.

.................................................................................................................

**c** I like this CD. – Why don't you buy it?

.................................................................................................................

**d** I could see him, but I couldn't hear him.

.................................................................................................................

**e** Do you know this book? – Yes, I have read it.

.................................................................................................................

**f** Where is Paul? – I haven't seen him.

.................................................................................................................

**g** Do you want this apple? – No, I don't want it.

.................................................................................................................

**h** Have you seen Petra and Ruth? – No, I haven't seen them.

.................................................................................................................

**i** Why don't you visit us? ......................................................................

**j** I met them in the park. ........................................................................

# Personal pronouns: indirect object

---

### What is an indirect object pronoun?
When a verb has two objects (a <u>direct</u> one and an <u>indirect</u> one), the **indirect object pronoun** is used instead of a noun to show the person or thing the action is intended to benefit or harm, for example, *me* in *He gave <u>me</u> a book; Can you get <u>me</u> a towel?*

---

## Using indirect object pronouns

➤ It is important to understand the difference between direct and indirect object pronouns, as they have different forms in German:

- an <u>indirect object</u> answers the question *who to?* or *who for?* and *to what?* or *for what?*
  He gave me a book. → *Who did he give the book to?* → me (=*indirect object pronoun*)
  Can you get me a towel? → *Who can you get a towel for?* → me (=*indirect object pronoun*)

- if something answers the question *what?* or *who?*, then it is the <u>direct object</u> and <u>NOT</u> the indirect object
  He gave me a book → *What did he give me?* → a book (=*direct object*)
  Can you get me a towel? → *What can you get me?* → a towel (=*direct object*)

➤ Here are the German indirect object pronouns in the dative case:

| Indirect Object Pronoun (Dative Case) | Meaning |
|---|---|
| mir | to/for me |
| dir | to/for you (*familiar*) |
| ihm | to/for him/it |
| ihr | to/for her/it |
| ihm | to/for it/him/her |
| einem | to/for one |
| uns | to/for us |
| euch | to/for you (*plural*) |
| ihnen | to/for them |
| Ihnen | to/for you (*polite*) |

| | |
|---|---|
| **Er hat <u>mir</u> das geschenkt.** | He gave me that as a present. |
| **Sie haben <u>ihnen</u> eine tolle Geschichte erzählt.** | They told them a great story. |

## Word order with indirect object pronouns

➤ Word order for indirect object pronouns is the same as for direct object pronouns. The pronoun usually comes directly after the verb, except with tenses like the perfect and modal verbs such as **wollen**.

| | |
|---|---|
| **Sie bringt <u>mir</u> das Schwimmen bei.** | She's teaching me how to swim. |
| **Sie hat es <u>ihm</u> gegeben.** | She gave it to him. |
| **Ich will <u>dir</u> etwas sagen.** | I want to tell you something. |

➤ When you have both a direct object pronoun AND an indirect object pronoun in the same sentence, the direct object pronoun or personal pronoun in the accusative <u>always</u> comes first. A good way of remembering this is to think of the following:

PAD = Pronoun Accusative Dative

| | |
|---|---|
| **Sie haben <u>es ihm</u> verziehen.** | They forgave him for it. |
| **Ich bringe <u>es dir</u> schon bei.** | I'll teach you. |

---

**KEY POINTS**

✔ The German indirect object pronouns are: **mir**, **dir**, **ihm**, **ihr**, **ihm**, **Ihnen** and **einem** in the singular, and **uns**, **euch**, **ihnen** and **Ihnen** in the plural.

✔ The indirect object pronoun comes after the verb, except with tenses like the perfect and when used with modal verbs such as **wollen**.

✔ The indirect object pronoun always comes after the direct object pronoun.

# Test yourself

**62** **Translate the following sentences into German.**

**a** Give him a banana. .................................................................................................

**b** Give us the keys. ....................................................................................................

**c** Bring me a chair. ....................................................................................................

**d** Tell me the truth. ...................................................................................................

**e** Give her the present. ..............................................................................................

**f** She didn't answer me. ............................................................................................

**g** He didn't give it to us. ............................................................................................

**h** She gave me a bottle of wine. ...............................................................................

**i** I send her money every week. ...............................................................................

**j** Can you tell me why you did that? ........................................................................

**63** **Match a sentence starting with a name to one starting with a pronoun.**

**a** Martina schrieb ihrer Schwester einen Brief.       Sie schrieb uns eine Karte.

**b** Sophie schrieb Peter und mir eine Karte.       Er schickte ihnen ein Paket.

**c** Marius schickte seiner Mutter ein Paket.       Sie schrieb ihm einen Brief.

**d** Gisela schrieb ihrem Chef einen Brief.       Sie schrieb ihr einen Brief.

**e** Peter schickte Frank und Lina ein Paket.       Er schickte ihr ein Paket.

**64** **Fill the gap with the correct indirect object pronoun. The first one has been done for you.**

**a** Hast du es deinen Eltern gesagt? – Ja, ich habe es ........*ihnen*...... gesagt.

**b** Sprichst du oft mit deinem Bruder? – Nein, ich spreche nicht oft mit ......................... .

**c** Gefällt die der Garten? – Ja, er gefällt ........................ .

**d** Hat Peter dir die CD geschenkt? – Ja, er hat sie ........................ geschenkt.

**e** Gibst du Petra ein Glas Milch? – Ja, ich gebe es ........................ .

**f** Hast du Herrn Becker den Brief gegeben? – Ja, ich habe ihn ........................ gegeben.

**g** Hast du Martin und Gerd das Geld gegeben? – Ja, ich habe es ........................ gegeben.

**h** Haben Sie mir etwas zu sagen? – Nein, ich habe ........................ nichts zu sagen.

**i** Schreibst du deinen Eltern eine Weihnachtskarte? – Ja, ich schreibe ........................ eine Weihnachtskarte.

**j** Gibst du mir die Schlüssel? – Ja, ich gebe sie ........................ .

# Personal pronouns: after prepositions

➤ When a personal pronoun is used after a preposition and refers to a person, the personal pronoun is in the case required by the preposition. For example, the preposition **mit** is always followed by the dative case.

**Ich bin <u>mit ihm</u> spazieren gegangen.**     I went for a walk with him.

➤ When a thing rather than a person is referred to, **da-** is added at the beginning of the preposition:

**Manuela hatte ein Messer geholt**     Manuela had brought a knife and was about
**und wollte <u>damit</u> den Kuchen**        to cut the cake with it.
**schneiden.**

*i* Note that before a preposition beginning with a vowel, the form **dar-** + preposition is used.

**Lege es bitte <u>darauf</u>.**     Put it there please.

➤ The following prepositions are affected in this way:

| Preposition | Preposition + da or dar |
|---|---|
| an | <u>da</u>ran |
| auf | <u>da</u>rauf |
| aus | <u>da</u>raus |
| bei | <u>da</u>bei |
| durch | <u>da</u>durch |
| für | <u>da</u>für |
| in | <u>da</u>rin |
| mit | <u>da</u>mit |
| nach | <u>da</u>nach |
| neben | <u>da</u>neben |
| über | <u>da</u>rüber |
| unter | <u>da</u>runter |
| zwischen | <u>da</u>zwischen |

⇨ *For more information on **Prepositions**, see page 210.*

*i* Note that these combined forms are also used after verbs followed by prepositions.

**sich erinnern an** + accusative case =     to remember
**Ich erinnere mich nicht <u>daran</u>.**     I don't remember (it).

## Grammar Extra!

After certain prepositions used to express movement, that is **aus** (meaning *out* or *from*), **auf** (meaning *on*) and **in** (meaning *in* or *into*), combined forms with **hin** and **her** are used to give more emphasis to the action being carried out.

| Preposition | hin or her + Preposition |
|---|---|
| aus | hinaus/heraus |
| auf | hinauf/herauf |
| in | hinein/herein |

| | |
|---|---|
| **Er ging die Treppe leise <u>hinauf</u>.** | He went up the stairs quietly. |
| **Endlich fand sie unser Zelt und kam <u>herein</u>.** | She finally found our tent and came inside. |
| **Sie öffnete die Reisetasche und legte die Hose <u>hinein</u>.** | She opened the bag and put in her trousers. |

### KEY POINTS

✔ When a personal pronoun referring to a person is used after a preposition, the personal pronoun is in the case required by the preposition.

✔ When a personal pronoun referring to a thing is used after a preposition, the construction **da(r)-** + preposition is used.

# Test yourself

**65** **Translate the following sentences into German.**

**a** It's for her. ...................................................................................................

**b** They came without him. ................................................................................

**c** I went with him. ...........................................................................................

**d** That's between you and me. .........................................................................

**e** Everyone except me saw it. ..........................................................................

**f** The plane is flying above us. ........................................................................

**g** Have you heard from him? ...........................................................................

**h** I did it for her. .............................................................................................

**i** The vase is on the table. ..............................................................................

**j** We are flying to Cologne. ............................................................................

**66** **Fill the gap with the appropriate preposition + _da_ or _dar_. The first one has been done for you.**

**a** Denkst du an die Schlüssel? – Ja ich denke ..... *daran* ...... .

**b** Hast du über meinen Vorschlag nachgedacht? – Ja, ich habe ......................... nachgedacht.

**c** Ist die Tasche unter dem Tisch? – Ja, sie ist ......................... .

**d** Steht der Stuhl neben dem Tisch? – Ja, er steht ......................... .

**e** Hast du aus deinen Fehlern gelernt? – Ja, ich habe ......................... gelernt.

**f** Was ist zwischen den Bergen? – Es ist ein Tal ......................... .

**g** Steigst du auf die Leiter? – Ja, ich steige ......................... .

**h** Führt der Weg über die Wiese? – Ja, er führt ......................... .

**i** Schwimmen die Fische im Aquarium? – Ja, sie schwimmen ......................... .

**j** Gehst du nach dem Essen spazieren? – Ja, ich gehe ......................... spazieren.

**67** **Match the German with its English translation.**

| | |
|---|---|
| **a** Gib es ihr nicht. | Show them to me. |
| **b** Zeige sie mir. | Don't give it to her. |
| **c** Sag ihm das nicht. | Tell me why. |
| **d** Kauf es für sie. | Don't tell him that. |
| **e** Sag mir warum. | Buy it for her. |

# Possessive pronouns

---

### What is a possessive pronoun?

In English you can say *This is my car* or *This car is mine*. In the first sentence *my* is a possessive adjective. In the second, *mine* is a possessive pronoun.

A **possessive pronoun** is one of the words *mine, yours, hers, his, ours* or *theirs*, which are used instead of a noun to show that one thing or person belongs to another, for example, *Ask Carol if this pen is hers*.

---

➤ German possessive pronouns are the same words as the possessive adjectives **mein**, **dein**, **sein**, **ihr**, **unser**, **euer**, **ihr**, **Ihr**, with the same endings, EXCEPT in the masculine nominative singular, the neuter nominative singular and the neuter accusative singular, as shown below.

| | Possessive Adjective | Meaning | Possessive Pronoun | Meaning |
|---|---|---|---|---|
| **Masculine Nominative Singular** | Das ist <u>mein</u> Wagen | That is my car | <u>Dieser Wagen</u> ist <u>meiner</u> | That car is mine |
| **Neuter Nominative Singular** | Das ist <u>mein</u> Buch | That is my book | <u>Dieses Buch</u> ist <u>meins</u> | That book is mine |
| **Neuter Accusative Singular** | Sie hat <u>mein</u> Buch genommen | She has taken my book | Sie hat <u>meins</u> genommen | She has taken mine |

➤ Here is the German possessive pronoun **meiner**, meaning *mine*, in all its forms:

| Case | Masculine Singular | Feminine Singular | Neuter Singular | All Genders Plural |
|---|---|---|---|---|
| **Nominative** | mein<u>er</u> | mein<u>e</u> | mein(e)s | mein<u>e</u> |
| **Accusative** | mein<u>en</u> | mein<u>e</u> | mein(e)s | mein<u>e</u> |
| **Genitive** | mein<u>es</u> | mein<u>er</u> | mein<u>es</u> | mein<u>er</u> |
| **Dative** | mein<u>em</u> | mein<u>er</u> | mein<u>em</u> | mein<u>en</u> |

*i* Note that the nominative and accusative neuter forms only of all the possessive pronouns are often pronounced without the last **-e**, for example **meins** instead of **meines**.

| | |
|---|---|
| **Der Wagen da drüben ist <u>meiner</u>.** | The car over there is mine. |
| **Er ist kleiner als <u>deiner</u>.** | It is smaller than yours. |
| **Das ist besser als <u>meins</u>!** | That's better than mine! |
| **Das Haus nebenan ist schöner als <u>seins</u>.** | The house next door is nicer than his. |
| **Meine Jacke war teurer als <u>ihre</u>.** | My jacket was more expensive than hers. |

---

For further explanation of grammatical terms, please see pages viii-xii.

*ⓘ* Note that **deiner**, meaning *yours (familiar)*, **seiner**, *meaning his/its*, **ihrer**, meaning *hers/its/theirs*, **Ihrer**, meaning *yours (polite)*, **unserer**, meaning *ours* and **euerer**, meaning *yours (plural familiar)* have the same endings as **meiner**.

> *Tip*
> **Unserer**, meaning *ours* is often pronounced **unsrer** and **euerer**, meaning *yours (plural familiar)* is often pronounced **eurer**. This pronunciation is occasionally reflected in writing.

| Case | Masculine Singular | Feminine Singular | Neuter Singular | All Genders Plural |
|---|---|---|---|---|
| **Nominative** | uns(e)rer | uns(e)re | uns(e)res | uns(e)re |
| **Accusative** | uns(e)ren | uns(e)re | uns(e)res | uns(e)re |
| **Genitive** | uns(e)res | uns(e)rer | uns(e)res | uns(e)rer |
| **Dative** | uns(e)rem | uns(e)rer | uns(e)rem | uns(e)ren |

| Case | Masculine Singular | Feminine Singular | Neuter Singular | All Genders Plural |
|---|---|---|---|---|
| **Nominative** | eu(e)rer | eu(e)re | eu(e)res | eu(e)re |
| **Accusative** | eu(e)ren | eu(e)re | eu(e)res | eu(e)re |
| **Genitive** | eu(e)res | eu(e)rer | eu(e)res | eu(e)rer |
| **Dative** | eu(e)rem | eu(e)rer | eu(e)rem | eu(e)ren |

**War euer Urlaub billiger als <u>unsrer</u>?**     Was your holiday cheaper than ours?

*ⓘ* Note the translation of *of mine*, *of yours* etc, where the personal pronoun in the dative is used:

**Er ist ein Freund von <u>mir</u>.**     He is a friend of mine.
**Ich habe eine CD von <u>dir</u> bei mir**     I have a CD of yours at home.
  **zu Hause.**

> ### KEY POINTS
> ✔ German possessive pronouns have the same form and endings as the possessive adjectives **mein**, **dein**, **sein**, **ihr**, **unser**, **euer**, **ihr**, **Ihr**, except in the masculine nominative singular, the neuter nominative singular and the neuter accusative singular.
> ✔ The nominative and accusative neuter forms of all the possessive pronouns are often pronounced without the last **-e**, for example **meins** instead of **meines**.
> ✔ **Unserer**, meaning *ours* is often pronounced **unsrer** and **euerer**, meaning *yours (plural familiar)* is often pronounced **eurer**. This pronunciation is occasionally reflected in writing.

# Test yourself

**68** **Translate the following sentences into German using the relevant possessive pronoun.**

a This car is mine. ........................................................................................................

b Is this bike yours? ......................................................................................................

c These pencils are hers. .............................................................................................

d Are these books yours or mine?

........................................................................................................................................

e Paul and Leo, these chairs are yours.

........................................................................................................................................

f This house is ours. .....................................................................................................

g These clothes are theirs. ..........................................................................................

h This room is his. .........................................................................................................

i The house is yours (*plural*). ....................................................................................

j These two newspapers are mine. ...........................................................................

**69** **Complete the sentence with the correct form of the possessive pronoun.**

a Gehören die Sachen deinem Mann? – Ja, es sind .......................... .

b Gehört die Katze euren Nachbarn? – Ja es ist .......................... .

c Ist das Ihr Haus? – Nein, es ist nicht .......................... .

d Gehört der Hund dir und deinen Eltern? – Ja, es ist .......................... .

e Ist das die Adresse deiner Schwester? – Ja, es ist .......................... .

f Gehört das Auto eurem Lehrer? – Ja, es ist .......................... .

g Sind das deine 5 Euro? – Ja, es sind .......................... .

h Ist das die Tasche deiner Freundin? – Nein, es ist nicht .......................... .

i Ist das Ihre Tasse Kaffee? – Ja, es ist .......................... .

j Gehört die Wohnung mir und meiner Mutter? – Ja, es ist .......................... .

# Test yourself

**70** **Fill the gap by inserting the correct possessive form of the pronoun.**

**a** Eure Wohnung ist größer als ................................ . **[wir]**

**b** Mein Auto ist teurer als ............................. . **[du]**

**c** Mein Lehrer ist netter als ............................. . **[du]**

**d** Dein Bruder ist größer als ............................. . **[er]**

**e** Unser Computer ist besser als ............................. . **[ihr]**

**f** Ihr Haus ist schöner als ............................. . **[er]**

**g** Mein Job wird besser bezahlt als ............................. . **[Sie]**

**h** Unser Gepäck ist schwerer als ............................. . **[sie]**

**i** Unsere Mannschaft spielt besser als ............................. . **[ihr]**

**j** Dein Fernseher hat mehr Programme als ............................. . **[ich]**

# Indefinite pronouns

---

## What is an indefinite pronoun?
An **indefinite pronoun** is one of a small group of pronouns such as *everything*, *nobody* and *something* which are used to refer to people or things in a general way without saying exactly who or what they are.

---

➤ In German, the indefinite pronouns **jemand** (meaning *someone*, *somebody*) and **niemand** (meaning *no-one*, *nobody*) are often used in speech without any endings. In written German, the endings are added.

| Case | Indefinite Pronoun |
|------|-------------------|
| **Nominative** | jemand/niemand |
| **Accusative** | jemand<u>en</u>/niemand<u>en</u> |
| **Genitive** | jemand<u>(e)s</u>/niemand<u>(e)s</u> |
| **Dative** | jemand<u>em</u>/niemand<u>em</u> |

| | |
|---|---|
| **Ich habe es jemand<u>em</u> gegeben.** | I gave it to someone. |
| **Jemand hat es genommen.** | Someone has taken it. |
| **Sie hat niemand<u>en</u> gesehen.** | She didn't see anyone. |
| **Ich bin unterwegs niemand<u>em</u> begegnet.** | I didn't meet anyone on the way. |

---

*Tip*
If you want to express the sense of *somebody or other*, use **irgendjemand** which is declined like **jemand**.

**Ich habe es irgendjemand<u>em</u>**      I gave it to somebody or other.
**gegeben.**

---

➤ The indefinite pronoun **keiner** has the same endings as the article **kein, keine, kein** except in the nominative masculine and nominative and accusative neuter forms, and can be used to refer to people or things. When referring to people it means *nobody*, *not ... anybody* or *none* and when referring to things, it means *not ... any* or *none*.

| Case | Masculine Singular | Feminine Singular | Neuter Singular | All Genders Plural |
|------|-------------------|-------------------|-----------------|--------------------|
| **Nominative** | kein<u>er</u> | kein<u>e</u> | kein<u>s</u> | kein<u>e</u> |
| **Accusative** | kein<u>en</u> | kein<u>e</u> | kein<u>s</u> | kein<u>e</u> |
| **Genitive** | kein<u>es</u> | kein<u>er</u> | kein<u>es</u> | kein<u>er</u> |
| **Dative** | kein<u>em</u> | kein<u>er</u> | kein<u>em</u> | kein<u>en</u> |

| | | |
|---|---|---|
| **Ich kenne hier kein<u>en</u>.** | I don't know anybody here. | |
| **Kein<u>er</u> weiß Bescheid über ihn.** | Nobody knows about him. | |
| **Das trifft auf kein<u>en</u> zu.** | That does not apply to anybody. | |
| **Er wollte ein Stück Schokolade,** | He wanted a piece of chocolate, but I didn't | |
| **  aber ich hatte kein<u>e</u>.** | have any. | |
| **„Hast du Geld?" – „Nein, gar kein<u>s</u>."** | "Have you got any money?" – "No, none | |
| | at all." | |

➤ The indefinite pronoun **einer** (meaning *one*) only has a singular form and can also be used to refer to people or things.

| Case | Masculine Singular | Feminine Singular | Neuter Singular |
|---|---|---|---|
| **Nominative** | einer | eine | ein(e)s |
| **Accusative** | einen | eine | ein(e)s |
| **Genitive** | eines | einer | eines |
| **Dative** | einem | einer | einem |

| | |
|---|---|
| **Sie trifft sich mit <u>einem</u> ihrer** | She's meeting one of her old friends from |
| **  alten Studienfreunde.** | university. |

**Ich brauche nur <u>einen</u>** (e.g. **einen Wagen, einen Pullover** etc) OR
**Ich brauche nur <u>eine</u>** (e.g. **eine Blume, eine Tasche** etc) OR
**Ich brauche nur <u>eins</u>** (e.g. **ein Buch, ein Notizbuch** etc) I only need one.

---

### KEY POINTS

✔ **Jemand** and **niemand** can be used without endings in spoken German but have endings added in written German.

✔ **Keiner** has the same endings as the article **kein**, **keine**, **kein** except in the nominative masculine and nominative and accusative neuter forms, and refers to people or things.

✔ **Einer** only has a singular form and refers to people or things.

# Test yourself

**71** **Fill the gap with the correct form of *jemand* or *niemand*.**

**a** Wo ist das Buch? Hast du es ............................. gegeben?

**b** Er lebt allein, und lässt ............................. in sein Haus.

**c** Es soll ein Geheimnis bleiben, deshalb habe ich es ............................. erzählt.

**d** Es ist schon spät; ob wohl noch ............................. kommt?

**e** Ich möchte allein sein, ich will ............................. sehen.

**f** Ich habe dreimal bei ihr angerufen, aber ............................. meldet sich.

**g** Es waren Einbrecher im Haus, haben Sie ............................. gesehen?

**h** Ich weiß nicht, wie das funktioniert; ich muss es mir von ............................. zeigen lassen.

**i** War irgendjemand im Haus? – Nein, es war ............................. da.

**j** Du darfst kein Geld aus der Kasse nehmen, ohne ............................. zu fragen.

**72** **Match the related items.**

| | |
|---|---|
| **a** Das Telefon ist kaputt. | Er hat kein Geld. |
| **b** Ich lebe allein. | Keiner hat mir geholfen. |
| **c** Er ist arm. | Er hat jemanden gefragt. |
| **d** Ich habe die Hausaufgaben allein gemacht. | Keiner kann anrufen. |
| **e** Er weiß Bescheid. | Niemand wohnt bei mir. |

**73** **Cross out the forms that are not correct.**

| | |
|---|---|
| **a** Ich bin ... begegnet. | niemandem/keinem/jemanden/einen |
| **b** Es war ... da. | keiner/keine/eine/niemanden |
| **c** Hast du ... gesehen? | keiner/einen/jemandem/keinen |
| **d** Ich will ... besuchen. | jemanden/keiner/keinen/einer |
| **e** Ich kenne dort ... | keiner/niemanden/jemanden/keinen |
| **f** Er hat es ... gegeben. | keins/jemandem/keinen/keinem |
| **g** Sie hat ... genommen. | keine/keinen/keinem/keiner |
| **h** Ich brauche ... | keinen/einem/eine/keins |
| **i** Sie hat ... mitgebracht. | keinen/keine/einem/jemanden |
| **j** Ich will ... sehen. | niemanden/jemandem/einer/keinen |

# Reflexive pronouns

> **What is a reflexive pronoun?**
> A **reflexive pronoun** is an object pronoun such as *myself, yourself, himself, herself* and *ourselves* that forms part of German reflexive verbs like **sich waschen** (meaning *to wash*) or **sich setzen** (meaning *to sit down*). A reflexive verb is a verb whose subject and object are the same and whose action is 'reflected back' to its subject.

➤ German reflexive pronouns have two forms: accusative (for the direct object pronoun) and dative (for the indirect object pronoun), as follows:

| Accusative Form | Dative Form | Meaning |
|---|---|---|
| mich | mir | myself |
| dich | dir | yourself (*familiar*) |
| sich | sich | himself/herself/itself |
| uns | uns | ourselves |
| euch | euch | yourselves (*plural*) |
| sich | sich | themselves |
| sich | sich | yourself/yourselves (*polite*) |

| | |
|---|---|
| **Er hat <u>sich</u> rasiert.** | He had a shave. |
| **Du hast <u>dich</u> gebadet.** | You had a bath. |
| **Ich will es <u>mir</u> zuerst überlegen.** | I'll have to think about it first. |

☑ Note that unlike personal pronouns and possessives, the polite forms have no capital letter.

| | |
|---|---|
| **Setzen Sie <u>sich</u> bitte.** | Please take a seat. |
| **Nehmen Sie <u>sich</u> ruhig etwas Zeit.** | Take your time. |

➤ The reflexive pronoun usually follows the first verb in the sentence, with certain exceptions:

**Sie wird <u>sich</u> darüber freuen.**   She'll be pleased about that.

- If the subject and verb are swapped round in the sentence, and the subject is a personal pronoun, then the reflexive pronoun must come AFTER the personal pronoun.
**Darüber wird sie <u>sich</u> freuen.**   She'll be pleased about that.

- If the sentence is made of up two parts or clauses, then the reflexive pronoun comes AFTER the subject in the second clause.
**Ich frage mich, ob sie <u>sich</u> darüber freuen wird.**   I wonder if she'll be pleased about that.

⇨ For more information on **Word order**, see page 242.
⇨ For more information on **Reflexive verbs**, see page 138.

➤ Unlike English, reflexive pronouns are also used after prepositions when the pronoun 'reflects back' to the subject of the sentence.

| | |
|---|---|
| **Er hatte nicht genug Geld bei <u>sich</u>.** | He didn't have enough money on him. |
| **Hatten Sie nicht genug Geld bei <u>sich</u>?** | Didn't you have enough money on you? |

➤ Another use of reflexive pronouns in German is with transitive verbs where the action is performed for the benefit of the subject, as in the English phrase: I bought *myself* a new hat. The pronoun is not always translated in English.

| | |
|---|---|
| **Ich hole <u>mir</u> einen Kaffee.** | I'm going to get (myself) a coffee. |
| **Sie hat <u>sich</u> eine neue Jacke gekauft.** | She bought (herself) a new jacket. |

➤ Reflexive pronouns are usually used in German where *each other* and *one another* would be used in English.

| | |
|---|---|
| **Wir sind <u>uns</u> letzte Woche begegnet.** | We met (each other) last week. |

☑ Note that **einander**, (meaning *one another*, *each other*), which does not change in form, may be used instead of a reflexive pronoun in such cases.

| | |
|---|---|
| **Wir kennen <u>uns</u> schon.** OR | We already know each other. |
| **Wir kennen <u>einander</u> schon.** | |

➤ After prepositions, **einander** is always used instead of a reflexive pronoun. The preposition and **einander** are then joined to form one word.

| | |
|---|---|
| **Sie redeten <u>miteinander</u>.** | They were talking to each other. |

➤ In English, pronouns used for emphasis are the same as normal reflexive pronouns, for example, *I did it myself*. In German **selbst** or, in informal spoken language, **selber** are used instead of reflexive pronouns for emphasis. They never change their form and are always stressed, regardless of their position in the sentence:

| | |
|---|---|
| **Ich <u>selbst</u> habe es nicht gelesen, aber ...** | I haven't read it *myself*, but ... |

---

**KEY POINTS**

✔ German reflexive pronouns have two forms: accusative for the direct object pronoun and dative for the indirect object pronoun.

✔ Reflexive pronouns are also used after prepositions when the pronoun 'reflects back' to the subject of the sentence.

✔ Reflexive pronouns are usually used in German where *each other* or *one another* would be used in English, but **einander** can be used as an alternative and is always used after prepositions.

✔ **Selbst** or, in informal spoken German, **selber** are used instead of reflexive pronouns for emphasis.

---

For further explanation of grammatical terms, please see pages viii-xii.

**74** **Fill the gap with the correct reflexive pronoun.**

**a** Das muss ich ......................... erst noch überlegen.

**b** Er hat ......................... über das Geschenk gefreut.

**c** Wir haben ......................... bei ihr bedankt.

**d** Ich kann ......................... nicht daran erinnern.

**e** Ich frage ......................... , warum er das gemacht hat.

**f** Schämt ihr ......................... denn gar nicht?

**g** Dafür interessiert er ......................... nicht.

**h** Du regst ......................... immer so schnell auf.

**i** Sie haben ......................... lange nicht gesehen.

**j** Freust du ......................... denn gar nicht?

**75** **Translate the following sentences into German, using a reflexive pronoun.**

**a** We were talking to each other. ..................................................................

**b** They met each other on Monday.

.................................................................................................................

**c** We were very pleased about that. ............................................................

**d** They already knew each other. ................................................................

**e** I had a bath. ..............................................................................................

**f** I ask myself whether it is a good idea.

.................................................................................................................

**g** Do you remember my brother? ................................................................

**h** We have to hurry. .....................................................................................

**i** Shall I get myself a cup of tea? ................................................................

**j** Are you interested in cars? ......................................................................

**76** **Match the two columns.**

| | |
|---|---|
| **a** Ich bemühe | mir |
| **b** Er rasiert | dich |
| **c** Du setzt | dir |
| **d** Ich erlaube es | mich |
| **e** Du wünschst | sich |

# Relative pronouns

---

### What is a relative pronoun?

In English a **relative pronoun** is one of the words *who, which* and *that* (and the more formal *whom*). These pronouns are used to introduce information that makes it clear which person or thing is being talked about, for example, *The man who has just come in is Ann's boyfriend; The vase that you broke was quite valuable.*

Relative pronouns can also introduce further information about someone or something, for example, *Peter, who is a brilliant painter, wants to study art; Jane's house, which was built in 1890, needs a lot of repairs.*

---

➤ In German the most common relative pronouns **der**, **den**, **dessen**, **dem** etc have the same forms as the definite article, except in the dative plural and genitive singular and plural. They are declined as follows:

| Case | Masculine Singular | Feminine Singular | Neuter Singular | All Genders Plural |
|------|--------------------|-------------------|-----------------|--------------------|
| **Nominative** | der | die | das | die |
| **Accusative** | den | die | das | die |
| **Genitive** | dessen | deren | dessen | deren |
| **Dative** | dem | der | dem | denen |

➤ Relative pronouns must agree in gender and number with the noun to which they refer, but the case they have depends on their function in the relative clause. The relative clause is simply the part of the sentence in which the relative pronoun appears. Relative clauses are <u>ALWAYS</u> separated by commas from the rest of the sentence.

- In the following example, the relative pronoun **den** is in the accusative because it is the direct object in the relative clause.

**Der Mann, <u>den</u> ich gestern gesehen habe, kommt aus Zürich.**

The man that I saw yesterday comes from Zürich.

- In this second example, the relative pronoun **dessen** is in the genitive because it is used to show that something belongs to someone.

**Das Mädchen, <u>dessen</u> Fahrrad gestohlen worden ist.**

The girl whose bike was stolen.

---

*Tip*

In English we often miss out the object pronouns *who, which* and *that*. For example, we can say both *the friends that I see most*, or *the friends I see most*, and *the house which we want to buy*, or *the house we want to buy*. In German you can <u>NEVER</u> miss out the relative pronoun in this way.

**Die Frau, mit <u>der</u> ich gestern gesprochen habe, kennt deine Mutter.**

The woman I spoke to yesterday knows your mother.

---

For further explanation of grammatical terms, please see pages viii-xii.

ℹ️ Note that the genitive forms are used in relative clauses in much the same way as in English, but to translate *one of whom*, *some of whom* use the following constructions.

| | |
|---|---|
| **Das Kind, <u>dessen</u> Fahrrad gestohlen worden war, fing an zu weinen.** | The child <u>whose</u> bicycle had been stolen started to cry. |
| **Die Kinder, von <u>denen</u> einige schon lesen konnten, ...** | The children, some of <u>whom</u> could already read, ... |
| **Meine Freunde, von <u>denen</u> einer ...** | My friends, one of <u>whom</u> ... |

---

*Grammar Extra!*

When a relative clause is introduced by a preposition, the relative pronoun can be replaced by **wo-** or **wor-** if the noun or pronoun it stands for refers to an object or something abstract. The full form of the pronoun plus preposition is much more common.

| | |
|---|---|
| **Das Buch, <u>woraus</u> ich vorgelesen habe, gehört dir.** | The book I read aloud from belongs to you. |
| OR | |
| **Das Buch, <u>aus dem</u> ich vorgelesen habe, gehört dir.** | |

---

➤ In German **wer** and **was** are normally used as interrogative pronouns (meaning *who?* and *what?*) to ask questions. They can also be the subject of a sentence or a relative pronoun. For example, *he who, a woman who, anyone who, those who* etc.

| | |
|---|---|
| **<u>Wer</u> das glaubt, ist verrückt.** | Anyone who believes that is mad. |
| **<u>Was</u> du gestern gekauft hast, steht dir ganz gut.** | The things you bought yesterday really suit you. |

ℹ️ Note that **was** is the relative pronoun used in set expressions with certain neuter forms. For example:

| | |
|---|---|
| **alles, was ...** | everything which |
| **das, was ...** | that which |
| **nichts, was ...** | nothing that |
| **vieles, was ...** | a lot that |
| **wenig, was ...** | little that |
| **Nichts, <u>was</u> er sagte, hat gestimmt.** | Nothing that he said was true. |
| **Das, <u>was</u> du jetzt machst, ist unpraktisch.** | What you are doing now is impractical. |
| **Mit allem, <u>was</u> du gesagt hast, sind wir einverstanden.** | We agree with everything you said. |

## KEY POINTS

✔ The most common relative pronouns **der**, **den**, **dessen**, **dem** etc have the same forms as the definite article, except in the dative plural and genitive singular and plural.

✔ Relative pronouns must agree in gender and number with the noun to which they refer, but take their case from their function in the relative clause.

✔ In German you can <u>NEVER</u> miss out the relative pronoun, unlike in English.

✔ Relative clauses are always separated by commas from the rest of the sentence.

✔ **Wer** and **was** are normally used as interrogative pronouns but can also be the subject of a sentence or a relative pronoun.

# Test yourself

**77** **Translate the following phrases into German.**

**a** the woman that I saw yesterday

.................................................................................................................

**b** the man whose car is red ........................................................................

**c** the family that lives here ........................................................................

**d** the car that I want to buy ........................................................................

**e** my brothers, one of whom is a doctor

.................................................................................................................

**f** the man that I love ...................................................................................

**g** the friend (*male*) that I'm writing to ....................................................

**h** the children who are playing in the street

.................................................................................................................

**i** the dress that costs most ........................................................................

**j** the friends that we visited ......................................................................

**78** **Match the noun with the description.**

**a** der Stuhl               an der sie leidet

**b** das Kind                über die ich nachdenke

**c** der Freund              von dem ich sprach

**d** die Probleme            auf dem ich sitze

**e** die Krankheit           auf den ich vertraue

**79** **Fill the gap with the correct relative pronoun. The first one has been done for you.**

**a** Das ist der Mann, mit ......*dem*...... ich gestern gesprochen habe.

**b** Die Frau, ........................ Hund Fifi heißt, ist sehr nett.

**c** Das sind die Kinder, für ........................ ich Geschenke kaufen muss.

**d** Ich sprach mit dem Jungen, ........................ Ball verschwunden ist.

**e** Wie heißt die Frau, mit ........................ er gerade spricht?

**f** Das ist das Auto, für ........................ ich so viel bezahlt habe.

**g** Meine Brüder, ........................ ich viel zu verdanken habe, leben in Indien.

**h** Fußball ist der Sport, ........................ ich am liebsten mag.

**i** Die Leute, ........................ wir das Geld gegeben haben, sind verreist.

**j** Das Kind, ........................ Haar rot ist, geht heute schwimmen.

**80** **Translate the following phrases using *was*. The first one has been done for you.**

**a** everything that he said *alles, was er gesagt hat*

**b** nothing that she saw

**c** what she is doing now

**d** everything he has read

**e** a lot of what he thinks

**f** little that he does

**g** that which is really important

**h** many things that you said

**i** everything we have bought

**j** nothing that we said

# Interrogative pronouns

---

### What is an interrogative pronoun?
This is one of the words *who*, *whose*, *whom*, *what* and *which* when they are used instead of a noun to ask questions, for example, *What*'s happening?; *Who*'s coming?

---

## Wer? and was?

➤ **Wer** and **was** only have a singular form.

| Case | Persons | Things |
|------|---------|--------|
| **Nominative** | wer? | was? |
| **Accusative** | wen? | was? |
| **Genitive** | wessen? | – |
| **Dative** | wem? | – |

- They can be used in direct questions.
  **Wer hat es gemacht?**              Who did it?
  **Mit wem bist du gekommen?**        Who did you come with?
  **Wo ist der Kugelschreiber, mit**   Where is the pen you wrote it with?
  **dem du es geschrieben hast?**

- They can also be used in indirect questions.
  **Ich weiß nicht, wer es gemacht hat.**   I don't know who did it.
  **Sie wollte wissen, mit wem sie**         She wanted to know who she was to
  **fahren sollte.**                            travel with.

## Interrogative pronouns with prepositions

➤ When used with prepositions, **was** usually becomes **wo-** and is combined with the preposition to form one word. Where the preposition begins with a vowel, **wor-** is used instead.
  **Wodurch ist es zerstört worden?**   How was it destroyed?
  **Worauf sollen wir sitzen? Es gibt**  What should we sit on?
  **keine Stühle.**                         There aren't any chairs.

## Was für ein?, welcher?

➤ These are used to mean *what kind of ...?* and *which one?* and are declined like the definite article.
  „**Er hat jetzt ein Auto**" –          "He has a car now." –
  „**Was für eins hat er gekauft?**"      "What kind (of one) did he buy?"
  **Welches hast du gewollt?**           Which one did you want?

⇨  For more information on **Words declined like the definite article**, see page 37.

➤ They can refer to people or things and require the appropriate endings.

**Für welchen** (e.g. **welchen Job, welchen Whisky** etc) **hat sie sich entschieden?** OR
**Für welches** (e.g. **welches Haus, welches Buch** etc) **hat sie sich entschieden?** OR
**Für welche** (e.g. **welche Person, welche Jacke** etc) **hat sie sich entschieden?**
Which one did she choose?

---

**KEY POINTS**

✔ The interrogative pronouns **wer** and **was** can be used for direct and indirect questions and only have a singular form.

✔ When used with prepositions, **was** becomes **wo-**, or **wor-** when the preposition begins with a vowel.

✔ **Was für ein?** and **welcher?** are used to mean *what kind of ...?* and *which one?*

---

# Test yourself

**81** **Complete the following sentences with the correct interrogative pronoun. The first one has been done for you.**

**a** .......*Wem*......... hast du das Buch gegeben?

**b** Ich weiß nicht, für ........................ dieses Geschenk ist.

**c** Weißt du, ........................ der Mörder ist?

**d** Ich kann mich nicht erinnern, mit ........................ er gekommen ist.

**e** Ich möchte gern wissen, ........................ Kind das ist.

**f** ........................ hat er besucht?

**g** Wissen Sie, ........................ dieses Auto kostet?

**h** ........................ von euch geht in diese Schule?

**i** Mit ........................ möchtest du ins Kino gehen?

**j** Ich weiß nicht, ........................ ich sagen soll.

**82** **Translate the following sentences into German.**

**a** Whose bike is that? ...........................................................................

**b** Who have you invited? ...........................................................................

**c** What's that? ...........................................................................

**d** Who told you? ...........................................................................

**e** Who did you come with? ...........................................................................

**f** Whose book is this? (use **gehören**) ...........................................................................

**g** What do these apples cost? ...........................................................................

**h** Who did you buy this car from? ...........................................................................

**i** How many would you like? ...........................................................................

**j** Whose house did you visit? ...........................................................................

# Verbs

---

## What is a verb?
A **verb** is a 'doing' word which describes what someone or something does, what someone or something is, or what happens to them, for example, *be, sing, live*.

---

## Weak, strong and mixed verbs

➤ Verbs are usually used with a noun, with a pronoun such as *I, you* or *she*, or with somebody's name. They can relate to the present, the past and the future; this is called their <u>tense</u>.

⇨ *For more information on* **Nouns** *and* **Pronouns**, *see pages 1 and 89.*

➤ Verbs are either:

- <u>weak</u>: their forms follow a set pattern. These verbs may also be called <u>regular</u>.

- <u>strong</u> and <u>irregular</u>: their forms change according to different patterns.
OR
- <u>mixed</u>: their forms follow a mixture of the patterns for weak and strong verbs.

➤ English verbs have a <u>base form</u> (the form of the verb without any endings added to it, for example, *walk*). This is the form you look up in a dictionary. The base form can have *to* in front of it, for example, *to walk*. This is called the <u>infinitive</u>.

➤ German verbs also have an infinitive, which is the form shown in a dictionary; most weak, strong and mixed verbs end in **-en**. For example, **holen** (meaning *to fetch*) is weak, **helfen** (meaning *to help*) is strong and **denken** (meaning *to think*) is mixed. All German verbs belong to one of these groups. We will look at each of these three groups in turn on the next few pages.

➤ English verbs have other forms apart from the base form and infinitive: a form ending in *-s* (*walks*), a form ending in *-ing* (*walking*), and a form ending in *-ed* (*walked*).

➤ German verbs have many more forms than this, which are made up of endings added to a <u>stem</u>. The stem of a verb can usually be worked out from the infinitive and can change, depending on the tense of the verb and who or what you are talking about.

➤ German verb endings also change, depending on who or what you are talking about: **ich** (*I*), **du** (*you* (informal)), **er/sie/es** (*he/she/it*), **Sie** (*you* (formal)) in the singular, or **wir** (*we*), **ihr** (*you* (informal)), **Sie** (*you* (formal)) and **sie** (*they*) in the plural. German verbs also have different forms depending on whether you are referring to the present, future or past.

⇨ *For* **Verb Tables**, *see supplement.*

---

**KEY POINTS**

✔ German verbs have different forms depending on what noun or pronoun they are used with, and on their tense.

✔ They are made up of a stem and an ending. The stem is based on the infinitive and can change in form.

✔ All German verbs fit into one of three patterns or conjugations: weak (and regular), strong (and irregular) or mixed (a mixture of the two).

# The present tense

---

## What is the present tense?
The **present tense** is used to talk about what is true at the moment, what happens regularly and what is happening now, for example, *I'm a student*, *I travel to college by train*, *I'm studying languages*.

---

## Using the present tense

➤ In English there are two forms of the present tense. One is used to talk about things happening now and the other is used for things that happen all the time. In German, you use the same form for both of these.

- things that are happening now
  **Es regnet.**                    It's raining.
  **Sie spielen Fußball.**          They're playing football.

- things that happen all the time, or things that you do as a habit
  **Hier regnet es viel.**          It rains a lot here.
  **Samstags spielen sie Fußball.** They play football on Saturdays.

➤ In German there are three alternative ways of emphasizing that something is happening now:

- present tense + an adverb
  **Er kocht gerade das Abendessen.**   He's cooking dinner.

- **beim** + an infinitive being used as a noun
  **Ich bin beim Bügeln.**          I am ironing.

- **eben/gerade dabei sein zu** (meaning *to be in the process of*) + an infinitive
  **Sie ist gerade dabei, eine E-Mail zu schreiben.**   She is just writing an email.

➤ In English you can also use the present tense to talk about something that is going to happen in the near future. You can do the same in German.
  **Morgen spiele ich Tennis.**     I'm going to play tennis tomorrow.
  **Wir nehmen den Zug um zehn Uhr.**   We're getting the ten o'clock train.

> Tip
> Although English sometimes uses parts of the verb *to be* to form the present tense of other verbs (for example, *I am listening*, *she's talking*). German <u>NEVER</u> uses the verb **sein** in this way.
> When using **seit** or **seitdem** to describe an action which began in the past and is continuing in the present, the present tense is used in German, where in English a verb form with *have* or *has* is used.
>
> **Ich <u>wohne</u> <u>seit</u> drei Jahren hier.**  I <u>have been living</u> here for three years.
>
> **<u>Seit</u> er krank <u>ist</u>, hat er uns nicht besucht.**  He hasn't visited us <u>since</u> he's been ill.
>
> **<u>Seitdem</u> sie am Gymnasium <u>ist</u>, hat sie kaum mehr Zeit.**  Since she's been going to grammar school, she's hardly had any time.
>
> ⓘ Note that if the action is finished, the perfect tense is used in German.
>
> **<u>Seit</u> seinem Unfall <u>habe</u> ich ihn nur ein einziges Mal <u>gesehen</u>.**  I <u>have</u> only <u>seen</u> him once since his accident.

## Forming the present tense of weak verbs

➤ Nearly all weak verbs in German end in **-en** in their infinitive form. This is the form of the verb you find in the dictionary, for example, **spielen**, **machen**, **holen**. Weak verbs are regular and their changes follow a set pattern or conjugation.

➤ To know which form of the verb to use in German, you need to work out what the stem of the verb is and then add the correct ending. The stem of most verbs in the present tense is formed by chopping the **-en** off the infinitive.

| Infinitive | Stem (without -en) |
|---|---|
| **spielen** (*to play*) | spiel- |
| **machen** (*to make*) | mach- |
| **holen** (*to fetch*) | hol- |

➤ Where the infinitive of a weak verb ends in **-eln** or **-ern**, only the **-n** is chopped off to form the stem.

| Infinitive | Stem (without -n) |
|---|---|
| **wandern** (*to hillwalk*) | wander- |
| **segeln** (*to sail*) | segel- |

➤ Now you know how to find the stem of a verb, you can add the correct ending. Which one you choose will depend on whether you are referring to **ich**, **du**, **er**, **sie**, **es**, **wir**, **ihr**, **Sie** or **sie**.

➯ *For more information on **Pronouns**, see page 89.*

➤ Here are the present tense endings for weak verbs ending in **-en**:

| Pronoun | Ending | Add to Stem, e.g. spiel- | Meanings |
|---|---|---|---|
| ich | -e | ich spiel<u>e</u> | I play<br>I am playing |
| du | -st | du spiel<u>st</u> | you play<br>you are playing |
| er<br>sie<br>es | -t | er spiel<u>t</u><br>sie spiel<u>t</u><br>es spiel<u>t</u> | he/she/it plays<br>he/she/it is<br>playing |
| wir | -en | wir spiel<u>en</u> | we play<br>we are playing |
| ihr | -t | ihr spiel<u>t</u> | you (*plural*) play<br>you are playing |
| sie<br><br>Sie | -en | sie spiel<u>en</u><br><br>Sie spiel<u>en</u> | they play<br>they are playing<br>you (*polite*) play<br>you are playing |

**Sie <u>macht</u> ihre Hausaufgaben.**     She's doing her homework.
**Er <u>holt</u> die Kinder.**     He's fetching the children.

🛈 Note that you add **-n**, not **-en** to the stem of weak verbs ending in **-ern** and **-eln** to get the **wir**, **sie** and **Sie** forms of the present tense.

| Pronoun | Ending | Add to Stem, e.g. wander- | Meanings |
|---|---|---|---|
| wir | -n | wir wander<u>n</u> | we hillwalk<br>we are hillwalking |
| sie<br><br>Sie | -n | sie wander<u>n</u><br><br>Sie wander<u>n</u> | they hillwalk<br>they are hillwalking<br>you (*polite*) hillwalk<br>you are hillwalking |

**Sie wandern gern, oder?**     You like hillwalking, don't you?
**Im Sommer wander<u>n</u> wir fast jedes**     In the summer we go hillwalking most
  **Wochenende.**     weekends.

➤ If the stem of a weak verb ends in **-d** or **-t**, an extra **-e** is added before the usual endings in the **du**, **er**, **sie**, **es** and **ihr** parts of the verb to make pronunciation easier.

| Pronoun | Ending | Add to Stem, e.g. red- | Meanings |
|---|---|---|---|
| du | -est | du red<u>est</u> | you talk<br>you are talking |
| er<br>sie<br>es | -et | er red<u>et</u><br>sie red<u>et</u><br>es red<u>et</u> | he/she/it talks<br>he/she/it is talking |
| ihr | -et | ihr red<u>et</u> | you (*plural*) talk<br>you are talking |

**Du red<u>est</u> doch die ganze Zeit über deine Arbeit!**   You talk about your work all the time!

| Pronoun | Ending | Add to Stem, e.g. arbeit- | Meanings |
|---|---|---|---|
| du | -est | du arbeit<u>est</u> | you work<br>you are working |
| er<br>sie<br>es | -et | er arbeit<u>et</u><br>sie arbeit<u>et</u><br>es arbeit<u>et</u> | he/she/it works<br>he/she/it is working |
| ihr | -et | ihr arbeit<u>et</u> | you (*plural*) work<br>you are working |

**Sie arbeit<u>et</u> übers Wochenende.**   She's working over the weekend.
**Ihr arbeit<u>et</u> ganz schön viel.**   You work a lot.

➤ If the stem of a weak verb ends in **-m** or **-n**, this extra **-e** is added to make pronunciation easier. If the **-m** or **-n** has a consonant in front of it, the **-e** is added, except if the consonant is **l**, **r** or **h**, for example **lernen**.

| Pronoun | Ending | Add to Stem, e.g. atm- | Meanings |
|---|---|---|---|
| du | -est | du atm<u>est</u> | you breathe<br>you are breathing |
| er<br>sie<br>es | -et | er atm<u>et</u><br>sie atm<u>et</u><br>es atm<u>et</u> | he/she/it breathes<br>he/she/it is breathing |
| ihr | -et | ihr atm<u>et</u> | you (*plural*) breathe<br>you are breathing |

**Du atm<u>est</u> ganz tief.**   You're breathing very deeply.

| Pronoun | Ending | Add to Stem, e.g. lern- | Meanings |
|---|---|---|---|
| du | -st | du lern<u>st</u> | you learn<br>you are learning |
| er<br>sie<br>es | -t | er lern<u>t</u><br>sie lern<u>t</u><br>es lern<u>t</u> | he/she/it learns<br>he/she/it is learning |
| ihr | -t | ihr lern<u>t</u> | you (*plural*) learn<br>you are learning |

**Sie lern<u>t</u> alles ganz schnell.**　　　　She learns everything very quickly.

> **KEY POINTS**
> ✔ Weak verbs are regular and most of them form their present tense stem by losing the **-en** from the infinitive.
> ✔ The present tense endings for weak verbs ending in **-en** are:
> **-e**, **-st**, **-t**, **-en**, **-t**, **-en**, **-en**.
> ✔ If the stem of a weak verb ends in **-d**, **-t**, **-m** or **-n**, an extra **-e** is added before the endings to make pronunciation easier.

# Test yourself

**83** **Translate the following sentences into German.**

**a** They are playing football. ................................................................

**b** He works in a factory. ................................................................

**c** We are doing our homework. ................................................................

**d** She loves you. ................................................................

**e** We are learning a lot. ................................................................

**f** It is raining outside. ................................................................

**g** We are painting a picture. ................................................................

**h** I thank you for your help. ................................................................

**i** She is looking for her keys. ................................................................

**j** He collects stamps. ................................................................

**84** **Match the two columns.**

**a** er              zeichnet

**b** Sie            zeichnet

**c** ich            zeichnest

**d** ihr            zeichne

**e** du            zeichnen

**85** **Fill the gap with the correct form of the present tense.**

**a** Wir ............................ Blumen im Garten. **[pflücken]**

**b** Das Buch ............................ von einem alten Mann. **[handeln]**

**c** Viele Äpfel ............................ am Baum. **[hängen]**

**d** Die Werkstatt ............................ mein Auto. **[reparieren]**

**e** Mein Bruder ............................ in einer Kneipe. **[jobben]**

**f** ............................ ihr gern Musik? **[hören]**

**g** Der Ball ............................ unter das Sofa. **[rollen]**

**h** Meine Mutter ............................ immer meine Hemden. **[bügelt]**

**i** Herr Müller, ............................ Sie oft ihren Computer? **[benutzen]**

**j** Du ............................ nie dein Zimmer auf. **[räumen]**

# Forming the present tense of strong verbs

➤ The present tense of most strong verbs is formed with the same endings that are used for weak verbs.

| Pronoun | Ending | Add to Stem, e.g. sing- | Meanings |
|---|---|---|---|
| ich | -e | ich singe | I sing<br>I am singing |
| du | -st | du singst | you sing<br>you are singing |
| er<br>sie<br>es | -t | er singt<br>sie singt<br>es singt | he/she/it sings<br>he/she/it is singing |
| wir | -en | wir singen | we sing<br>we are singing |
| ihr | -t | ihr singt | you (*plural*) sing<br>you are singing |
| sie<br><br>Sie | -en | sie singen<br><br>Sie singen | they sing<br>they are singing<br>you (*polite*) sing<br>you are singing |

**Sie singen in einer Gruppe.**       They sing in a band.

➤ However, the vowels in stems of most strong verbs change for the **du** and **er/sie/es** forms. The vowels listed below change as shown in nearly all cases:

| | | |
|---|---|---|
| long **e** | → | **ie** (*see* **sehen**) |
| short **e** | → | **i** (*see* **helfen**) |
| **a** | → | **ä** (*see* **fahren**) |
| **au** | → | **äu** (*see* **laufen**) |
| **o** | → | **ö** (*see* **stoßen**) |

- long **e** → **ie**

| Pronoun | Ending | Add to Stem, e.g. seh- | Meanings |
|---|---|---|---|
| ich | -e | ich seh<u>e</u> | I see<br>I am seeing |
| du | -st | du s<u>ie</u>h<u>st</u> | you see<br>you are seeing |
| er<br>sie<br>es | -t | er s<u>ie</u>h<u>t</u><br>sie s<u>ie</u>h<u>t</u><br>es s<u>ie</u>h<u>t</u> | he/she/it sees<br>he/she/it is seeing |
| wir | -en | wir seh<u>en</u> | we see<br>we are seeing |
| ihr | -t | ihr seh<u>t</u> | you (*plural*) see<br>you are seeing |
| sie<br><br>Sie | -en | sie seh<u>en</u><br><br>Sie seh<u>en</u> | they see<br>they are seeing<br>you (*polite*) see<br>you are seeing |

**S<u>ie</u>h<u>st</u> du fern?**          Are you watching TV?

- short **e** → **i**

| Pronoun | Ending | Add to Stem, e.g. helf- | Meanings |
|---|---|---|---|
| ich | -e | ich helf<u>e</u> | I help<br>I am helping |
| du | -st | du h<u>i</u>lf<u>st</u> | you help<br>you are helping |
| er<br>sie<br>es | -t | er h<u>i</u>lf<u>t</u><br>sie h<u>i</u>lf<u>t</u><br>es h<u>i</u>lf<u>t</u> | he/she/it helps<br>he/she/it is helping |
| wir | -en | wir helf<u>en</u> | we help<br>we are helping |
| ihr | -t | ihr helf<u>t</u> | you (*plural*) help<br>you are helping |
| sie<br><br>Sie | -en | sie helf<u>en</u><br><br>Sie helf<u>en</u> | they help<br>they are helping<br>you (*polite*) help<br>you are helping |

**Heute h<u>i</u>lf<u>t</u> er beim Kochen.**          He's helping with the cooking today.

- a → ä

| Pronoun | Ending | Add to Stem, e.g. fahr- | Meanings |
|---|---|---|---|
| ich | -e | ich fahr<u>e</u> | I drive<br>I am driving |
| du | -st | du f<u>ä</u>hr<u>st</u> | you drive<br>you are driving |
| er<br>sie<br>es | -t | er f<u>ä</u>hrt<br>sie f<u>ä</u>hrt<br>es f<u>ä</u>hrt | he/she/it drives<br>he/she/it is driving |
| wir | -en | wir fahr<u>en</u> | we drive<br>we are driving |
| ihr | -t | ihr fahrt | you (*plural*) drive<br>you are driving |
| sie<br><br>Sie | -en | sie fahr<u>en</u><br><br>Sie fahr<u>en</u> | they drive<br>they are driving<br>you (*polite*) drive<br>you are driving |

**Am Samstag f<u>ä</u>hr<u>t</u> sie nach Italien.**     She's driving to Italy on Saturday.

- au → äu

| Pronoun | Ending | Add to Stem, e.g. lauf- | Meanings |
|---|---|---|---|
| ich | -e | ich lauf<u>e</u> | I run<br>I am running |
| du | -st | du l<u>äu</u>f<u>st</u> | you run<br>you are running |
| er<br>sie<br>es | -t | er l<u>äu</u>ft<br>sie l<u>äu</u>ft<br>es l<u>äu</u>ft | he/she/it runs<br>he/she/it is running |
| wir | -en | wir lauf<u>en</u> | we run<br>we are running |
| ihr | -t | ihr lauf<u>t</u> | you (*plural*) run<br>you are running |
| sie | -en | sie lauf<u>en</u> | they run<br>they are running |
| Sie | | Sie lauf<u>en</u> | you (*polite*) run<br>you are running |

**Er l<u>äu</u>f<u>t</u> die 100 Meter in Rekordzeit.**     He runs the 100 metres in record time.

- o → ö

| Pronoun | Ending | Add to Stem, e.g. stoß- | Meanings |
|---------|--------|-------------------------|----------|
| ich | -e | ich stoße | I push<br>I am pushing |
| du | -st | du stößt | you push<br>you are pushing |
| er<br>sie<br>es | -t | er stößt<br>sie stößt<br>es stößt | he/she/it pushes<br>he/she/it is pushing |
| wir | -en | wir stoßen | we push<br>we are pushing |
| ihr | -t | ihr stoßt | you (*plural*) push<br>you are pushing |
| sie<br><br>Sie | -en | sie stoßen<br><br>Sie stoßen | they push<br>they are pushing<br>you (*polite*) push<br>you are pushing |

**Pass auf, dass du nicht an den Tisch stößt.**   Watch that you don't bump into the table.

ⓘ Note that strong AND weak verbs whose stem ends in **-s**, **-z**, **-ss** or **-ß** (such as **stoßen**) add **-t** rather than **-st** to get the **du** form in the present tense. However, if the stem ends in **-sch**, the normal **-st** is added.

| Verb | Stem | Du Form |
|------|------|---------|
| wachsen | wachs- | wächst |
| waschen | wasch- | wäschst |

---

### KEY POINTS
✔ Strong verbs have the same endings in the present tense as weak verbs.
✔ The vowel or vowels of the stem of strong verbs change(s) in the present for the **du** and **er/sie/es** forms.

# Test yourself

**86** **Fill the gap with the correct form of the present tense.**

**a** Wir ............................... heute Abend ins Theater. **[gehen]**

**b** Ihr ............................... eurem Vater bei der Arbeit. **[helfen]**

**c** Ich ............................... euch nach dem Kino nach Hause. **[fahren]**

**d** Ich ............................... Sie, das nicht zu tun. **[bitten]**

**e** Diese Blume ............................... nach Honig. **[riechen]**

**f** Martina ............................... im Schulchor. **[singen]**

**g** Wir ............................... unsere Wäsche selbst. **[waschen]**

**h** Ich ............................... dir, die Stadt zu verlassen. **[raten]**

**i** Mein Vater ............................... mich dazu. **[zwingen]**

**j** Immer wenn ich von der Schule ............................... , steht das Essen auf dem Tisch.
**[kommen]**

**87** **Translate the following sentences into German.**

**a** My brother helps her with her homework.

...............................................................................................................

**b** My father drives me to school. .....................................................................

**c** We are growing very fast. .............................................................................

**d** You are riding on a horse. (use **du**) ..............................................................

**e** Do you see the bird on the tree? ...................................................................

**f** I always eat rolls for breakfast. ....................................................................

**g** They are offering us 2000 euros for the car.

...............................................................................................................

**h** On Sunday we're going on holiday. ...............................................................

**i** Will you help me? (use **du**) ..........................................................................

**j** Will you give us some more time? (use **Sie**)

...............................................................................................................

# Test yourself

**88** **Complete the following sentences with the correct form of the present tense. Note that a vowel change is required in each case.**

  **a** Wohin ............................. du mit dem Motorrad? **[fahren]**

  **b** Er ............................. sich selbst im Spiegel. **[sehen]**

  **c** Ich ............................. abends nie lange aufbleiben. **[dürfen]**

  **d** Sonntags ............................. er immer bis 10 Uhr. **[schlafen]**

  **e** Was ............................. heute im Kino? **[laufen]**

  **f** Sie ............................. ihre kleine Schwester an der Hand. **[halten]**

  **g** Es ............................. aus, als ob es bald regnet. **[sehen]**

  **h** Er ............................. morgens immer um 7 Uhr aufstehen. **[müssen]**

  **i** Seine Mutter ............................. ein buntes Kleid. **[tragen]**

  **j** ............................. du dich mit ihm nach der Schule? **[treffen]**

## Forming the present tense of mixed verbs

➤ There are nine mixed verbs in German. They are very common and are formed according to a mixture of the rules already explained for weak and strong verbs.

➤ The nine mixed verbs are:

| Mixed Verb | Meaning | Mixed Verb | Meaning | Mixed Verb | Meaning |
|---|---|---|---|---|---|
| brennen | to burn | kennen | to know | senden | to send |
| bringen | to bring | nennen | to name | wenden | to turn |
| denken | to think | rennen | to run | wissen | to know |

➤ The present tense of mixed verbs has the same endings as weak verbs and has no vowel or consonant changes in the stem: **ich bringe**, **du bringst**, **er/sie/es bringt**, **wir bringen**, **ihr bringt**, **sie bringen**, **Sie bringen**.

| | |
|---|---|
| **Sie bringt mich nach Hause.** | She's bringing me home. |
| **Bringst du mir etwas mit?** | Will you bring something for me? |

*i* Note that the present tense of the most important strong, weak and mixed verbs is shown in the Verb Tables.

⇨ For **Verb Tables**, *see supplement.*

---

**KEY POINTS**

✔ There are nine mixed verbs in German.
✔ The present tense of mixed verbs has the same endings as weak verbs and has no vowel or consonant changes in the stem.

---

# Test yourself

**89** **Fill the gap with the correct present tense form of one of the nine mixed verbs.**

**a** Mach das Feuer aus, sonst ........................ gleich das ganze Haus. **[brennen]**

**b** Mein Mann ........................ mir zum Geburtstag immer Blumen mit. **[bringen]**

**c** Ich ........................ mich immer an meine Schwester, wenn ich Hilfe brauche. **[wenden]**

**d** Ihr ........................ viel zu schnell, wir haben doch Zeit! **[rennen]**

**e** Ich ........................ meine Katze Sammy. **[nennen]**

**f** Meine Kinder ........................ mir zu Weihnachten ein Paket mit Geschenken. **[senden]**

**g** Sie setzt sich an den Computer und ........................ eine CD. **[brennen]**

**h** ........................ Sie diesen Mann? **[kennen]**

**i** Ich ........................ überhaupt nichts über Napoleon. **[wissen]**

**j** Woran ........................ du gerade? **[denken]**

**90** **Match the sentences that have a connection.**

**a** Wir rufen die Feuerwehr.                 Ich kenne ihn nicht.

**b** Ich muss mich beeilen.                   Ich bringe ihr ein Geschenk.

**c** Ich habe ihn noch nie gesehen.          Ich nenne ihm meinen Namen.

**d** Er fragt mich, wer ich bin.             Das Haus brennt.

**e** Ich bin meiner Freundin dankbar.        Ich renne zur Schule.

# Reflexive verbs

---

## What is a reflexive verb?

A **reflexive verb** is one where the subject and object are the same, and where the action 'reflects back' on the subject. Reflexive verbs are used with a reflexive pronoun such as *myself, yourself* and *herself* in English, for example, *I washed myself; He shaved himself.*

---

## Using reflexive verbs

➤ In German, reflexive verbs are much more common than in English, and many are used in everyday German. Reflexive verbs consist of two parts: the reflexive pronoun **sich** (meaning *himself, herself, itself, themselves* or *oneself*) and the infinitive of the verb.

 ➪ *For more information on **Reflexive pronouns**, see page 111.*

## Forming the present tense of reflexive verbs

➤ Reflexive verbs are often used to describe things you do (to yourself) every day or that involve a change of some sort (getting dressed, sitting down, getting excited, being in a hurry).

➤ The reflexive pronoun is either the direct object in the sentence, which means it is in the accusative case, or the indirect object in the sentence, which means it is in the dative case. Only the reflexive pronouns used with the **ich** and **du** forms of the verb have separate accusative and dative forms.

| Accusative Form | Dative Form | Meaning |
|---|---|---|
| mich | mir | myself |
| dich | dir | yourself (*familiar*) |
| sich | sich | himself/herself/itself |
| uns | uns | ourselves |
| euch | euch | yourselves (*plural*) |
| sich | sich | themselves |
| sich | sich | yourself/yourselves (*polite*) |

➤ The present tense forms of a reflexive verb work in just the same way as an ordinary verb, except that the reflexive pronoun is used as well.

➤ Below you will find the present tense of the common reflexive verbs **sich setzen** (meaning *to sit down*) which has its reflexive pronoun in the accusative and **sich erlauben** (meaning *to allow oneself*) which has its reflexive pronoun in the dative.

| Reflexive Forms | Meaning |
|---|---|
| ich setze mich | I sit (myself) down |
| du setzt dich | you sit (yourself) down |
| er/sie/es setzt sich | he/she/it sits down |
| wir setzen uns | we sit down |
| ihr setzt euch | you (*plural familiar*) sit down |
| sie setzen sich | they sit down |
| Sie setzen sich | you (*polite form*) sit down |

**Ich setze <u>mich</u> neben dich.**      I'll sit beside you.
**Sie setzen <u>sich</u> aufs Sofa.**      They sit down on the sofa.

| Reflexive Forms | Meaning |
|---|---|
| ich erlaube mir | I allow myself |
| du erlaubst dir | you allow yourself |
| er/sie/es erlaubt sich | he/she/it allows himself/herself/itself |
| wir erlauben uns | we allow ourselves |
| ihr erlaubt euch | you (*plural familiar*) allow yourselves |
| sie erlauben sich | they allow themselves |
| Sie erlauben sich | you (*polite form*) allow yourself |

**Ich erlaube <u>mir</u> jetzt ein Bier.**      Now I'm going to allow myself a beer.
**Er erlaubt <u>sich</u> ein Stück Kuchen.**      He's allowing himself a piece of cake.

➤ Some of the most common German reflexive verbs are listed here:

| Reflexive Verb with Reflexive Pronoun in Accusative | Meaning |
|---|---|
| sich anziehen | to get dressed |
| sich aufregen | to get excited |
| sich beeilen | to hurry |
| sich beschäftigen mit | to be occupied with |
| sich bewerben um | to apply for |
| sich erinnern an | to remember |
| sich freuen auf | to look forward to |
| sich interessieren für | to be interested in |
| sich irren | to be wrong |
| sich melden | to report (for duty etc) *or* to volunteer |
| sich rasieren | to shave |
| sich setzen *or* hinsetzen | to sit down |
| sich trauen | to dare |
| sich umsehen | to look around |

**Ich <u>ziehe</u> mich schnell <u>an</u> und**      I'll get dressed quickly and then we can go.
**dann gehen wir.**
**Wir müssen <u>uns beeilen</u>.**      We must hurry.

| Reflexive Verb with Reflexive Pronoun in Dative | Meaning |
|---|---|
| sich abgewöhnen | to give up (something) |
| sich ansehen | to have a look at |
| sich einbilden | to imagine (wrongly) |
| sich erlauben | to allow oneself |
| sich leisten | to treat oneself |
| sich vornehmen | to plan to do |
| sich vorstellen | to imagine |
| sich wünschen | to want |

| | |
|---|---|
| **Ich muss <u>mir</u> das Rauchen abgewöhnen.** | I must give up smoking. |
| **Sie kann <u>sich</u> ein neues Auto nicht leisten.** | She can't afford a new car. |
| **Was <u>wünscht</u> ihr <u>euch</u> zu Weihnachten?** | What do you want for Christmas? |

*i* Note that a direct object reflexive pronoun changes to an indirect object pronoun if another direct object is present.

| | |
|---|---|
| **Ich wasche <u>mich</u>.** | I'm having a wash. |
| **mich** = direct object reflexive pronoun | |
| **Ich wasche <u>mir</u> die Hände.** | I am washing my hands. |
| **mir** = indirect object reflexive pronoun | |
| **die Hände** = direct object | |

⇨ *For more information on **Pronouns**, see page 89.*

➤ Some German verbs which are not usually reflexive can be made reflexive by adding a reflexive pronoun.

| | |
|---|---|
| **Soll ich es melden?** | Should I report it? |
| **Ich habe <u>mich</u> gemeldet.** | I volunteered. |

⇨ *For more information on **Reflexive pronouns**, see page 111.*

---

**KEY POINTS**

✔ A reflexive verb is made up of a reflexive pronoun and a verb.
✔ The direct object pronouns in the accusative are **mich**, **dich**, **sich**, **uns**, **euch**, **sich**, **sich**.
✔ The indirect object pronouns in the dative are **mir**, **dir**, **sich**, **uns**, **euch**, **sich**, **sich**.

---

# Test yourself

**91** **Fill the gap with the reflexive pronoun *mir* or *mich* as appropriate.**

    **a** Ich kann ........................ nicht daran erinnern.

    **b** Das kann ich ........................ überhaupt nicht vorstellen.

    **c** Ich bilde ........................ nicht ein, genauso klug zu sein wie du.

    **d** Ich freue ........................ sehr auf deinen Besuch.

    **e** Ich sehe ........................ das Bild etwas genauer an.

    **f** Bist du allein hier? Ich setze ........................ zu dir.

    **g** Ich beschäftige ........................ schon lange mit dieser Frage.

    **h** Ich glaube, ich bewerbe ........................ um die neue Stelle.

    **i** Ich nehme ........................ vor, immer pünktlich zu sein.

    **j** Ich gewöhne ........................ das Rauchen ab.

**92** **Translate the following sentences into German, using a reflexive verb.**

    **a** You have to hurry. ....................................................................

    **b** I'm looking forward to the summer holidays.

       ....................................................................

    **c** We're having a look at his new car.

       ....................................................................

    **d** My father always shaves before breakfast.

       ....................................................................

    **e** I'm never wrong. ....................................................................

    **f** What do you want for your birthday?

       ....................................................................

    **g** We are getting close to the castle. ....................................................................

    **h** I'm allowing myself an ice cream. ....................................................................

    **i** I don't dare to jump off the wall.

       ....................................................................

    **j** We look around in the village. ....................................................................

# Test yourself

**93** **Form a sentence using the elements given.**

**a** wäscht/die Hände/sich/er ......................................................

**b** mir/ich/neuen Computer/leiste/einen

......................................................

**c** sich/bildet/ein/er/was ......................................................

**d** gar nichts/an/ich/mich/erinnere

......................................................

**e** regst/so/immer/du/dich/auf ......................................................

**f** mich/meinen Geburtstag/ich/auf/freue

......................................................

**g** ich/neues Fahrrad/mir/ein/wünsche

......................................................

**h** die Bank/wir/auf/uns/setzen ......................................................

**i** kleine Pause/erlauben/wir/uns/eine

......................................................

**j** nähere/ich/der Stadt/mich ......................................................

# The imperative

---
**What is the imperative?**
An **imperative** is a form of the verb used when giving orders and instructions,
for example, *Shut the door!; Sit down!; Don't go!*
---

## Using the imperative

➤ In German, there are three main forms of the imperative that are used to give instructions or orders to someone. These correspond to the three different ways of saying *you*: **du**, **ihr** and **Sie**. However, it is only in the **Sie** form of the imperative that the pronoun usually appears – in the **du** and **ihr** forms, the pronoun is generally dropped, leaving only the verb.

| | |
|---|---|
| **Hör zu!** | Listen! |
| **Hören <u>Sie</u> zu!** | Listen! |

## Forming the present tense imperative

➤ Most weak, strong and mixed verbs form the present tense imperative in the following way:

| Pronoun | Form of Imperative | Verb Example | Meaning |
|---|---|---|---|
| **du** (*singular*) | verb stem (+ **e**) | **hol(e)!** | fetch! |
| **ihr** (*plural*) | verb stem + **t** | **holt!** | fetch! |
| **Sie** (*polite singular and plural*) | verb stem + **en** + **Sie** | **holen Sie!** | fetch! |

ⓘ Note that the **-e** of the **du** form is often dropped, but NOT where the verb stem ends, for example, in **chn-**, **fn-**, or **tm-**. In such cases, the **-e** is kept to make the imperative easier to pronounce.

| | |
|---|---|
| **Hör zu!** | Listen! |
| **Hol es!** | Fetch it! |
| BUT: | |
| **Öffn<u>e</u> die Tür!** | Open the door! |
| **Atm<u>e</u> richtig durch!** | Take a deep breath! |
| **Rechn<u>e</u> noch mal nach!** | Do your sums again! |

---

*Grammar Extra!*
Weak verbs ending in **-eln** or **-ern** also retain this **-e**, but the other **-e** in the stem itself is often dropped in spoken German.

| Verb | Meaning | Imperative | Meaning |
|---|---|---|---|
| **wandern** | to walk | **wand(e)re!** | walk! |
| **handeln** | to act | **hand(e)le!** | act! |

---

➤ Any vowel change in the present tense of a strong verb also occurs in the **du** form of its imperative and the **-e** mentioned above is generally not added. However, if this vowel change in the present tense involves adding an umlaut, this umlaut is NOT added to the **du** form of the imperative.

| Verb | Meaning | 2nd Person Singular | Meaning | 2nd Person Singular Imperative | Meaning |
|------|---------|---------------------|---------|-------------------------------|---------|
| **nehmen** | to take | **du nimmst** | you take | **nimm!** | take! |
| **helfen** | to help | **du hilfst** | you help | **hilf!** | help! |
| **laufen** | to run | **du läufst** | you run | **lauf(e)!** | run! |
| **stoßen** | to push | **du stößt** | you push | **stoß(e)!** | push! |

## Word order with the imperative

➤ An object pronoun is a word like **es** (meaning *it*), **mir** (meaning *me*) or **ihnen** (meaning *them/to them*) that is used instead of a noun as the object of a sentence. In the imperative, the object pronoun comes straight after the verb. However, you can have orders and instructions containing both <u>direct object</u> and <u>indirect object</u> pronouns. In these cases, the direct object pronoun always comes before the indirect object pronoun.

| | |
|---|---|
| **Hol mir das Buch!** | Fetch me that book! |
| **Hol es mir!** | Fetch me it! |
| **Holt mir das Buch!** | Fetch me that book! |
| **Holt es mir!** | Fetch me it! |
| **Holen Sie mir das Buch!** | Fetch me that book! |
| **Holen Sie es mir!** | Fetch me it! |

➪ *For more information on **Word order with indirect object pronouns**, see page 99.*

➤ In the imperative form of a reflexive verb such as **sich waschen** (meaning *to wash oneself*) or **sich setzen** (meaning *to sit down*), the reflexive pronoun comes immediately after the verb.

| Reflexive verb | Meaning | Imperative Forms | Meaning |
|----------------|---------|------------------|---------|
| **sich setzen** | to sit down | **setz <u>dich</u>!** | sit down! |
| | | **setzt <u>euch</u>!** | sit down! |
| | | **setzen Sie <u>sich</u>!** | do sit down! |

➪ *For more information on **Reflexive pronouns**, see page 111.*

➤ In verbs which have separable prefixes, the prefix comes at the end of the imperative.

| Verb with Separable Prefix | Meaning | Imperative Example | Meaning |
|----------------------------|---------|--------------------|---------|
| **zumachen** | to close | **Mach die Tür zu!** | Close the door! |
| **aufhören** | to stop | **Hör aber endlich auf!** | Do stop it! |

➪ *For more information on **Separable prefixes**, see page 150.*

For further explanation of grammatical terms, please see pages viii-xii.

## Other points about the imperative

➤ In German, imperatives are usually followed by an exclamation mark, unless they are not being used to give an order or instruction. For example, they can also be used where we might say *Can you...* or *Could you ...* in English.

| | |
|---|---|
| **Lass ihn in Ruhe!** | Leave him alone! |
| **Sagen Sie mir bitte, wie spät es ist.** | Can you tell me what time it is please? |

➤ The verb **sein** (meaning *to be*) is a strong, irregular verb. Its imperative forms are also irregular and the **du**, **Sie** and less common **wir** forms are not the same as the present tense forms of the verb.

| | |
|---|---|
| **Sei ruhig!** | Be quiet! |
| **Seid ruhig!** | Be quiet! |
| **Seien Sie ruhig!** | Be quiet! |

> *Tip*
>
> The words **auch**, **nur**, **mal** and **doch** are frequently used with imperatives to change their meanings in different ways, but are often not translated since they have no direct equivalent in English.
>
> | | |
> |---|---|
> | **Geh doch!** | Go on!/Get going! |
> | **Sag mal, wo warst du?** | Tell me, where were you? |
> | **Versuchen Sie es mal!** | Give it a try! |
> | **Komm schon!** | Do come./Please come. |
> | **Mach es auch richtig!** | Be sure to do it properly. |

---

*Grammar Extra!*

There are some alternatives to using the imperative in German:

• Infinitives (the *to* form of a verb) are often used instead of the imperative in written instructions or public announcements

| | |
|---|---|
| **Einsteigen!** | All aboard! |
| **Zwiebeln abziehen und in Ringe schneiden.** | Peel the onions and slice them. |

• Nouns, adjectives or adverbs can also be used as imperatives

| | |
|---|---|
| **Ruhe!** | Be quiet!/Silence! |
| **Vorsicht!** | Careful!/Look out! |

Some of these have become set expressions

| | |
|---|---|
| **Achtung!** | Listen!/Attention! |
| **Rauchen verboten!** | No smoking. |

---

**KEY POINTS**

✔ The imperative has four forms: **du**, **ihr**, **Sie** and **wir**.
✔ The forms are the same as the **ihr**, **Sie** and **wir** forms of the present tense for most strong, weak and mixed verbs, but the **du** form drops the **-st** present tense ending and sometimes adds an **-e** on the end.
✔ Any vowel change in the stem of a strong verb also occurs in the imperative, except if it involves adding an umlaut.
✔ Object pronouns always go after the verb, with the direct object pronoun coming before the indirect object pronoun.
✔ Reflexive pronouns also come after the verb, while separable verb prefixes come at the end of the imperative sentence.
✔ **Sein** has irregular imperative forms.

# Test yourself

**94** **Translate the following instructions into German. Assume you are addressing one person with whom you are on familiar terms.**

**a** Give me that! ......................................................................................................

**b** Give them to me! ...............................................................................................

**c** Don't say that! ...................................................................................................

**d** Go away! ...........................................................................................................

**e** Fetch me a coffee! .............................................................................................

**f** Listen to me! .....................................................................................................

**g** Speak to me! .....................................................................................................

**h** Open the door! ..................................................................................................

**i** Leave me alone! ................................................................................................

**j** Read the book! ..................................................................................................

**95** **Replace the highlighted command with the *Sie* form of the imperative. The first one has been done for you.**

**a** **Gib** mir das Buch! *Geben Sie* ......................

**b** **Lauf** ihr nicht nach! ......................................

**c** **Sei** endlich still! ...........................................

**d** **Lass** mich ausreden! ....................................

**e** **Mach** das Fenster auf! ..................................

**f** **Nimm dir** ein Glas! .......................................

**g** **Sag** mir warum! ...........................................

**h** **Hör** endlich auf! ...........................................

**i** **Wasch dir** die Hände! ..................................

**j** **Komm** endlich! ............................................

# Test yourself

**96 Cross out the items the speaker is not likely to be referring to.**

a Sprich mit ...!      deinem Vater/dem Bild/ihr/dem Lehrer

b Verlangen Sie ...!      Ihr Recht/das Geld zurück/den Hund/Gerechtigkeit

c Macht ...!      das Fenster auf/das Buch/schnell/Schluss

d Nimm ...!      den Brief/etwas Geduld/seine Hand/dir Zeit

e Holen Sie ...!      die Wand/Hilfe/das Geld/die Polizei

f Seid ...!      still/ruhig/günstig/langsam

g Versuchen Sie ...!      es nochmal/diesen Tee/den Ball/das Kind

h Setz dich ...!      in den Baum/auf die Bank/dorthin/neben sie

i Mach mir ...!      etwas Geduld/einen Kaffee/keine Sorgen/ein Buch

j Lassen Sie ...!      ihn los/sie fest/mich ausreden/uns gehen

**97 Match the sentences that have a connection.**

a Gehen wir nach Hause!      Er hat Durst.

b Hab ein bisschen Geduld!      Du gehst zu schnell.

c Sei still!      Sie kommt bestimmt gleich.

d Mach ihm einen Tee!      Du redest zu viel.

e Warte auf uns!      Es ist schon spät.

# Verb prefixes in the present tense

---

## What is a verb prefix?

In English, a **verb prefix** is a word such as *up* or *down* which is used with verbs to create new verbs with an entirely different meaning.

get → get up → get down
put → put up → put down
shut → shut up → shut down

---

➤ In German there is a similar system, but the words are put before the infinitive and joined to it:

**zu** (meaning *to*) + **geben** (meaning *to give*) = **zugeben** (meaning *to admit*)
**an** (meaning *on, to, by*) + **ziehen** (meaning *to pull*) = **anziehen** (meaning *to put on* or *to attract*)

➤ Prefixes can be found in strong, weak and mixed verbs. Some prefixes are always joined to the verb and never separated from it – these are called inseparable prefixes. However, the majority are separated from the verb in certain tenses and forms, and come at the end of the sentence. They are called separable prefixes.

## Inseparable prefixes

➤ There are eight inseparable prefixes in German, highlighted in the table of common inseparable verbs below:

| Inseparable Verb | Meaning | Inseparable Verb | Meaning |
|---|---|---|---|
| **be**schreiben | to describe | **ent**täuschen | to disappoint |
| **ge**hören | to belong | **ver**lieren | to lose |
| **emp**fangen | to receive | **er**halten | to preserve |
| **miss**trauen | to mistrust | **zer**legen | to dismantle |

ⓘ Note that when you pronounce an inseparable verb, the stress is NEVER on the inseparable prefix:

er*hal*ten
ver*lie*ren
emp*fan*gen
ver*ges*sen

**Das muss ich wirklich nicht ver*ges*sen.**   I really mustn't forget that.

## Separable prefixes

➤ There are many separable prefixes in German and some of them are highlighted in the table below which shows a selection of the most common separable verbs:

| Separable Verb | Meaning | Separable Verb | Meaning |
|---|---|---|---|
| **ab**fahren | to leave | **mit**machen | to join in |
| **an**kommen | to arrive | **nach**geben | to give way/in |
| **auf**stehen | to get up | **vor**ziehen | to prefer |
| **aus**gehen | to go out | **weg**laufen | to run away |
| **ein**steigen | to get on | **zu**schauen | to watch |
| **fest**stellen | to establish/see | **zurecht**kommen | to manage |
| **frei**halten | to keep free | **zurück**kehren | to return |
| **her**kommen | to come (here) | **zusammen**passen | to be well-suited; to go well together |
| **hin**legen | to put down | | |

**Der Zug fährt in zehn Minuten <u>ab</u>.**  The train is leaving in ten minutes.
**Ich stehe jeden Morgen früh <u>auf</u>.**  I get up early every morning.
**Sie gibt niemals <u>nach</u>.**  She'll never give in.

## Word order with separable prefixes

➤ In tenses consisting of one verb part only, for example the present and the imperfect, the separable prefix is placed at the end of the main clause.
   **Der Bus kam immer spät <u>an</u>.**  The bus was always late.

⇨ *For more information on **Separable prefixes** in the perfect tense, see page 155.*

➤ In subordinate clauses, the prefix is attached to the verb, which is then placed at the end of the subordinate clause.
   **Weil der Bus spät <u>an</u>kam,**  Because the bus arrived late, she missed
   **verpasste sie den Zug.**  the train.

⇨ *For more information on **Subordinate clauses**, see page 244.*

➤ In infinitive phrases using **zu**, the **zu** is inserted between the verb and its prefix to form one word.
   **Um rechtzeitig auf<u>zu</u>stehen, muss**  In order to get up on time I'll have to set
   **ich den Wecker stellen.**  the alarm.

⇨ *For more information on the **Infinitive**, see page 181.*

## Verb combinations

➤ Below you will see some other types of word which can be combined with verbs. These combinations are mostly written as two separate words (but some may also be written as one word) and behave like separable verbs:

- Noun + verb combinations

| | |
|---|---|
| **Ski fahren** | to ski |
| **Ich <u>fahre</u> gern <u>Ski</u>.** | I like skiing. |

| | |
|---|---|
| **Schlittschuh laufen** | to ice-skate |
| **Im Winter kann man <u>Schlittschuh laufen</u>.** | You can ice-skate in winter. |

- Infinitive + verb combinations

| | |
|---|---|
| **kennenlernen** (or **kennen lernen**) | to meet or to get to know |
| **Meine Mutter möchte dich kennenlernen.** | My mother wants to meet you. |
| **Er <u>lernt</u> sie nie richtig <u>kennen</u>.** | He'll never get to know her properly. |

| | |
|---|---|
| **sitzen bleiben** (or **sitzenbleiben**) | to remain seated |
| **<u>Bleiben</u> Sie bitte <u>sitzen</u>.** | Please remain seated. |

| | |
|---|---|
| **spazieren gehen** (or **spazierengehen**) | to go for a walk |
| **Er <u>geht</u> jeden Tag <u>spazieren</u>.** | He goes for a walk every day. |

- Adjective + verb combinations

| | |
|---|---|
| **bekannt machen** | to announce |
| **Die Regierung will das morgen <u>bekannt</u> <u>machen</u>.** | The government plans to announce it tomorrow. |

- Some adverb + verb combinations

| | |
|---|---|
| **gut riechen** | to smell good |
| **Das Essen <u>riecht</u> <u>gut</u>.** | The food smells good. |

- Verb combinations with **-seits**

| | |
|---|---|
| **abseitsstehen** | to stand apart |
| **Sie <u>steht</u> immer <u>abseits</u> von den anderen.** | She always stands apart from the others. |

- Prefix combinations with **sein**

| | |
|---|---|
| **auf sein** | to be open or to be up |
| **Das Fenster <u>ist</u> <u>auf</u>.** | The window is open. |
| **Die Geschäfte <u>sind</u> am Sonntag nicht <u>auf</u>.** | The shops are closed on Sundays. |
| **Sie <u>ist</u> noch nicht <u>auf</u>.** | She isn't up yet. |

| | |
|---|---|
| **zu sein** | to be shut |
| **Das Fenster <u>ist</u> <u>zu</u>.** | The window is shut. |

[*i*] Note that **auf** (meaning *open*) is another word for **geöffnet** and **zu** (meaning *shut* or *closed*) is another word for **geschlossen**.

---

### KEY POINTS

✔ Prefixes can be found in strong, weak and mixed verbs.
✔ Eight prefixes are inseparable and are never separated from the verb.
✔ Most prefixes are separable and are separated from the verb in certain tenses and forms and come at the end of the sentence.

# Test yourself

**98** Cross out the verbs that are unlikely to be combined with the prefix.

| | | |
|---|---|---|
| **a** | zu- | passen/sehen/steigen/machen |
| **b** | her- | geben/sprechen/kommen/schauen |
| **c** | hin- | sehen/riechen/legen/stellen |
| **d** | zurück- | gehen/geben/laufen/sprechen |
| **e** | zusammen- | kehren/passen/lernen/schieben |
| **f** | frei- | halten/lernen/geben/machen |
| **g** | mit- | geben/singen/kehren/machen |
| **h** | weg- | gehen/laufen/schauen/sprechen |
| **i** | an- | lesen/sprechen/machen/legen |
| **j** | nach- | sagen/sprechen/geben/lachen |

**99** Form a sentence, in the present tense, using the elements below. The first one has been done for you.

**a** ankommen/spät/heute/Bus/der

*Der Bus kommt heute spät an.* ................................................

**b** zu/zurückkehren/er/wann/uns

................................................

**c** Farben/nicht/diese/zusammenpassen

................................................

**d** das/ich/Buch/hier/hinlegen

................................................

**e** er/sehr/immer/aufstehen/morgens/früh

................................................

**f** ihr/du/immer/warum/nachgeben ................................................

**g** Platz/du/diesen/freihalten/mir

................................................

**h** Abend/mit/ausgehen/heute/Brigitte

................................................

**i** 1000 Euro/wir/auskommen/nicht/mit

................................................

**j** bitte/zuschauen/mir/nicht

................................................

# The perfect tense

> ### What is the perfect tense?
> The **perfect** is one of the verb tenses used to talk about the past, especially about a single, rather than a repeated action.
>
> | | |
> |---|---|
> | **Den Nachtisch habe ich schon gegessen.** | I've already eaten dessert. |

## Using the perfect tense

➤ The German perfect tense is the one generally used to translate an English form such as *I have finished*.

> I <u>have</u> finished the book.      **Ich <u>habe</u> das Buch zu Ende <u>gelesen</u>.**

➤ The perfect tense is also sometimes used to translate an English form such as *I gave*.

> I gave him my phone number.      **Ich <u>habe</u> ihm meine Nummer <u>gegeben</u>.**

> *Tip*
> When a specific time in the past is referred to, you use the perfect tense in German. In English you use the *-ed* form instead.
>
> | | |
> |---|---|
> | **Gestern Abend habe ich einen Krimi im Fernsehen gesehen.** | Last night I watched a thriller on TV. |

➤ The perfect tense is used with **seit** or **seitdem** to describe a completed action in the past, whereas the present tense is used to describe an action which started in the past and is still continuing in the present.

> <u>Seit</u> dem Unfall <u>habe</u> ich sie nur einmal <u>gesehen</u>.      I've only seen her once since the accident.

> ⇨ *For more information on this use of the **Present tense**, see page 124.*

## Forming the perfect tense

➤ Unlike the present and imperfect tenses, the perfect tense has <u>TWO</u> parts to it:

- the <u>present</u> tense of the irregular weak verb **haben** (meaning *to have*) or the irregular strong verb **sein** (meaning *to be*). They are also known as auxiliary verbs.

- a part of the main verb called the *past participle*, like *given, finished* and *done* in English.

➤ In other words, the perfect tense in German is like the form *I have done* in English.

| Pronoun | Ending | Present Tense | Meanings |
|---------|--------|---------------|----------|
| ich | -e | ich hab<u>e</u> | I have |
| du | -st | du ha<u>st</u> | you have |
| er<br>sie<br>es | -t | er ha<u>t</u><br>sie ha<u>t</u><br>es ha<u>t</u> | he/she/it has |
| wir | -en | wir hab<u>en</u> | we have |
| ihr | -t | ihr hab<u>t</u> | you (*plural*) have |
| sie<br>Sie | -en | sie hab<u>en</u><br>Sie hab<u>en</u> | they have<br>you (*polite*) have |

| Pronoun | Ending | Present Tense | Meanings |
|---------|--------|---------------|----------|
| ich | – | ich bin | I am |
| du | – | du bist | you are |
| er<br>sie<br>es | – | er ist<br>sie ist<br>es ist | he/she/it is |
| wir | – | wir sind | we are |
| ihr | – | ihr seid | you (*plural*) are |
| sie<br>Sie | –<br>– | sie sind<br>Sie sind | they are<br>you (*polite*) are |

## Forming the past participle

➤ To form the past participle of <u>weak</u> verbs, you add **ge-** to the beginning of the verb stem and **-t** to the end.

| Infinitive | Take off -en | Add ge- and -t |
|------------|--------------|----------------|
| **holen** (*to fetch*) | hol- | **geholt** |
| **machen** (*to do*) | mach- | **gemacht** |

🛈 Note that one exception to this rule is weak verbs ending in **-ieren**, which omit the **ge**.

**studieren** (*to study*)          **studiert** (*studied*)

➤ To form the past participle of <u>strong</u> verbs, you add **ge-** to the beginning of the verb stem and **-en** to the end. The vowel in the stem may also change.

| Infinitive | Take off -en | Add ge- and -en |
|------------|--------------|-----------------|
| **laufen** (*to run*) | lauf- | **gelaufen** |
| **singen** (*to sing*) | sing- | **ges<u>u</u>ngen** |

➤ To form the past participle of <u>mixed</u> verbs, you add **ge-** to the beginning of the verb stem and, like <u>weak</u> verbs, **-t** to the end. As with many strong verbs, the stem vowel may also change.

For further explanation of grammatical terms, please see pages viii-xii.

| Infinitive | Take off -en | Add ge- and -t |
|---|---|---|
| bringen (*to bring*) | bring- | gebracht |
| denken (*to think*) | denk- | gedacht |

➤ The perfect tense of <u>separable</u> verbs is also formed in the above way, except that the separable prefix is joined on to the front of the **ge-**: **ich habe die Flasche auf<u>ge</u>macht**, **du hast die Flasche auf<u>ge</u>macht** and so on.

➤ With <u>inseparable</u> verbs, the only difference is that past participles are formed without the **ge-**: **ich habe Kaffee <u>bestellt</u>**, **du hast Kaffee <u>bestellt</u>** and so on.

⇨ *For more information on **Separable** and **Inseparable verbs**, see pages 150 and 149.*

## Verbs that form their perfect tense with haben

➤ Most weak, strong and mixed verbs form their perfect tense with **haben**, for example **machen**:

| Pronoun | haben | Past Participle | Meaning |
|---|---|---|---|
| ich | habe | gemacht | I did, I have done |
| du | hast | gemacht | you did, you have done |
| er<br>sie<br>es | hat | gemacht | he/she/it did,<br>he/she/it has done |
| wir | haben | gemacht | we did, we have done |
| ihr | habt | gemacht | you (*plural familiar*)<br>did, you have done |
| sie<br>Sie | haben<br>haben | gemacht<br>gemacht | they did, they have done<br>you (*singular/plural formal*)<br>did, you have done |

| | |
|---|---|
| **Sie <u>hat</u> ihre Hausaufgaben schon <u>gemacht</u>.** | She has already done her homework. |
| **<u>Haben</u> Sie gut <u>geschlafen</u>?** | Did you sleep well? |
| **Er <u>hat</u> fleißig <u>gearbeitet</u>.** | He has worked hard. |

## haben or sein?

➤ <u>MOST</u> verbs form their perfect tense with **haben.**

| | |
|---|---|
| **Ich <u>habe</u> das schon <u>gemacht</u>.** | I've already done that. |
| **Wo <u>haben</u> Sie früher <u>gearbeitet</u>?** | Where did you work before? |

➤ With reflexive verbs the reflexive pronoun comes immediately after **haben**.

| | |
|---|---|
| **Ich <u>habe</u> <u>mich</u> heute Morgen geduscht.** | I had a shower this morning. |
| **Sie <u>hat</u> <u>sich</u> nicht daran erinnert.** | She didn't remember. |

⇨ *For more information on **Reflexive verbs**, see page 138.*

➤ There are two main groups of verbs which form their perfect tense with **sein** instead of **haben**, and most of them are strong verbs:

- verbs which take no direct object and are used mainly to talk about movement or a change of some kind, such as:

| | |
|---|---|
| **gehen** | to go |
| **kommen** | to come |
| **ankommen** | to arrive |
| **abfahren** | to leave |
| **aussteigen** | to get off |
| **einsteigen** | to get on |
| **sterben** | to die |
| **sein** | to be |
| **werden** | to become |
| **bleiben** | to remain |
| **begegnen** | to meet |
| **gelingen** | to succeed |
| **aufstehen** | to get up |
| **fallen** | to fall |

| | |
|---|---|
| **Gestern <u>bin</u> ich ins Kino <u>gegangen</u>.** | I went to the cinema yesterday. |
| **Sie <u>ist</u> heute Morgen ganz früh <u>abgefahren</u>.** | She left really early this morning. |
| **An welcher Haltestelle <u>sind</u> Sie <u>ausgestiegen</u>?** | Which stop did you get off at? |

- two verbs which mean *to happen*.

| | |
|---|---|
| **Was ist geschehen/passiert?** | What happened? |

⇨ Here are the perfect tense forms of a very common strong verb, **gehen**, in full:

| Pronoun | sein | Past Participle | Meanings |
|---|---|---|---|
| ich | bin | gegangen | I went, I have gone |
| du | bist | gegangen | you went, you have gone |
| er<br>sie<br>es | ist | gegangen | he/she/it went,<br>he/she/it has gone |
| wir | sind | gegangen | we went, we have gone |
| ihr | seid | gegangen | you (*plural familiar*) went,<br>you have gone |
| sie<br>Sie | sind<br>sind | gegangen<br>gegangen | they went, they have gone<br>you (*singular/plural formal*)<br>went, you have gone |

*i* Note that the perfect tense of the most important strong, weak and mixed verbs is shown in the Verb Tables.

⇨ For **Verb Tables**, *see supplement*.

**KEY POINTS**

✔ The perfect tense describes things that happened and were completed in the past.

✔ The perfect tense is formed with the present tense of **haben** or **sein** and a past participle.

✔ The past participle begins in **ge-** and ends in **-t** for weak verbs, in **ge-** and **-en** for strong verbs, often with a stem vowel change, and in **ge-** and **-t** for mixed verbs, often with a stem vowel change.

✔ Most verbs take **haben** in the perfect tense. Many strong verbs, especially those referring to movement or change, take **sein**.

# Test yourself

**100 Translate the following sentences into German.**

**a** We stayed at home yesterday.

.................................................................................................

**b** I have lost my keys.

.................................................................................................

**c** Sabine has bought two pairs of shoes.

.................................................................................................

**d** He gave me his phone number.

.................................................................................................

**e** I've already met her twice today.

.................................................................................................

**f** I slept badly last night.

.................................................................................................

**g** They went to the theatre yesterday.

.................................................................................................

**h** I've already seen the film.

.................................................................................................

**i** Who told you that?

.................................................................................................

**j** Have you done your homework? (use **ihr**)

.................................................................................................


**101 Complete the following sentences with the correct past participle.**

**a** Sie ist gestern in Urlaub ..................................... . **[fahren]**

**b** Der Kuchen ist mir wirklich gut ..................................... . **[gelingen]**

**c** Hast du mir ein Geschenk ..................................... ? **[mitbringen]**

**d** Unsere Mannschaft hat 4:2 ..................................... . **[verlieren]**

**e** Wir haben sofort die Polizei ..................................... . **[rufen]**

**f** Meine Großmutter ist letzte Woche ..................................... . **[sterben]**

**g** Ich habe letzte Nacht nicht gut ..................................... . **[schlafen]**

**h** An welcher Haltestelle bist du ..................................... ? **[aussteigen]**

**i** Wie viele CDs hast du ..................................... ? **[kaufen]**

**j** Ich bin gestern den ganzen Abend zu Hause ..................................... . **[sein]**

# Test yourself

**102 Fill the gap with the correct form of *haben* or *sein* as appropriate.**

**a** ........................ du gesehen, wohin er gegangen ist?

**b** Gestern ........................ ich um 6 Uhr aufgestanden.

**c** Der Zug ........................ vor fünf Minuten abgefahren.

**d** Im Café ........................ wir Kuchen gegessen.

**e** ........................ du an deine Hausaufgaben gedacht?

**f** Ich ........................ ihm gestern auf der Straße begegnet.

**g** Dieser Apfel ........................ vom Baum gefallen.

**h** ........................ Sie schon einmal in Bayern gewesen?

**i** Wir ........................ ihn gestern vom Bahnhof abgeholt.

**j** Er ........................ in München Chemie studiert.

# The imperfect tense

> **What is the imperfect tense?**
> The **imperfect tense** is one of the verb tenses used to talk about the past, especially in descriptions, and to say what used to happen, for example, It _was_ sunny at the weekend; I _used to walk_ to school.

## Using the imperfect tense

➤ The German imperfect tense is used:

- to describe actions in the past which the speaker feels have no link with the present

  **Er <u>kam</u> zu spät, um teilnehmen zu können.**      He <u>arrived</u> too late to take part.

- to describe what things were like and how people felt in the past

  **Ich <u>war</u> ganz traurig, als sie wegging.**      I <u>was</u> very sad when she left.

  **Damals <u>gab</u> es ein großes Problem mit Drogen.**      There <u>was</u> a big problem with drugs at that time.

- to say what used to happen or what you used to do regularly in the past

  **Wir <u>machten</u> jeden Tag einen Spaziergang.**      We <u>used to go for a walk</u> every day.

  **Samstags <u>spielte</u> ich Tennis.**      I <u>used to play tennis</u> on Saturdays.

> _i_   Note that if you want to talk about an event or action that took place and was completed in the past, you normally use the <u>perfect tense</u> in German conversation. The <u>imperfect tense</u> is normally used in written German.

> **Was <u>hast</u> du heute <u>gemacht</u>?**      What have you done today?

⇨ _For more information on the **Perfect tense**, see page 153._

➤ When using **seit** or **seitdem** to describe something that <u>had</u> happened or <u>had</u> been true at a point in the past, the imperfect is used in German, where in English a verb form with _had_ is used.

  **Sie <u>war</u> seit ihrer Heirat als Lehrerin beschäftigt.**      She <u>had</u> been working as a teacher since her marriage.

⇨ _For more information on the **Pluperfect tense**, see page 172._

> _Tip_
> Remember that you <u>NEVER</u> use the verb **sein** to translate _was_ or _were_ in forms like _was raining_ or _were looking_ and so on. You change the German verb ending instead.

## Forming the imperfect tense of weak verbs

➤ To form the imperfect tense of weak verbs, you use the same stem of the verb as for the present tense. Then you add the correct ending, depending on whether you are referring to **ich**, **du**, **er**, **sie**, **es**, **wir**, **ihr**, **sie** or **Sie**.

| Pronoun | Ending | Add to Stem, e.g. spiel- | Meanings |
|---------|--------|--------------------------|----------|
| ich | -te | ich spiel<u>te</u><br>I was playing | I played |
| du | -test | du spiel<u>test</u><br>you were playing | you played |
| er<br>sie<br>es | -te | er spiel<u>te</u><br>sie spiel<u>te</u>   he/she/it played<br>es spiel<u>te</u>   he/she/it were playing | he/she/it played |
| wir | -ten | wir spiel<u>ten</u><br>we were playing | we played |
| ihr | -tet | ihr spiel<u>tet</u><br>you were playing | you (*plural*) played |
| sie<br><br>Sie | -ten<br><br>Sie spiel<u>ten</u> | sie spiel<u>ten</u><br>they were playing<br>you (*polite*) played<br>you were playing | they played |

| | | |
|---|---|---|
| **Sie hol<u>te</u> ihn jeden Tag von der Arbeit ab.** | | She picked him up from work every day. |
| **Normalerweise mach<u>te</u> ich nach dem Abendessen meine Hausaufgaben.** | | I usually did my homework after dinner. |

➤ As with the present tense, some weak verbs change their spellings slightly when they are used in the imperfect tense.

● If the stem ends in **-d**, **-t**, **-m** or **-n** an extra **-e** is added before the usual imperfect endings to make pronunciation easier.

| Pronoun | Ending | Add to Stem, e.g. arbeit- | Meanings |
|---------|--------|---------------------------|----------|
| ich | -ete | ich arbeit<u>ete</u> | I worked<br>I was working |
| du | -etest | du arbeit<u>etest</u> | you worked<br>you were working |
| er<br>sie<br>es | -ete | er arbeit<u>ete</u><br>sie arbeit<u>ete</u><br>es arbeit<u>ete</u> | he/she/it worked<br>he/she/it was working |
| wir | -eten | wir arbeit<u>eten</u> | we worked<br>we were working |
| ihr | -etet | ihr arbeit<u>etet</u> | you (*plural*) worked<br>you were working |
| sie<br><br>Sie | -eten<br><br>-eten | sie arbeit<u>eten</u><br><br>Sie arbeit<u>eten</u> | they worked<br>they were working<br>you (*polite*) worked<br>you (*polite*) were working |

| | | |
|---|---|---|
| **Sie arbeit<u>ete</u> übers Wochenende.** | | She was working over the weekend. |
| **Ihr arbeit<u>etet</u> ganz schön viel.** | | You worked a lot. |

- If the **-m** or **-n** has one of the consonants **l**, **r** or **h** in front of it, the **-e** is not added as shown in the **du**, **er**, **sie** and **es**, and **ihr** forms below.

| Pronoun | Ending | Add to Stem, e.g. lern- | Meanings |
|---|---|---|---|
| du | -test | du lerntest | you learned<br>you were learning |
| er<br>sie<br>es | -te | er lernte<br>sie lernte<br>es lernte | he/she/it learned<br>he/she/it was learning |
| ihr | -tet | ihr lerntet | you (*plural*) learned<br>you were learning |

| | |
|---|---|
| **Sie lernte alles ganz schnell.** | She learned everything very quickly. |

## Forming the imperfect tense of strong verbs

➤ The main difference between strong verbs and weak verbs in the imperfect is that strong verbs have a vowel change and take a different set of endings. For example, let's compare **sagen** and **rufen**:

| | Infinitive | Meaning | Present | Imperfect |
|---|---|---|---|---|
| Weak | sagen | to say | er sagt | er sagte |
| Strong | rufen | to shout | er ruft | er rief |

➤ To form the imperfect tense of strong verbs you add the following endings to the stem, which undergoes a vowel change.

| Pronoun | Ending | Add to Stem, e.g. rief- | Meanings |
|---|---|---|---|
| ich | – | ich rief | I shouted<br>I was shouting |
| du | -st | du riefst | you shouted<br>you were shouting |
| er<br>sie<br><br>es | – | er rief<br>sie rief<br><br>es rief | he/she/it shouted<br>he/she/it were shouting |
| wir | -en | wir riefen | we shouted<br>we were shouting |
| ihr | -t | ihr rieft | you (*plural*) shouted<br>you were shouting |
| sie<br><br>Sie | -en | sie riefen<br><br>Sie riefen | they shouted<br>they were shouting<br>you (*polite*) shouted<br>you were shouting |

| | |
|---|---|
| **Sie rief mich immer freitags an.** | She always called me on Friday. |
| **Sie liefen die Straße entlang.** | They ran along the street. |
| **Als Kind sangst du viel.** | You used to sing a lot as a child. |

For further explanation of grammatical terms, please see pages viii-xii.

➤ As in other tenses, the verb **sein** is a very irregular strong verb since the imperfect forms seem to have no relation to the infinitive form of the verb: **ich war**, **du warst**, **er/sie/es war**, **wir waren**, **ihr wart**, **sie/Sie waren**.

## Forming the imperfect tense of mixed verbs

➤ The imperfect tense of mixed verbs is formed by adding the weak verb endings to a stem whose vowel has been changed as for a strong verb.

| Pronoun | Ending | Add to Stem, e.g. kann- | Meanings |
|---|---|---|---|
| ich | -te | ich k<u>ann</u>te | I knew |
| du | -test | du k<u>ann</u>test | you knew |
| er sie es | -te | er k<u>ann</u>te sie k<u>ann</u>te es k<u>ann</u>te | he/she/it knew |
| wir | -ten | wir k<u>ann</u>ten | we knew |
| ihr | -tet | ihr k<u>ann</u>tet | you (*plural*) knew |
| sie | -ten | sie k<u>ann</u>ten | they knew |
| Sie | | Sie k<u>ann</u>ten | you (*polite*) knew |

**Er kannte die Stadt nicht.**    He didn't know the town.

➤ **Bringen** (meaning *to bring*) and **denken** (meaning *to think*) have a vowel AND a consonant change in their imperfect forms

| | |
|---|---|
| **bringen** (*to bring*) | **denken** (*to think*) |
| **ich br<u>ach</u>te** | **ich d<u>ach</u>te** |
| **du br<u>ach</u>test** | **du d<u>ach</u>test** |
| **er/sie/es br<u>ach</u>te** | **er/sie/es d<u>ach</u>te** |
| **wir br<u>ach</u>ten** | **wir d<u>ach</u>ten** |
| **ihr br<u>ach</u>tet** | **ihr d<u>ach</u>tet** |
| **sie/Sie br<u>ach</u>ten** | **sie/Sie d<u>ach</u>ten** |

ⓘ Note that the imperfect tense of the most important strong, weak and mixed verbs is shown in the Verb Tables.

⇨ For **Verb Tables**, *see supplement*.

**KEY POINTS**

✔ The imperfect tense is generally used for things that happened regularly or for descriptions in the past, especially in written German.

✔ The imperfect of weak verbs is formed using the same stem of the verb as for the present tense + these endings: **-te**, **-test**, **-te**, **-ten**, **-tet**, **-ten**.

✔ If the stem of a weak verb ends in **-d**, **-t**, **-m** or **-n** an extra **-e** is added before the usual imperfect endings to make pronunciation easier.
If the **-m** or **-n** has one of the consonants **l**, **r** or **h** in front of it, the **-e** is not added.

✔ The imperfect tense of strong verbs is formed by adding the following endings to the stem, which undergoes a vowel change: **-**, **-st**, **-**, **-en**, **-t**, **-en**.

✔ The imperfect tense of mixed verbs is formed by adding the weak verb endings to a stem whose vowel has been changed as for a strong verb. The verbs **bringen** and **denken** also have a consonant change.

# Test yourself

**103** **Translate the following sentences into German.**

**a** We walked along the road. ...................................................................................

**b** They didn't know who he was. ...........................................................................

**c** She was prettier than her sister. ........................................................................

**d** Five friends of ours came for lunch. .................................................................

**e** We saw each other very often. ...........................................................................

**f** They said they wanted to go to the cinema.

...................................................................................................................................

**g** When I was a child, we had a house in the country.

...................................................................................................................................

**h** She was always losing her keys. ........................................................................

**i** The children loved their mother. ......................................................................

**j** When it started raining, we went to a café.

...................................................................................................................................

**104** **Replace the highlighted present tense with the imperfect.**

**a** Wir **rufen** um Hilfe. .............................................................................................

**b** Sie **wissen** sich nicht zu helfen. ........................................................................

**c** Ich **sehe** mir einen Dokumentarfilm im Fernsehen an. ...............................

**d** Die Bauern **verkaufen** ihr Gemüse auf dem Wochenmarkt. .........................

**e** Ich **denke** mir nichts Böses dabei. ...................................................................

**f** Wir **brauchen** einen Arzt. ..................................................................................

**g** Meine Eltern **verbringen** ihren Urlaub in Griechenland. ...............................

**h** Der Arbeitstag **fängt** um 8 Uhr an. ..................................................................

**i** Er **ist** mit einer Zahnärztin verheiratet. .........................................................

**j** Ich **kenne** ihn nicht. ..........................................................................................

**105** **Match the sentences that are connected.**

| | |
|---|---|
| **a** **Sie war verheiratet.** | Sie aß kein Fleisch. |
| **b** **Sie lebte auf dem Land.** | Sie arbeitete in einem Hotel. |
| **c** **Sie war Kellnerin.** | Sie ging oft in die Stadt einkaufen. |
| **d** **Sie war Vegetarierin.** | Ihre Eltern hatten einen Bauernhof. |
| **e** **Sie liebte teure Kleider.** | Ihr Mann hieß Günter. |

# The future tense

---

### What is the future tense?
The **future tense** is a verb tense used to talk about something that will happen or will be true.

---

## Using the future tense

➤ In English the future tense is often shown by *will* or its shortened form *'ll*.
    What <u>will</u> you do?
    The weather <u>will</u> be warm and dry tomorrow.
    He<u>'ll</u> be here soon.
    I<u>'ll</u> give you a call.

➤ Just as in English, you can use the present tense in German to refer to something that is going to happen in the future.

| | |
|---|---|
| **Wir <u>fahren</u> nächstes Jahr nach Griechenland.** | We're going to Greece next year. |
| **Ich <u>nehme</u> den letzten Zug heute Abend.** | I'm taking the last train tonight. |

➤ The future tense IS used however to:

- emphasize the future
    **Das <u>werde</u> ich erst nächstes Jahr machen <u>können</u>.**  I won't be able to do that until next year.

- express doubt or suppose something about the future
    **Wenn sie zurückkommt, <u>wird</u> sie mir bestimmt <u>helfen</u>.**  I'm sure she'll help me when she returns.

➤ In English we often use *going to* followed by an infinitive to talk about something that will happen in the immediate future. You CANNOT use the German verb **gehen** (meaning *to go*) followed by an infinitive in the same way. Instead, you use either the present or the future tense.

| | |
|---|---|
| **Das <u>wirst</u> du bereuen.** | You're going to regret that. |
| **Wenn er sich nicht beeilt, <u>verpasst</u> er den Zug.** | He's going to miss the train if he doesn't hurry up. |

## Forming the future tense

➤ The future tense has <u>TWO</u> parts to it and is formed in the same way for all verbs, be they weak, strong or mixed:

- the present tense of the strong verb **werden** (meaning *to become*), which acts as an <u>auxiliary verb</u> like **haben** and **sein** in the perfect tense

---

For further explanation of grammatical terms, please see pages viii-xii.

| Pronoun | Ending | Present Tense | Meanings |
|---------|--------|---------------|----------|
| ich | -e | ich werde | I become |
| du | -st | du wirst | you become |
| er<br>sie<br>es | – | er wird<br>sie wird<br>es wird | he/she/it becomes |
| wir | -en | wir werden | we become |
| ihr | -t | ihr werdet | you (*plural*) become |
| sie<br>Sie | -en<br>-en | sie werden<br>Sie werden | they become<br>you (*polite*) become |

- the infinitive of the main verb, which normally goes at the end of the clause or sentence.

| Pronoun | Present Tense | Infinitive of<br>of werden | Meanings<br>Main Verb |
|---------|---------------|-----------------|-----------------|
| ich | werde | holen | I will fetch |
| du | wirst | holen | you will fetch |
| er<br>sie<br>es | wird | holen | he/she/it will fetch |
| wir | werden | holen | we will fetch |
| ihr | werdet | holen | you (*plural*) will fetch |
| sie<br>Sie | werden | holen | they will fetch<br>you (*polite*) will fetch |

**Morgen <u>werde</u> ich mein Fahrrad <u>holen</u>.**    I'll fetch my bike tomorrow.
**Sie <u>wird</u> dir meine Adresse <u>geben</u>.**    She'll give you my address.
**Wir <u>werden</u> draußen <u>warten</u>.**    We'll wait outside.

🔟 Note that in reflexive verbs, the reflexive pronoun comes after the present tense of **werden**.

**Ich <u>werde</u> mich nächste Woche <u>vorbereiten</u>.**    I'll prepare next week.

---

### KEY POINTS

✔ You can use a present tense in German to talk about something that will happen or be true in the future, just as in English.
✔ The future tense is formed from the present tense of **werden** and the infinitive of the main verb.
✔ You CANNOT use **gehen** with an infinitive to refer to things that will happen in the immediate future.
✔ The future tense is used to emphasize the future and express doubt or suppose something about the future.

# Test yourself

**106 Translate the following sentences into German without using _werden_.**

    **a** I'll get up early tomorrow. ....................................................................................

    **b** I will arrive at 10 o'clock. ....................................................................................

    **c** You'll have to be careful. ....................................................................................

    **d** Andrea will be able to help you. ..........................................................................

    **e** We'll be going to Italy in August. .........................................................................

    **f** Tomorrow after breakfast I'll go for a swim.

        ....................................................................................

    **g** I'll go home by train. ............................................................................................

    **h** She'll call you at the weekend. ............................................................................

    **i** Will you be in Berlin next week? ...........................................................................

    **j** We'll go to the museum tomorrow. ......................................................................

**107 Fill the gap with the appropriate form of _werden_.**

    **a** Wenn sie aus Köln zurückkommt, ........................ sie mich bestimmt besuchen.

    **b** Ich ........................ mich um die Kinder kümmern.

    **c** Wo ........................ du deine Ferien verbringen?

    **d** Wegen der Wirtschaftskrise ........................ es noch viele Probleme geben.

    **e** Wenn wir erst mal Kinder haben, ........................ wir uns ein größeres Haus kaufen müssen.

    **f** Was du heute getan hast, ........................ du noch bereuen.

    **g** Er ........................ gleich kommen.

    **h** Nächstes Jahr ........................ ihr beide 15 Jahre alt sein.

    **i** Ich hoffe, dass es Ihnen auch weiterhin gut gehen ........................ .

    **j** Dafür ........................ die Kinder dir ewig dankbar sein.

**108 Match the sentences that are connected.**

| | |
|---|---|
| **a** Morgen gewinnen wir im Lotto. | Wir werden in den Ferien zu Hause bleiben. |
| **b** Ich habe mich verschlafen. | Wir werden heiraten. |
| **c** Wir lieben uns sehr. | Ich werde zu spät zur Schule kommen. |
| **d** Wir haben kein Geld, um zu verreisen. | Ich werde zur Universität gehen. |
| **e** Ich will studieren. | Wir werden reich sein. |

# The conditional

---

## What is the conditional?

The **conditional** is a verb form used to talk about things that would happen or that would be true under certain conditions, for example, *I would help you if I could*. It is also used to say what you would like or need, for example, *Could you give me the bill?*

---

## Using the conditional

➤ You can often recognize a conditional in English by the word *would* or its shortened form *'d*.
   I <u>would</u> be sad if you left.
   If you asked him, he<u>'d</u> help you.

➤ In German, the conditional is also used to express *would*.

| | |
|---|---|
| Ich <u>würde</u> dir schon <u>helfen</u>, ich **habe aber keine Zeit.** | I <u>would</u> help you, but I don't have the time. |
| Was <u>würden</u> Sie an meiner Stelle <u>tun</u>? | What <u>would</u> you do in my position? |

## Forming the conditional

➤ The conditional has <u>TWO</u> parts to it and is formed in the same way for all verbs, be they weak, strong or mixed:

• the **würde** form or subjunctive of the verb **werden** (meaning *to become*)

• the infinitive of the main verb, which normally goes at the end of the clause.

| Pronoun | Subjunctive of werden | Infinitive of Main Verb | Meanings |
|---|---|---|---|
| ich | würde | holen | I would fetch |
| du | würdest | holen | you would fetch |
| er sie es | würde | holen | he/she/it would fetch |
| wir | würden | holen | we would fetch |
| ihr | würdet | holen | you (*plural*) would fetch |
| sie Sie | würden | holen | they would fetch you (*polite*) would fetch |

| | |
|---|---|
| **Das <u>würde</u> ich nie <u>machen</u>.** | I would never do that. |
| **<u>Würdest</u> du mir etwas Geld <u>leihen</u>?** | Would you lend me some money? |
| **<u>Würden</u> Sie jemals mit dem Rauchen <u>aufhören</u>?** | Would you ever stop smoking? |

[i] Note that you have to be careful not to mix up the present tense of **werden**, used to form the future tense, and the subjunctive of **werden**, used to form the conditional. They look similar.

| Future use | Conditional use |
|---|---|
| **ich werde** | ich würde |
| **du wirst** | du würdest |
| **er/sie/es wird** | er/sie/es würde |
| **wir werden** | wir würden |
| **ihr werdet** | ihr würdet |
| **sie/Sie werden** | sie/Sie würden |

**KEY POINTS**

✔ The conditional tense is formed from the subjunctive or **würde** part of **werden** and the infinitive of the main verb.

✔ The future tense is often confused with the conditional.

# Test yourself

**109 Fill the gap with the appropriate form of *würde*.**

**a** Ich ......................... heute Abend gern ausgehen.

**b** ......................... ihr so nett sein, mir zu helfen?

**c** Wir ......................... uns sehr freuen, Sie bei uns begrüßen zu können.

**d** Bis zum Schluss war unklar, wie der Prozess ausgehen ......................... .

**e** Herr Bergmann, Sie ......................... gut daran tun, dieses Angebot anzunehmen.

**f** Sie ......................... ihr Leben für ihre Kinder geben.

**g** ......................... du mir 500 Euro leihen?

**h** Ich wusste, dass es so kommen ......................... .

**i** Wenn sie bloß auf mich hören ......................... !

**j** ......................... Sie mir bitte das Buch geben?

**110 Translate the following sentences into German.**

**a** How much would you pay for that car?

...............................................................................

**b** Would you please stop talking? ...............................................

**c** What would his father say? .....................................................

**d** The children would like it here. .............................................

**e** I would buy it but I have no money.

...............................................................................

**f** Would you ever do anything like that?

...............................................................................

**g** If I had a camera I would take photos.

...............................................................................

**h** What would you do? ..............................................................

**i** I told him that I would do it.

...............................................................................

**j** I would help him if I had the time.

...............................................................................

# The pluperfect tense

> ### What is the pluperfect tense?
> The **pluperfect** is a verb tense which describes something that had happened or had been true at a point in the past, for example, *I'd forgotten to finish my homework*.

## Using the pluperfect tense

➤ You can often recognize a pluperfect tense in English by a form like *I had arrived*, *you'd fallen*.

| | |
|---|---|
| Sie **waren** schon **weggefahren**. | They <u>had</u> already <u>left</u>. |
| Diese Bücher **hatten** sie schon **gelesen**. | They <u>had</u> already <u>read</u> these books. |
| Meine Eltern **waren** schon ins Bett **gegangen**. | My parents <u>had gone</u> to bed already. |

🔢 Note that when translating *had done/had been doing* in conjunction with **seit/seitdem**, you use the imperfect tense in German.

| | |
|---|---|
| Sie **machte** es seit Jahren. | She <u>had been doing</u> it for years. |

⇨ *For more information on the Imperfect tense, see page 160.*

## Forming the pluperfect tense

➤ Like the perfect tense, the pluperfect tense in German has <u>two</u> parts to it:

- the <u>imperfect</u> tense of the verb **haben** (meaning *to have*) or **sein** (meaning *to be*)

- the past participle

➤ If a verb takes **haben** in the perfect tense, then it will take **haben** in the pluperfect too. If a verb takes **sein** in the perfect, then it will take **sein** in the pluperfect.

⇨ *For more information on the Imperfect tense and the Perfect tense, see pages 160 and 153.*

## Verbs taking haben

➤ Here are the pluperfect tense forms of **holen** (meaning *to fetch*) in full.

| Pronoun | haben | Past Participle | Meanings |
|---|---|---|---|
| ich | hatte | geholt | I had fetched |
| du | hattest | geholt | you had fetched |
| er<br>sie<br>es | hatte | geholt | he/she/it had fetched |
| wir | hatten | geholt | we had fetched |
| ihr | hattet | geholt | you (*plural*) had fetched |
| sie | hatten | geholt | they had fetched |
| Sie | | | you (*polite*) had fetched |

**Ich <u>hatte</u> schon mit ihm <u>gesprochen</u>.**   I had already spoken to him.

## Verbs taking sein

➤ Here are the pluperfect tense forms of **reisen** (meaning *to travel*) in full.

| Pronoun | sein | Past Participle | Meanings |
|---|---|---|---|
| ich | war | gereist | I had travelled |
| du | warst | gereist | you had travelled |
| er<br>sie<br>es | war | gereist | he/she/it had travelled |
| wir | waren | gereist | we had travelled |
| ihr | wart | gereist | you (*plural*) had travelled |
| sie<br>Sie | waren | gereist | they had travelled<br>you (*polite*) had travelled |

**Sie <u>war</u> sehr spät <u>angekommen</u>.**   She had arrived very late.

---

### KEY POINTS

✔ The pluperfect tense describes things that had happened or were true at a point in the past before something else happened.

✔ It is formed with the imperfect tense of **haben** or **sein** and the past participle.

✔ Verbs which take **haben** in the perfect tense will take **haben** in the pluperfect tense, and those which take **sein** in the perfect tense will take **sein** in the pluperfect tense.

# Test yourself

**111**  **Fill the gap with an appropriate past participle.**

**a** Sie waren mit dem Auto gekommen, aber zu Fuß nach Hause ......................... .
   **[gehen]**

**b** Er war hungrig, denn er hatte noch nicht zu Abend ......................... . **[essen]**

**c** Ich hatte sie schon zweimal ......................... , aber sie wollte mir nicht antworten.
   **[fragen]**

**d** Gestern war er mit dem Fahrrad ......................... und hatte einen Unfall gehabt.
   **[fahren]**

**e** Ich hatte lange darüber ......................... , aber die Antwort fiel mir nicht ein.
   **[nachdenken]**

**f** Er hatte dem Reporter ein Interview ......................... . **[geben]**

**g** Mit ihrem Besuch hatte ich nicht mehr ......................... , denn es war schon sehr spät.
   **[rechnen]**

**h** Wir waren mit dem Flugzeug in den Urlaub ......................... **[fliegen]**

**i** Das lange Warten hatte ihn müde ......................... **[machen]**

**j** Ich hatte gerade die Kinder ins Bett ......................... , als es klingelte. **[bringen]**

**112**  **Translate the following sentences into German.**

**a** He still hadn't seen that film.

.............................................................................................................

**b** They had never been to Ireland before. .................................................

**c** We had already decided to sell the house.

.............................................................................................................

**d** She had never worked there before. .......................................................

**e** He had drunk a lot. ..................................................................................

**f** She had already asked him about it. .......................................................

**g** I had noticed it immediately. ..................................................................

**h** He had often seen her in the supermarket.

.............................................................................................................

**i** I had not expected that. ..........................................................................

**j** I hadn't seen him for a long time.

.............................................................................................................

# The subjunctive

---

### What is the subjunctive?
The **subjunctive** is a verb form that is used in certain circumstances to express some sort of feeling, or to show there is doubt about whether something will happen or whether something is true. It is only used occasionally in modern English, for example, *If I were you, I wouldn't bother; So be it.*

---

## Using the subjunctive

➤ In German, subjunctive forms are used much more frequently than in English, to express uncertainty, speculation or doubt.

**Es könnte doch wahr sein.** It could be true.

➤ Subjunctives are also commonly used in <u>indirect speech</u>, also known as <u>reported</u> <u>speech</u>. What a person asks or thinks can be reported <u>directly</u>:

**Sie sagte: „Er kennt deine Schwester"** She said, "He <u>knows</u> your sister"
OR <u>indirectly</u>:
**Sie sagte, er kenne meine Schwester.** She said he <u>knew</u> my sister.

[*i*] Note that the change from direct to indirect speech is indicated by a change of tense in English, but is shown by a change to the subjunctive form in German.

---

*Grammar Extra!*

➤ There are two ways of introducing indirect speech in German, as in English.

• The conjunction **dass** (meaning *that*) begins the clause containing the indirect speech and the verb goes to the end of the clause.

**Sie hat uns gesagt, dass sie** She told us that she spoke Italian.
  **Italienisch spreche**.

• **dass** is dropped and normal word order applies in the second clause – the verb comes directly after the subject.

**Sie hat uns gesagt, sie spreche** She told us she spoke Italian.
  **Italienisch.**

---

➤ If you want to express a possible situation in English, for example, *I would be happy if you came*, you use '*if*' followed by the appropriate tense of the verb. In German you use the conjunction **wenn** followed by a subjunctive form of the verb.

[*i*] Note that the verb <u>ALWAYS</u> goes to the end of a clause beginning with **wenn**.

• **wenn** (meaning *if, whenever*)
**Wenn du käm(e)st** (*subjunctive*), **wäre** (*subjunctive*) **ich froh.**
OR
**Wenn du käm(e)st, würde ich froh sein.** I would be happy if you came.

ⓘ Note that the main clause can either have a subjunctive form or the conditional form.

**Wenn es mir nicht <u>gefiele</u>, würde ich**     If I wasn't happy with it, I wouldn't pay for it.
**es nicht bezahlen.**
OR
**Wenn es mir nicht <u>gefiele</u>, bezahlte**
(subjunctive) **ich es nicht.**

> ### Tip
> The imperfect forms of **bezahlen**, and of all weak verbs, are exactly the same as the imperfect subjunctive forms, so it's better to use a conditional tense to avoid confusion.

➤ **wenn ... nur** (meaning *if only*), **selbst wenn** (meaning *even if* or *even though*) and **wie** (meaning *how*) work in the same way as **wenn**. This means that the normal word order is changed and the verb comes at the end of the clause.

- **wenn ... nur**
  **<u>Wenn</u> wir <u>nur</u> erfolgreich <u>wären</u>!**     If only we were successful!

- **selbst wenn**
  **<u>Selbst wenn</u> er etwas <u>wüsste</u>,**     Even if he knew about it, he wouldn't
  **würde er nichts sagen.**     say anything.

- **wie**, expressing uncertainty
  **Er wunderte sich, <u>wie</u> es ihr wohl**     He wondered how she was.
  **<u>ginge</u>.**

➤ Unlike **wenn** and **wie** etc, the word order does not change after **als** (meaning *as if* or *as though*) when it is used in conditional clauses: it is immediately followed by the verb.
  **Sie sah aus, <u>als sei</u> sie krank.**     She looked as if she were ill.

> ### Tip
> It is quite common to hear the subjunctive used when someone is asking you something politely, for example, the person serving you in a shop might ask:
>
> **<u>Wäre</u> da sonst noch etwas?**     Will there be anything else?

## Forming the present subjunctive

➤ The three main forms of the subjunctive are the <u>present subjunctive</u>, the <u>imperfect subjunctive</u> and the <u>pluperfect subjunctive</u>.

➤ The present subjunctive of weak, strong and mixed verbs has the same endings:

| Pronoun | Present Subjunctive: Weak and Strong Verb Endings |
|---|---|
| ich | -e |
| du | -est |
| er/sie/es | -e |
| wir | -en |
| ihr | -et |
| sie/Sie | -en |

- **holen** (weak verb, meaning *to fetch*)
  **ich hole** — I fetch
  **du holest** — you fetch

- **fahren** (strong verb, meaning *to drive, to go*)
  **ich fahre** — I drive, I go
  **du fahrest** — you drive, you go

- **denken** (mixed verb, meaning *to think*)
  **ich denke** — I think
  **du denkest** — you think

> *Tip*
> The present and the present subjunctive endings are exactly the same for the **ich**, **wir** and **sie/Sie** forms.

## Forming the imperfect subjunctive

➤ The imperfect subjunctive is very common and is not always used to describe actions in the past. It can, for example, express the future.

**Wenn ich nur früher kommen könnte!** — If only I could come earlier!

➤ The imperfect tense and the imperfect subjunctive of weak verbs are identical.

| Pronoun | Imperfect/Imperfect Subjunctive | Meaning |
|---|---|---|
| ich | holte | I fetched |
| du | holtest | you fetched |
| er/sie/es | holte | he/she/it fetched |
| wir | holten | we fetched |
| ihr | holtet | you (*plural*) fetched |
| sie/Sie | holten | they/you (*polite*) fetched |

➤ The imperfect subjunctive of strong verbs is formed by adding the following endings to the stem of the imperfect. If there is an **a**, **o** or **u** in this stem, an umlaut is also added to it.

| Pronoun | Imperfect Subjunctive: Strong Verb Endings |
|---|---|
| ich | -e |
| du | -(e)st |
| er/sie/es | -e |
| wir | -en |
| ihr | -(e)t |
| sie/Sie | -en |

*(i)* Note that you add the **-e** to the **du** and **ihr** parts of the verb if it makes pronunciation easier, for example:

**du stieß<u>est</u>**          you pushed
**ihr stieß<u>et</u>**          you pushed

| Pronoun | Imperfect Subjunctive | Meaning |
|---|---|---|
| ich | gäb<u>e</u> | I gave |
| du | gäb<u>(e)st</u> | you gave |
| er/sie/es | gäb<u>e</u> | he/she/it gave |
| wir | gäb<u>en</u> | we gave |
| ihr | gäb<u>(e)t</u> | you (*plural*) gave |
| sie/Sie | gäb<u>en</u> | they/you (*polite*) gave |

➤ The imperfect subjunctive forms of the mixed verbs **brennen**, **kennen**, **senden**, **nennen**, **rennen** and **wenden** add weak verb imperfect endings to the stem of the verb, which DOES NOT change the vowel. The imperfect subjunctive forms of the remaining mixed verbs **bringen**, **denken** and **wissen** are also the same as the imperfect with one major difference: not only does the stem vowel change, but an umlaut is also added to the **a** or **u**. However, all of these forms are rare, with the conditional tense being used much more frequently instead.

**Wenn ich du wäre, <u>würde</u> ich <u>rennen</u>.**
INSTEAD OF
**Wenn ich du wäre, <u>rennte</u> ich.**          If I were you, I would run.
**Ich <u>würde</u> so etwas nie <u>denken</u>!**
INSTEAD OF
**Ich <u>dächte</u> so etwas nie!**          I would never think such a thing!

⇨ *For more information on the **Conditional**, see page 169.*

*Grammar Extra!*

The pluperfect subjunctive is formed from the imperfect subjunctive of **haben** or **sein** + the past participle. This subjunctive form is frequently used to translate the English structure 'If I had done something, ...'

| | |
|---|---|
| **Wenn ich Geld gehabt hätte**, | If I had had money, |
| **wäre ich gereist**. | I would have travelled. |

---

## KEY POINTS

✔ In German, subjunctive forms are used much more frequently than in English, to express uncertainty, speculation or doubt.

✔ Subjunctive forms are commonly used in indirect speech and in conditional sentences.

✔ The present subjunctive of weak, strong and mixed verbs have the same endings.

✔ The imperfect tense and the imperfect subjunctive of weak verbs are identical.

✔ The imperfect subjunctive of strong verbs is formed by adding the endings **-e**, **-(e)st**, **-e**, **-en**, **-(e)t**, **-en** to the stem of the imperfect and often has an umlaut change.

✔ The imperfect subjunctive of mixed verbs is rare and the conditonal form of **würde** + infinitive is normally used instead.

# Test yourself

**113** **Replace the highlighted words with indirect speech. The first one has been done for you.**

**a** Er sagte: „**Ich spreche** Französisch." _Er sagte, er spreche Französisch._

**b** Sie sagte: „**Ich komme** morgen." ...................................................

**c** Sie sagte: „**Er hat** keine Manieren." ...................................................

**d** Er erklärte: „**Ich bin** eigentlich aus Kanada." ...................................................

**e** Er sagte: „**Ich habe** viel Geld." ...................................................

**f** Sie sagten: „**Wir sind** weit gereist." ...................................................

**g** Er meinte: „**Ich trage** keine Schuld daran." ...................................................

**h** Sie sagte: „**Ich weiß** es nicht." ...................................................

**i** Er erklärte: „**Ich werde** das nicht tun." ...................................................

**j** Sie meinte: „**Ich bin** nicht allwissend." ...................................................

**114** **Match the pronoun with the present or imperfect subjunctive.**

**a** du                 gäben

**b** er                  geben

**c** Sie                 gebet

**d** wir                 gebest

**e** ihr                 gäbe

# The infinitive

> **What is the infinitive?**
> The **infinitive** is the 'to' form of the verb, for example, *to go*, and is the form you look up in a dictionary. It is the **-en** form of the verb in German.

## Using the infinitive

➤ **zu** is used with the infinitive:

- after other verbs
  **Ich versuchte <u>zu</u> kommen.**        I tried <u>to come</u>.

- after adjectives
  **Es war leicht <u>zu</u> sehen.**        It was easy <u>to see</u>.
  **Es ist schwierig <u>zu</u> verstehen.**    It's hard <u>to understand</u>.

- after nouns
  **Ich habe keine Zeit, <u>zu</u> gehen.**    I don't have the time <u>to go</u>.
  **Ich habe keine Lust, heute**        I don't want to <u>work today</u>.
    **<u>zu</u> arbeiten.**

➤ The infinitive is used <u>without</u> **zu** after the following:

- modal verbs, such as **können** (meaning *to be able, can*)
  **Sie kann gut schwimmen.**        She can swim very well.

⇨ *For more information on **Modal verbs**, see page 184.*

> *Tip*
> The English *–ing* form is often translated by the German infinitive,
> as shown in some of the examples below.
>
> - the verbs **lassen** (meaning *to let, to leave*), **bleiben** (meaning *to stay*) and
>   **gehen** (meaning *to go*)
>   **Sie <u>ließen</u> uns <u>warten</u>.**        They kept us waiting.
>   **Sie <u>blieb</u> <u>sitzen</u>.**        She remained seated.
>   **Er <u>ging</u> <u>einkaufen</u>.**        He went shopping.
>
> - verbs of perception such as **hören** (meaning *to hear, to listen (to)*) and
>   **sehen** (meaning *to see, to watch*)
>   **Ich <u>sah</u> ihn <u>kommen</u>.**        I saw him coming.
>   **Er <u>hörte</u> sie <u>singen</u>.**        He heard her singing.

➤ The infinitive can be used to give an order or instruction.
    **Bitte nicht in diesen Zug <u>einsteigen</u>!**    Please don't board this train!

➤ It can also be used as a noun with a capital letter. It is always neuter.

**rauchen** = to smoke

**Sie hat <u>das Rauchen</u> aufgegeben.**     She's given up smoking.

---

**KEY POINTS**

✔ The infinitive is the 'to' form of the verb, the one you look up in a dictionary.

✔ **zu** is used with the infinitive after other verbs, adjectives and nouns.

✔ The infinitive is used WITHOUT **zu** after certain verbs, mostly modal verbs.

✔ The infinitive can be used to give an order or instruction.

✔ It can be used as a noun with a capital letter and is always neuter.

---

**115** **Translate the following sentences into German using the infinitive.**

**a** I saw him walking along the street.

.................................................................................................

**b** I heard her talking. ......................................................................

**c** Do you see them coming? ............................................................

**d** Please do not smoke! ..................................................................

**e** Let's go shopping! .......................................................................

**f** I don't have the time to do my homework.

.................................................................................................

**g** Please remain seated! (use **Sie**) ...............................................

**h** He can run very well. ...................................................................

**i** Will you visit him tomorrow? .......................................................

**j** His English is easy to understand.

.................................................................................................

**116** **Fill the gap with *zu* if required, otherwise leave blank.**

**a** Es ist sehr schwierig, ihn ........................ überzeugen.

**b** Ich kann Sie leider nicht ........................ verstehen.

**c** Er darf nicht mit auf den Spielplatz ........................ kommen.

**d** Ich habe dazu nichts ........................ sagen.

**e** Du solltest morgen einkaufen ........................ fahren.

**f** Du musst das nicht unbedingt ........................ machen.

**g** Ich würde dich gern davon ........................ überzeugen.

**h** Es war schwer für ihn, das Problem ........................ sehen.

**i** Möchtest du ein Glas Wein ........................ trinken?

**j** Hast du Lust, zum Bäcker ........................ gehen?

# Modal verbs

---

## What are modal verbs?

**Modal verbs** are used to <u>modify</u> or <u>change</u> other verbs to show such things as *ability*, *permission* or *necessity*. For example, *He <u>can</u> swim*; *<u>May</u> I come?*; *We <u>ought to go</u>*.

---

## Using modal verbs

➤ In German, the modal verbs are **dürfen**, **können**, **mögen**, **müssen**, **sollen** and **wollen**.

➤ Modal verbs are different from other verbs in their conjugation, which is shown in the Verb Tables.

⇨ For **Verb Tables**, see supplement.

➤ Here are the main uses of **dürfen**:

- Meaning *to be allowed to* or *may*
  **<u>Darfst</u> du mit ins Kino kommen?**     Are you allowed to/can you come to the cinema with us?

- Meaning *must not* or *may not*
  **Ich <u>darf</u> keine Schokolade essen.**     I mustn't eat any chocolate.

- Expressing politeness
  **<u>Darf</u> ich?**     May I?

➤ Here are the main uses of **können**:

- Meaning *to be able to* or *can*
  **Wir <u>können</u> es nicht schaffen.**     We can't make it.

- Meaning *would be able to* or *could*
  **<u>Könntest</u> du morgen hinfahren?**     Could you go there tomorrow?

- As a more common, informal alternative to **dürfen**, with the meaning *to be allowed to* or *can*
  **<u>Kann</u> ich/<u>Darf</u> ich einen Kaffee haben?**   Can I/May I have a coffee?

- Expressing possibility
  **Das <u>kann</u> sein.**     That may be so.
  **Das <u>kann</u> nicht sein.**     That can't be true.

➤ Here are the main uses of **mögen**:

- Meaning *to like*, when expressing likes and dislikes
  **<u>Magst</u> du Schokolade?**     Do you like chocolate?
  **Sie <u>mögen</u> es nicht.**     They don't like it.

---

- Meaning *would like to*, when expressing wishes and polite requests
  **Möchtest du sie besuchen?**           Would you like to visit her?
  **Möchten Sie etwas trinken?**          Would you like something to drink?

- Expressing possibility or probability
  **Es mag sein, dass es falsch war.**    It may well be that it was wrong.

➤ Here are the main uses of **müssen**:

- Meaning *to have to* or *must* or *need to*
  **Sie musste jeden Tag um sechs**       She had to get up at six o'clock every day.
  **aufstehen.**

- Certain common, informal uses
  **Muss das sein?**                      Is that really necessary?
  **Den Film muss man gesehen haben.**    That film is worth seeing.

  ⓘ Note that you can use a negative form of **brauchen** (meaning *to need*) instead of **müssen** for *don't have to* or *need not*

  **Das brauchst du nicht zu sagen.**     You don't have to say that.

➤ Here are the main uses of **sollen**:

- Meaning *ought to* or *should*
  **Das sollten Sie sofort machen.**      You ought to do that straight away.
  **Sie wusste nicht, was sie tun sollte.**  She didn't know what to do.
                                            (*what she should do*)

- Meaning *to be (supposed) to* where someone else has asked you to do something
  **Du sollst deine Freundin anrufen.**   You are to/should phone your girlfriend
                                            (*she has left a message asking you to ring*).

- Meaning *to be said to be*
  **Sie soll sehr reich sein.**           I've heard she's very rich./She is said to be
                                            very rich.

➤ Here are the main uses of **wollen**:

- Meaning *to want* or *to want to*
  **Sie will Lkw-Fahrerin werden.**       She wants to be a lorry driver.

- As a common, informal alternative to **mögen**, meaning *to want* or *wish*
  **Willst du eins?**                     Do you want one?
  **Willst du/Möchtest du etwas trinken?** Do you want/Would you like something
                                            to drink?

- Meaning *to be willing to*
  **Er will nichts sagen.**               He refuses to say anything.

- Expressing something you previously intended to do
  **Ich wollte gerade anrufen.**          I was just about to phone.

# Modal verb forms

➤ Modal verbs have unusual present tenses:

| dürfen | können | mögen |
|---|---|---|
| ich darf | ich kann | ich mag |
| du darfst | du kannst | du magst |
| er/sie/es darf | er/sie/es kann | er/sie/es mag |
| wir dürfen | wir können | wir mögen |
| ihr dürft | ihr könnt | ihr mögt |
| sie/Sie dürfen | sie/Sie können | sie/Sie mögen |

| müssen | sollen | wollen |
|---|---|---|
| ich muss | ich soll | ich will |
| du musst | du sollst | du willst |
| er/sie/es muss | er/sie/es soll | er/sie/es will |
| wir müssen | wir sollen | wir wollen |
| ihr müsst | ihr sollt | ihr wollt |
| sie/Sie müssen | sie/Sie sollen | sie/Sie wollen |

➤ In tenses consisting of one verb part, the infinitive of the verb used with the modal comes at the end of the sentence or clause.

**Sie <u>kann</u> sehr gut <u>schwimmen</u>.**    She is a very good swimmer.

---

*Grammar Extra!*

In sentences with modal verbs where the other verb expresses movement, it can be dropped if there is an adverb or adverbial phrase to show movement instead.

**Ich <u>muss</u> <u>nach Hause</u>.**    I must go home.
**Die Kinder <u>sollen</u> jetzt <u>ins Bett</u>.**    The children have to go to bed now.

⇨ *For more information on **Adverbs**, see page 74.*

---

### KEY POINTS

✔ Modal verbs are used to <u>modify</u> the meaning of other verbs.
✔ In German, the modal verbs are **dürfen**, **können**, **mögen**, **müssen**, **sollen** and **wollen**.
✔ Modal verbs are different from other verbs in their conjugation.

# Test yourself

**117** **Modify the sentences using the modal verb given. The first one has been done for you.**

**a** Ich trinke keinen Alkohol. **(dürfen)** *Ich darf keinen Alkchol trinken.*

**b** Sie ist sehr schön. **(sollen)** ............................................................

**c** Sie wird einmal Ärztin. **(wollen)** ............................................................

**d** Isst du etwas? **(mögen)** ............................................................

**e** Du fragst ihn nicht. **(brauchen)** ............................................................

**f** Wir gewinnen das Spiel nicht. **(können)**

............................................................

**g** Ich bin um 6 Uhr zu Hause. **(müssen)**

............................................................

**h** Ich komme mit in die Ausstellung. **(dürfen)**

............................................................

**i** Das stelle ich mir vor. **(können)** ............................................................

**j** Da staunt man nur. **(können)** ............................................................

**118** **Translate the following sentences into German.**

**a** He was just about to leave. ............................................................

**b** First you should turn the light on.

............................................................

**c** Would you like a cup of tea? ............................................................

**d** Do you like peppermint tea? ............................................................

**e** Do you always have to be late? ............................................................

**f** He always wants to be right. ............................................................

**g** He is said to be a good actor. ............................................................

**h** Could we visit her tomorrow? ............................................................

**i** Are you allowed to go out at night?

............................................................

# Test yourself

**119 Cross out the unlikely options.**

| | | |
|---|---|---|
| a | Ich ... kein Eis. | will/soll/mag/möchte |
| b | ... du etwas trinken? | Willst/Kannst/Sollst/Magst |
| c | Er ... sehr arm sein. | kann/soll/muss/will |
| d | Was ... du? | sollst/möchtest/willst/musst |
| e | ... du ihn? | Kannst/Magst/Willst/Musst |
| f | Das ... nicht sein. | kann/darf/muss/will |
| g | ... du mitkommen? | Sollst/Darfst/Kannst/Willst |
| h | ... ich? | Darf/Will/Kann/Mag |
| i | Ich ... schwimmen gehen. | mag/darf/will/muss |
| j | ... das sein? | Muss/Soll/Will/Kann |

# Impersonal verbs

## What is an impersonal verb?

An **impersonal verb** is one that does not relate to a real person or thing and where the subject is represented by *it*, for example, *It's going to rain*; *It's ten o'clock*.

➤ In German, <u>impersonal verbs</u> are used with **es** (meaning *it*) and the third person singular form of the verb.

| | |
|---|---|
| **Es regnet.** | It's raining. |
| **Es gibt ein Problem.** | There's a problem. |

➤ Here are the most common impersonal verbs. In some of these expressions it is possible to drop the **es**, in which case a personal pronoun such as **mich** or **mir** begins the clause. For example:

**Es ist mir egal, ob er mitkommt.**
OR
**Mir ist egal, ob er mitkommt**          I don't care if he comes with us.

⇨ *For more information on **Personal pronouns**, see page 89.*

➤ These expressions are marked with a * in the list below.

- **Es freut mich, dass/zu**                I am glad that/to.
  **Es freut mich, dass du gekommen bist.**    I'm pleased that you have come.
  **Es freut mich, Sie in unserer Stadt**      I'm pleased to welcome you to our town.
    **begrüßen zu dürfen.**

- **Es gefällt mir.**                     I like it.
  **Es gefällt mir gar nicht.**           I don't like it at all.

- **Es geht mir gut/schlecht.**           I'm fine/not too good.

- **Es geht nicht.**                      It's not possible.

- **es geht um**                          it's about
  **Es geht um die Liebe.**               It's about love.

- **es gelingt mir (zu)**                 I succeed (in)
  **Es ist mir gelungen, ihn zu überzeugen.**   I managed to convince him.

- **es handelt sich um**                  it's a question of
  **Es handelt sich um Zeit und Geld.**   It's a question of time and money.

- **Es hängt davon ab.**                  It depends.
  **Es hängt davon ab, ob ich arbeiten muss.**   It depends whether I have to work or not.

- **Es hat keinen Zweck.**                There's no point.

- **es ist mir egal (ob)***               it's all the same to me (if)
  **Es ist mir egal, ob du kommst**       I don't care if you come or not.
    **oder nicht.**

- es ist möglich(, dass)
  **Es is doch möglich, dass sie ihr
  Handy nicht dabei hat.**

  it's possible (that)
  It's always possible she doesn't have her
  mobile with her.

- es ist nötig
  **Es wird nicht nötig sein, mir
  Bescheid zu sagen.**

  it's necessary
  It won't be necessary to let me know.

- es ist schade(, dass)
  **Es ist schade, dass sie nicht kommt.**

  it's a pity (that)
  It's a pity (that) she isn't coming.

- **Es ist mir warm** OR **Es ist mir kalt\*.**

  I'm warm OR I'm cold.

- **Es klingelt.**

  Someone's ringing the bell OR The phone
  is ringing.

  **Es hat gerade geklingelt.**

  The bell just went OR The phone just rang.

- **Es klopft.**

  Someone's knocking (at the door).

- es kommt darauf an(, ob)
  **Es kommt darauf an, ob ich
  arbeiten muss.**

  it all depends (whether)
  It all depends whether I have to work.

- **Es lohnt sich (nicht).**
  **Ich weiß nicht, ob es sich lohnt oder
  nicht.**

  It's (not) worth it.
  I don't know if it's worth it or not.

- **Es macht nichts.**

  It doesn't matter.

- es macht nichts aus
  **Macht es dir etwas aus, wenn wir
  morgen gehen?**

  it makes no difference
  Would you mind if we went tomorrow?

- es stimmt, dass …
  **Es stimmt, dass sie keine Zeit hat.**

  it's true that …
  It's true that she doesn't have any time.

- es tut mir leid(, dass) …

  I'm sorry(that) …

- **Wie geht es (dir)?**

  How are you?

- **Mir wird schlecht\*.**

  I feel sick.

➤ All weather verbs are impersonal.

| Infinitive | Expression | Meaning |
|---|---|---|
| donnern und blitzen | es donnert und blitzt | there's thunder and lightning |
| frieren | es friert | it's freezing |
| gießen | es gießt | it's pouring |
| regnen | es regnet | it's raining |
| schneien | es schneit | it's snowing |
| sein | es ist warm/kalt | it's cold/warm |

**KEY POINTS**

✔ Impersonal verbs are used with **es** (meaning *it*) and the third person singular form of the verb.

✔ All weather verbs are impersonal.

# Test yourself

**120 Match the two statements.**

a Es schneit.                      Wir werden nass.

b Es regnet.                      Gleich kommt der Blitz.

c Es donnert.                   Zieh deinen Mantel aus.

d Es ist warm.                  Es ist 3 Grad unter null.

e Es friert.                      Wir können einen Schneemann bauen.

**121 Translate the following sentences into German. Begin each sentence with Es.**

a It's all the same to me if you're rich or poor.

..................................................................................................

b I don't mind if we eat at 6 o'clock. ...........................................

c I'm sorry that you had to wait (use **Sie**).

..................................................................................................

d It's true that I'm only 16. ...........................................................

e It won't be necessary to visit her tomorrow.

..................................................................................................

f There's no point discussing it any further.

..................................................................................................

g It depends whether he has time or not.

..................................................................................................

h I don't care if we arrive two hours late.

..................................................................................................

i I'm pleased to see you. ..............................................................

j It's a pity that the weather's so bad.

..................................................................................................

**122 Match the statement and the reply.**

a Sie haben mich beleidigt.       Das ist mir egal.

b Wir haben das Spiel verloren.  Das geht nicht.

c Ich will mit Regine ins Kino gehen.  Das ist schade.

d Du gehst zur Tür?               Es tut mir leid.

e Er ist dir immer noch böse.    Es hat geklingelt.

# There is/There are

➤ There are two main ways of expressing this in German.

## Es gibt

- This is always used in the singular form and is followed by a singular or plural object in the accusative case.

  **Es gibt zu viele Probleme dabei.** There are too many problems involved.
  **Es gibt keinen besseren Wein.** There is no better wine.

- **Es gibt** is used to refer to things of a general nature.

  **Es gibt bestimmt Regen.** It's definitely going to rain.
  **Wenn wir zu spät kommen,** If we arrive late, there'll be trouble.
  **gibt es Ärger.**

- It is often used informally.

  **Was gibts (=gibt es) zu essen?** What is there to eat?
  **Was gibts?** What's wrong?, What's up?
  **So was gibts doch nicht!** That's impossible!

## Es ist/es sind

- Here, the **es** simply introduces the real subject of the sentence, so if the subject is plural, **es sind** is used. The subject is in the nominative case.

  **Es sind kaum Leute da.** There are hardly any people there.

- Where the subject and verb swap places in the clause or sentence, the **es** is dropped.

  **Da sind kaum Leute.** There are hardly any people there.

- *i* Note that **es gibt** is frequently used instead of **es ist/es sind** in the above two examples.

- **Es ist** or **es sind** are used to refer to a temporary situation.

  **Es war niemand da.** There was no-one there.

- They are also used to begin a story.

  **Es war einmal eine Königin.** Once upon a time there was a Queen ...

---

**KEY POINT**

✔ In German there are two main ways of translating *there is/there are*: **es gibt** and **es ist/es sind**.

---

# Test yourself

**123** **Fill the gap with *gibt*, *sind* or *ist* as appropriate.**

**a** Es ........................ 20.000 Menschen im Stadion.

**b** In der Wüste ........................ es keinen Schnee.

**c** Ich will eine Rede halten, aber es ........................ niemand da.

**d** Es ........................ nichts was ich lieber mag als Brokkoli.

**e** Ich reise gern nach Schottland, aber es ........................ so viele Mücken.

**f** Meinst du, es ........................ heute noch Regen?

**g** Es ........................ nichts im Kühlschrank.

**h** Ich würde gern schlafen gehen, aber es ........................ noch zu viele Gäste da.

**i** Ich habe Durst, aber es ........................ kein Bier da.

**j** ........................ es etwas zu essen?

**124** **Match the two statements.**

**a** **Es ist kein Bier da.**          Ich habe kein Kleingeld.

**b** **Es sind viele Dosen im Automaten.**   Dann müssen wir eben Wasser trinken.

**c** **Es ist jemand an der Tür.**       Ich habe aber Durst.

**d** **Es gibt kein Wasser in der Wüste.**   Ich habe nichts gehört.

**e** **Es gibt nichts zu trinken.**       Vielleicht müssen wir verdursten.

# Use of es as an anticipatory object

➤ The object of many verbs can be a clause beginning with **dass** (meaning *that*) or an infinitive with **zu**.

| | |
|---|---|
| **Er wusste, <u>dass</u> wir pünktlich kommen würden.** | He knew that we would come on time. |
| **Sie fing an <u>zu</u> lachen.** | She began to laugh. |

➤ With some verbs, **es** is often used as the object to anticipate this clause or infinitive phrase.

**Er hatte <u>es</u> abgelehnt, mitzukommen.**  He refused to come.

➤ When the **dass** clause or infinitive phrase begins the sentence, **es** is not used in the main clause. Instead, it can be replaced by the pronoun **das** (meaning *that*).

| | |
|---|---|
| **<u>Dass</u> es Karla war, <u>das</u> haben wir ihr verschwiegen.** | We did not tell her that it was Karla. |

🛈 Note that **dass** is a subordinating conjunction and **das** is a demonstrative pronoun.

⇨ *For more information on **Subordinating conjunctions**, see page 238.*

➤ The following common verbs <u>usually</u> have the **es** object.

- **es ablehnen, zu ...**                                           to refuse to

- **es aushalten, zu tun/dass ...**                         to stand doing
  **Ich halte <u>es</u> nicht mehr aus, bei ihnen zu arbeiten.**          I can't stand working for them any longer.

- **es ertragen, zu tun/dass ...**                          to bear doing
  **Ich ertrage <u>es</u> nicht, dass sie mir widerspricht.**             I can't bear her contradicting me.

- **es leicht haben, zu ...**                                   to find it easy to
  **Sie hatte <u>es</u> nicht leicht, sie zu überreden.**          She didn't have an easy job persuading them.

- **es nötig haben, zu ...**                                   to need to
  **Ich habe <u>es</u> nicht nötig, mit dir darüber zu reden.**           I don't have to talk to you about it.

- **es satt haben, zu ...**                                     to have had enough of (doing)
  **Ich habe <u>es</u> satt, englische Verben zu lernen.**          I've had enough of learning English verbs.

- **es verstehen, zu ...**                                      to know how to
  **Sie versteht <u>es</u>, Autos zu reparieren.**          She knows about repairing cars.

➤ The following common verbs <u>often</u> have the **es** object.

- **es jemandem anhören/ansehen, dass ...**                   to tell by listening to/looking at someone that
  **Man hörte <u>es</u> ihm an, dass er kein Deutscher war.**          You could tell by listening to him that he wasn't German.

- es bereuen, zu tun/dass ...
  **Ich bereue es nicht, dass ich
  gekommen bin.**

  to regret doing/that
  I don't regret coming.

- es jemandem verbieten, zu ...
  **Ihre Mutter hat es ihr verboten,
  dort hinzugehen.**

  to forbid someone to
  Her mother forbade her to go there.

- es wagen, zu ...
  **Er wagte es nicht, ein neues Auto
  zu kaufen.**

  to dare to
  He didn't dare buy a new car.

---

### KEY POINTS

✔ The object of many verbs can be a clause beginning with **dass** (meaning *that*) or an infinitive with **zu**.

✔ With some verbs, **es** is used as the object to anticipate this clause or infinitive phrase.

✔ When the **dass** clause or infinitive phrase begins the sentence, **es** is not used in the main clause. Instead, it can be replaced by the pronoun **das** (meaning *that*).

---

# Test yourself

**125** **Match the two phrases to form a complete sentence.**

| | | |
|---|---|---|
| **a** | Er versteht es, | dass er sie ständig beleidigt. |
| **b** | Ich habe es satt, | die Leute zu betrügen. |
| **c** | Sie wagt es nicht, | jeden Tag zur Schule zu gehen. |
| **d** | Ich bereue es, | mir zu widersprechen. |
| **e** | Sie erträgt es nicht, | dass ich ihn geheiratet habe. |

**126** **Translate the following sentences into German, remembering to use *es* in the main clause. The first one has been done for you.**

**a** She didn't have an easy job keeping the family together.

*Sie hatte es nicht leicht, die Familie zusammenzuhalten.*

**b** I don't need to listen to your arguments.

................................................................................

**c** He knows about persuading people.

................................................................................

**d** He refuses to have lunch with us. ................................................

**e** I can't bear him leaving me. ......................................................

**f** You can tell by listening to him that he's from Bavaria.

................................................................................

**g** His mother forbids him to visit his girlfriend.

................................................................................

**h** I don't regret giving them the money.

................................................................................

**i** She didn't dare tell him the truth.

................................................................................

**j** He knows how to program computers.

................................................................................

# Verbs followed by prepositions

➤ Some English verbs must be followed by prepositions for certain meanings, for example, *to wait for*, *to ask for*. This also happens in German:

| | |
|---|---|
| **sich sehnen <u>nach</u>** | to long <u>for</u> |
| **warten <u>auf</u>** | to wait <u>for</u> |
| **bitten <u>um</u>** | to ask <u>for</u> |

---

*Tip*

As you can see from the examples above, the preposition that is used in German is not always the same as the one that is used in English. Whenever you learn a new verb, try to learn which preposition is used after it too.

➤ As in English, using different prepositions with a verb creates completely different meanings.

| | |
|---|---|
| **bestehen** | to pass (a test etc) |
| **bestehen <u>aus</u>** | to consist of |
| **bestehen <u>auf</u>** | to insist on |
| **sich freuen <u>auf</u>** | to look forward to |
| **sich freuen <u>über</u>** | to be pleased about |

*[i]* Note that you occasionally need to use a preposition with a German verb whose English equivalent does not have one.

| | |
|---|---|
| **diskutieren <u>über</u>** | to discuss |

---

➤ Prepositions used with these verbs behave like normal prepositions and affect the case of the following noun in the normal way. For instance, with verbs followed by **für** the accusative case is always used.

| | |
|---|---|
| **sich interessieren für** | to be interested in |
| **Sie interessiert sich nicht <u>für den neuen</u> Wagen.** | She isn't interested in the new car. |

➤ A verb plus preposition is not always followed by a noun or pronoun. It can also be followed by a clause containing another verb. This is often used to translate an *–ing* form in English and is dealt with in one of two ways.

- If the verbs in both parts of the sentence have the same subject, **da-** or **dar-** is added to the beginning of the preposition and the following verb becomes an infinitive used with **zu**.

| | |
|---|---|
| **Ich freue mich sehr <u>darauf</u>, mal wieder mit ihr <u>zu</u> arbeiten.** | I am looking forward to work<u>ing</u> with her again. |

- If the subject is not the same for both verbs, a **dass** (meaning *that*) clause is used.

| | |
|---|---|
| **Ich freue mich <u>darauf</u>, <u>dass</u> du morgen kommst.** | I am looking forward to you com<u>ing</u> tomorrow. |

# Verbs followed by a preposition + the accusative case

➤ The following list contains the most common verbs followed by a preposition plus the accusative case:

- **sich amüsieren über**
  **Sie haben sich <u>über</u> ihn amüsiert.**

  to laugh at
  They laughed at him.

- **sich ärgern über**

  to get annoyed about/with

- **sich bewerben um**
  **Sie hat sich <u>um</u> die Stelle als Direktorin beworben.**

  to apply for
  She applied for the position of director.

- **bitten um**

  to ask for

- **denken an**
  **<u>Daran</u> habe ich gar nicht mehr gedacht.**

  to be thinking of
  I'd forgotten about that.

- **denken über**
  **Wie denkt ihr <u>darüber</u>?**

  to think about, hold an opinion of
  What do you think about it?

- **sich erinnern an**

  to remember

- **sich freuen auf**

  to look forward to

- **sich freuen über**
  **Ich freue mich sehr <u>über</u> den neuen Job.**

  to be pleased about
  I'm very pleased about the new job.

- **sich gewöhnen an**

  to get used to

- **sich interessieren für**
  **Sie interessiert sich sehr <u>für</u> Politik.**

  to be interested in
  She's very interested in politics.

- **kämpfen um**

  to fight for

- **sich kümmern um**
  **Kannst du dich <u>um</u> meine Pflanzen kümmern?**

  to take care of, see to
  Can you see to my plants?

- **nachdenken über**
  **Er hatte schon lange <u>darüber</u> nachgedacht.**

  to think about
  He had been thinking about it for a long time.

- **sich unterhalten über**

  to talk about

- **sich verlassen auf**
  **Kann sie sich <u>auf</u> ihn verlassen?**

  to rely on, depend on
  Can she rely on him?

- **warten auf**

  to wait for

# Verbs followed by a preposition + the dative case

➤ The following list contains the most common verbs followed by a preposition plus the dative case:

- **abhängen von**
  **Das hängt <u>von</u> der Zeit ab, die**
  **uns noch bleibt.**

  to depend on
  That depends how much time we
    have left.

- **sich beschäftigen mit**
  **Sie beschäftigen sich im Moment**
  **<u>mit</u> dem neuen Haus.**

  to occupy oneself with
  They're busy with their new house at
    the moment.

- **bestehen aus**

  to consist of

- **leiden an/unter**
  **Sie hat lange <u>an</u> dieser Krankheit**
  **gelitten.**

  to suffer from
  She suffered from this illness for
    a long time.

- **riechen nach**

  to smell of

- **schmecken nach**
  **Es schmeckt <u>nach</u> Zimt.**

  to taste of
  It tastes of cinnamon.

- **sich sehnen nach**

  to long for

- **sterben an**
  **Sie ist <u>an</u> Krebs gestorben.**

  to die of
  She died of cancer.

- **teilnehmen an**
  **Du solltest <u>am</u> Wettbewerb**
  **teilnehmen.**

  to take part in
  You should take part in the competition.

- **träumen von**

  to dream of

- **sich verabschieden von**
  **Ich habe mich noch nicht <u>von</u>**
  **ihm verabschiedet.**

  to say goodbye to
  I haven't said goodbye to him yet.

- **sich verstehen mit**
  **Sie versteht sich ganz gut <u>mit</u> ihr.**

  to get along with, get on with
  She gets on really well with her.

---

## KEY POINTS

✔ German prepositions after verbs are often not the same as the ones used in English.
✔ Using different prepositions with a verb creates completely different meanings.
✔ German verbs occasionally use prepositions where their English equivalents don't.
✔ Prepositions used with verbs behave like normal prepositions and affect the case of the following noun.

---

For further explanation of grammatical terms, please see pages viii–xii.

# Test yourself

**127 Translate the following sentences into German.**

**a** Can you look after my cat when I'm on holiday?

.............................................................................................................

**b** He's interested in her CD collection. ...........................................................

**c** They were talking about politics. .................................................................

**d** The workers are fighting for their rights.

.............................................................................................................

**e** I don't know if I can rely on you. ..................................................................

**f** I'm always thinking of my sister. ...................................................................

**g** I asked her for a bit more time. .....................................................................

**h** I can't get used to living in a big city. ...........................................................

**i** I'm still waiting for a reply. ...........................................................................

**j** I'm looking forward to my birthday. ..............................................................

**128 Fill the gap with the correct form of an appropriate verb. All of them are followed by a preposition plus the dative case.**

**a** Ich ............................. mich nach meiner Kindheit.

**b** Er ............................. sich nicht gut mit seinen Eltern.

**c** Sie ist an Lungenentzündung ............................. .

**d** Ich ............................. oft von meinem nächsten Urlaub.

**e** Probier mal die Suppe, sie ............................. nach Koriander.

**f** Ich habe mich am Bahnhof von meinem Bruder ............................. .

**g** Unsere Wohnung ............................. aus vier Zimmern.

**h** Das ............................. davon ab, wie viel du dafür bezahlst.

**i** In der Schule ............................. wir uns gerade mit Shakespeare.

**j** Sie ............................. schon seit drei Jahren an dieser Krankheit.

**129 Match the two columns.**

| | |
|---|---|
| **a Ich kümmere mich** | von ihr |
| **b Ich sehne mich** | um sie |
| **c Ich interessiere mich** | über sie |
| **d Ich träume** | für sie |
| **e Ich ärgere mich** | nach ihr |

# Verbs followed by the dative case

## Verbs with a direct and indirect object

➤ Some verbs are generally used with a <u>direct object</u> and an <u>indirect object</u>. For example, in the English sentence, *She gave me a book*, the direct object of *gave* is *a book* and would be in the accusative case in German, and *me* (= *to me*) is the indirect object and would be in the dative case in German.

> **Sie gab <u>mir</u> ein Buch.**　　　　　She gave me a book.
> direct object = **ein Buch**
> indirect object = **mir**

➤ In German, as in English, this type of verb is usually concerned with giving or telling someone something, or with doing something for someone else.

> **Sie erzählte ihm eine Geschichte.**　　She told him a story.
> direct object = **eine Geschichte**
> indirect object = **ihm**

> ⓘ Note that the normal word order after such verbs is for the direct object to follow the indirect, EXCEPT where the direct object is a personal pronoun.

> **Kaufst du <u>mir</u> <u>das Buch</u>?**　　　　Will you buy me the book?
> BUT
> **Kaufst du <u>es mir</u>?**　　　　　　　Will you buy it for me?

> ⇨ *For more information on **Direct** and **Indirect object pronouns**, see pages 94 and 98.*

➤ Here are some of the most common examples of verbs which are used with both a direct and an indirect object:

- **anbieten**　　　　　　　　　　　to offer
  **Sie bot <u>ihr</u> die Arbeitsstelle an.**　She offered her the job.

- **bringen**　　　　　　　　　　　to bring
  **Bringst du <u>mir</u> eins?**　　　　　Will you bring me one?

- **beweisen**　　　　　　　　　　to prove
  **Können Sie es <u>mir</u> beweisen?**　　Can you prove it to me?

- **fehlen**　　　　　　　　　　　to be absent *or* missing
  **<u>Mir</u> fehlt das nötige Geld.**　　　I don't have enough money.

- **geben**　　　　　　　　　　　to give
  **Gib <u>mir</u> das sofort!**　　　　　Give me that now!

- **schenken**　　　　　　　　　　to give (as a present)
  **Ich schenke <u>ihr</u> einen Computer**　　I'm giving her a computer for her birthday.
  　**zum Geburtstag.**

- **schreiben**　　　　　　　　　　to write
  **Schreib <u>ihm</u> mal einen Brief.**　　Write him a letter sometime.

- **zeigen**　　　　　　　　　　　to show
  **Zeig es <u>mir</u>!**　　　　　　　Show me it!

For further explanation of grammatical terms, please see pages viii-xii.

# Verbs with their object in the dative

➤ Certain verbs in German, such as **helfen** (meaning *to help*) can ONLY be followed by an object in the dative case.

➤ Here are some of the most common ones.

- **begegnen**
  **Er ist <u>seinem</u> Freund in der Stadt begegnet.**

  to bump into, meet
  He bumped into his friend in town.

- **gehören**
  **<u>Wem</u> gehört dieses Buch?**

  to belong to
  Whose book is this?

- **helfen**
  **Er wollte <u>ihr</u> nicht helfen.**

  to help
  He refused to help her.

- **danken**
  **Ich danke <u>dir</u>!**

  to thank
  Thank you!

- **schaden**
  **Rauchen schadet <u>der</u> Gesundheit**

  to damage
  Smoking is bad for your health.

- **schmecken**
  **Das Essen hat <u>ihnen</u> gut geschmeckt.**

  to taste
  They enjoyed the meal.

- **trauen**
  **Ich traue <u>dir</u> nicht.**

  to trust
  I don't trust you.

---

### KEY POINTS

✔ Some German verbs are usually used with a direct AND an indirect object.
✔ The indirect object is ALWAYS in the dative case.
✔ The normal word order after such verbs is for the direct object to follow the indirect, EXCEPT where the direct object is a personal pronoun.
✔ Certain German verbs can only be followed by an object in the dative case.

# Test yourself

**130** **Form a sentence using the elements below. Use the imperfect tense throughout.**

**a** mir/zeigen/sie/ihre Hausaufgaben

.......................................................................................................

**b** bringen/ein Bier/mir/er .......................................................................

**c** können/ihm/es/leider/beweisen/ich/nicht

.......................................................................................................

**d** sie/zum Geburtstag/das Handy/mir/kaufen

.......................................................................................................

**e** erzählen/alles/ihren Mann/über/mir/sie

.......................................................................................................

**f** eine Karte/dem/aus/schreiben/Urlaub/ihm/Sandra

.......................................................................................................

**g** geben/ihm/sie/einen Scheck .............................................................

**h** sie/ein Glas/mir/anbieten/Apfelsaft .................................................

**i** mir/Weihnachten/ein Fahrrad/zu/schenken/er

.......................................................................................................

**j** den Weg/Wanderer/zeigen/uns/die

.......................................................................................................

**131** **Translate the following sentences into German. Use verbs which are followed by an object in the dative case.**

**a** Who does this computer belong to? .................................................

**b** Do you really trust him? ....................................................................

**c** Did you enjoy your lunch? .................................................................

**d** I can't help you. .................................................................................

**e** I bumped into him in a pub.

.......................................................................................................

**f** Too much sun is bad for your skin. ...................................................

**g** This money doesn't belong to me. ....................................................

**h** I'd like to thank you for your help.

.......................................................................................................

**i** Are you enjoying the soup? ...............................................................

**j** I met my colleague while shopping.

# The passive

---

### What is the passive?
The **passive** is the form of the verb that is used when the subject of the verb is the person or thing that is affected by the action, for example, *I was given, we were told, it had been made.*

---

## Using the passive

➤ In a normal, or *active* sentence, the subject of the verb is the person or thing that carries out the action described by the verb. The object of the verb is the person or thing that the verb happens to.

> Ryan (*subject*) hit (*active verb*) me (*object*).

➤ In English, as in German, you can turn an active sentence round to make a passive sentence.

> I (*subject*) was hit (*passive verb*) by Ryan (*agent*).

➤ Very often, however, you cannot identify who is carrying out the action indicated by the verb.

> I was hit in the face.
> The trees will be chopped down.
> I've been chosen to represent the school.

## Forming the passive

➤ In English we use the verb *to be* with the past participle (*was hit, was given*) to form the passive and the word *by* usually introduces the agent. In German the passive is formed using **werden** and the past participle, while the agent is introduced by

- **von**, for a person, animal or organisation
  **Das Kind <u>wurde von</u> einem Hund <u>gebissen</u>.**          The child was bitten by a dog.

- **durch**, for a thing
  **Die Tür <u>wurde durch</u> den Wind <u>geöffnet</u>.**          The door was opened by the wind.

  ⇨ *For more information on the **Past participle**, see page 154.*

➤ Here is the present tense of the verb **sehen** (meaning *to see*) in its passive form.

| | |
|---|---|
| **ich werde gesehen** | I am seen |
| **du wirst gesehen** | you are seen |
| **er/sie/es wird gesehen** | he/she/it is seen |
| **wir werden gesehen** | we are seen |
| **ihr werdet gesehen** | you (*plural*) are seen |
| **sie/Sie werden gesehen.** | they/you (*formal*) are seen |

> **Tip**
> *There is/there are* can be translated by a verb in the passive tense in German.
> **Es wird immer viel getrunken** | There is always a lot of drinking at
> **auf seiner Party.** | his party.

➤ You can form other tenses of the passive by changing the tense of the verb **werden**, for example, the imperfect passive.

> **ich wurde gesehen** | I was seen

⇨ *For more information on the* **Imperfect tense**, *see page* 160.

> **Tip**
> There is a very important difference between German and English in sentences containing an <u>indirect object</u>. In English we can quite easily turn a normal (active) sentence with an indirect object into a passive sentence.
>
> **Active**
> Someone (*subject*) gave (*active verb*) me (*indirect object*) a book (*direct object*).
>
> **Passive**
> I (*subject*) was given (*passive verb*) a book (*direct object*).
>
> In German, an indirect object can <u>NEVER</u> become the subject of a passive verb. Instead, the indirect object must remain in the dative case, with either the direct object becoming the subject of the passive sentence OR use of an impersonal passive construction.
> **Ein Buch** (*subject*) **wurde mir geschenkt.**

## Avoiding the passive

➤ Passives are not as common in German as in English. There are <u>three</u> main ways that German speakers express the same idea.

- by using the pronoun **man** (meaning *they* or *one*) with a normal, active verb
  **Man hatte es mir schon gesagt.** | I had already been told.

  ⓘ Note that **man** is not always translated as *they* or *one*.

  **Man hatte es schon verkauft.** | It had already been sold.

- by using **sich lassen** plus a verb in the infinitive
  **Das <u>lässt sich</u> machen.** | That can be done.

- by using an active tense where the agent of the action is known
  **Susi <u>schenkte</u> ihr ein Auto.** | Susi gave her a car.
  INSTEAD OF
  **Ihr wurde von Susi ein Auto geschenkt.** | She was given a car by Susi.

**KEY POINTS**

✔ The present tense of the passive is formed by using the present tense of **werden** with the past participle.

✔ In German, an indirect object can <u>NEVER</u> become the subject of a passive verb.

✔ You can often avoid a passive construction by using the pronoun **man** or **sich lassen** plus an infinitive or an active tense where the agent is known.

# Test yourself

**132 Complete the passive construction by inserting the past participle.**

**a** Das Endspiel wurde von 10 Millionen Menschen weltweit ............................... .
**[sehen]**

**b** Von wem wurde dieser Roman ............................... ? **[schreiben]**

**c** Die Verdächtigen sind jetzt von der Polizei ............................... worden. **[verhaften]**

**d** Das Theaterstück wurde 1985 ............................... **[uraufführen]**

**e** Vor Spielbeginn wurde ..............................., wer beginnen sollte. **[auslosen]**

**f** Der Preisträger wurde in einer Rede ............................... **[ehren]**

**g** Sie wurd zur Ehrenbürgerin der Stadt ............................... **[ernennen]**

**h** Der Verbrecher wurde zu 8 Jahren Gefängnis ............................... **[veurteilen]**

**i** Ihm wurde kein Verschulden ............................... **[nachweisen]**

**j** Er wurde aus politischen Motiven ............................... **[umbringen]**

**133 Transform the active sentence into a passive construction. The first one has been done for you.**

**a** Demonstranten störten die Veranstaltung.
*Die Veranstaltung wurde von Demonstranten gestört.*

**b** Die Bank kündigte seinen Kredit.
............................................................................................

**c** Man teilte ihm mit, dass er gehen musste.
............................................................................................

**d** Die Zöllner untersuchten den Koffer sehr genau.
............................................................................................

**e** Die Theaterleitung setzte das Stück ab.
............................................................................................

**f** Alle Sender strahlten die Eröffnungszeremonie aus.
............................................................................................

**g** Die Behörde warf ihm finanzielle Unregelmäßigkeiten vor.
............................................................................................

**h** Die Opposition zwang die Regierung zum Rücktritt.
............................................................................................

# Test yourself

**i** Man schätzte die Besucherzahl auf 20.000

..................................................................................................................................

**j** Gestern kündigte ihr der Vermieter die Wohnung.

..................................................................................................................................


**134** **Create a passive sentence in the past tense using the elements below.**

**a** der Krieg/beenden/1918 ...........................................................................................

**b** die Frage/einvernehmlich/klären ........................................................................

**c** den Schülern/ein Lob/erteilen ............................................................................

**d** das Buch/allgemein/loben ....................................................................................

**e** das Gesetz/Parlament/einstimmig/verabschieden

..................................................................................................................................

**f** auf der Party/viel/tanzen ......................................................................................

**g** das Geld/gleichmäßig/verteilen ..........................................................................

**h** der Vorschlag/zustimmend/aufnehmen

..................................................................................................................................

**i** drei Minister/Kanzler/entlassen

..................................................................................................................................

**j** der Beginn/Veranstaltung/drei Uhr/festsetzen

..................................................................................................................................

# Prepositions

---

### What is a preposition?

A **preposition** is a word such as *at, for, with, into* or *from*, which is usually followed by a noun, pronoun or, in English, a word ending in *-ing*. Prepositions show how people and things relate to the rest of the sentence, for example,
*She's <u>at</u> home; a tool <u>for</u> cutting grass; it's <u>from</u> David.*

---

## Using prepositions

➤ Prepositions are used in front of nouns and pronouns (such as *me, him, the man* and so on), and show the relationship between the noun or pronoun and the rest of the sentence. Some prepositions can be used before verb forms ending in *-ing* in English.

I showed my ticket <u>to</u> the inspector.
Come <u>with</u> me.
This brush is really good <u>for</u> cleaning shoes.

⇨ *For more information on **Nouns** and **Pronouns**, see pages 1 and 89.*

➤ In English, a preposition does not affect the word or phrase it introduces, for example:

| | |
|---|---|
| the inspector | <u>to</u> the inspector |
| me | <u>with</u> me |
| cleaning shoes | <u>for</u> cleaning shoes |

➤ In German, however, the noun following a preposition must be put into the accusative, genitive or dative case.

> *Tip*
> It is important to learn each preposition with the case or cases it governs.

## Prepositions followed by the dative case

➤ Some of the most common prepositions taking the dative case are:
**aus, außer, bei, gegenüber, mit, nach, seit, von, zu**

- **aus**                                                    *out of, from*
  **Er trinkt <u>aus</u> der Flasche.**          He is drinking out of the bottle.
  **Sie kommt <u>aus</u> Essen.**                 She comes from Essen.

- **außer**                                                 *out of; except*
  **Der Fahrstuhl war <u>außer</u> Betrieb.**   The lift was out of order.
  **Der Patient ist jetzt <u>außer</u> Gefahr.**  The patient is out of danger now.
  **Alle <u>außer</u> mir kamen zu spät.**      All except me came too late.

- **bei**                                                     *at the home/shop/work etc of; near*
  **Feiern wir <u>bei</u> uns?**                      Shall we celebrate at our house?
  **<u>Bei</u> uns in Schottland ist das kein Problem.**   At home in Scotland that isn't a problem.

| | |
|---|---|
| **Er ist noch <u>beim</u> Friseur.** | He is still at the hairdresser's. |
| **Er wohnt immer noch <u>bei</u> seinen Eltern.** | He still lives with his parents. |
| **Riegel ist <u>bei</u> Freiburg.** | Riegel is near Freiburg. |

*[i]* Note that **bei** plus the definite article can be shortened to **beim**.

➪ *For more information on* **Shortened forms of prepositions**, *see page 229.*

| | |
|---|---|
| • gegenüber | *opposite; towards* |
| **Er wohnt uns <u>gegenüber</u>.** | He lives opposite us. |
| **Sie ist mir <u>gegenüber</u> immer sehr freundlich gewesen.** | She has always been very friendly towards me. |

*[i]* Note that when used as a preposition, **gegenüber** is placed <u>AFTER</u> a pronoun, but can be placed <u>BEFORE</u> or <u>AFTER</u> a noun.

| | |
|---|---|
| • mit | *with* |
| **Er ging <u>mit</u> seinen Freunden spazieren.** | He went for a walk with his friends. |

| | |
|---|---|
| • nach | *after; to* |
| **<u>Nach</u> zwei Stunden kam er wieder.** | He returned two hours later. |
| **Sie ist <u>nach</u> London gereist.** | She went to London. |
| **Ihrer Sprache <u>nach</u> ist sie Süddeutsche.** | From the way she talks I would say she is from southern Germany. |

*[i]* Note that when **nach** means *according to*, as in the last example, it can be placed <u>AFTER</u> the noun.

| | |
|---|---|
| • seit | *since; for (of time)* |
| **<u>Seit</u> er krank ist, spielt er nicht mehr Fußball.** | He's stopped playing football since he became ill. |

*[i]* Note that after *seit*, meaning *for*, we use the <u>present tense</u> in German, but the <u>perfect tense</u> in English.

| | |
|---|---|
| **Ich <u>wohne</u> <u>seit</u> zwei Jahren in Frankfurt.** | <u>I've been living</u> in Frankfurt for two years. |
| **Sie <u>arbeitet</u> <u>seit</u> acht Jahren bei uns.** | <u>She's been working</u> for us for eight years. |

➪ *For more information on* **Tenses used with seit**, *see page 125.*

| | |
|---|---|
| • von | *from; about; by (when used in the passive tense)* |
| **<u>Von</u> Berlin sind wir weiter nach Krakau gefahren.** | From Berlin we went on to Krakow. |
| **Ich weiß nichts <u>von</u> ihm.** | I know nothing about him. |
| **Sie ist <u>von</u> unseren Argumenten überzeugt worden.** | She was convinced by our arguments. |

➪ *For more information on the* **Passive**, *see page 205.*

ⓘ Note that **von** can be used as a common alternative to the genitive case.

| | |
|---|---|
| **Die Mutter <u>von</u> diesen Mädchen ist Künstlerin.** | The mother of these girls is an artist. |
| **Sie ist eine Freundin <u>von</u> Alexander.** | She is a friend of Alexander's. |

⇨ *For more information on the* **Genitive case***, see page 12.*

- **zu**            *to; for*
  **Er ging <u>zum</u> Arzt.**        He went to the doctor's.
  **Wir sind <u>zum</u> Essen eingeladen.**    We're invited for a meal.

ⓘ Note that **zu** plus the definite article can be shortened to **zum** or **zur**.

⇨ *For more information on* **Shortened forms of prepositions***, see page 229.*

---

*Grammar Extra!*
Some of the above prepositions are also used as separable verb prefixes, that is the part at the beginning of a separable German verb.

| | |
|---|---|
| <u>aus</u>**halten** | to endure |
| **Ich halte es nicht mehr <u>aus</u>.** | I can't stand it any longer. |
| | |
| **(jemandem) <u>bei</u>stehen** | to stand by (somebody) |
| **Er stand seinem Freund <u>bei</u>.** | He stood by his friend. |
| | |
| <u>gegenüber</u>**stehen** | to have an attitude towards |
| **Er steht ihnen kritisch <u>gegenüber</u>.** | He has a critical attitude towards them. |
| | |
| **jemanden <u>mit</u>nehmen** | to give somebody a lift |
| **Nimmst du mich bitte <u>mit</u>?** | Will you give me a lift, please? |
| | |
| <u>nach</u>**machen** | to copy |
| **Sie macht mir alles <u>nach</u>.** | She copies everything I do. |
| | |
| <u>zu</u>**machen** | to shut |
| **Mach die Tür <u>zu</u>!** | Shut the door! |

⇨ *For more information on* **Separable verbs***, see page 150.*

---

**KEY POINTS**
- ✔ **gegenüber**, **aus**, **bei**, **mit**, **nach**, **seit**, **von**, **zu**, **außer** are the most common prepositions used with the dative case.
- ✔ Each of them has several different possible meanings, depending on the context they are used in.
- ✔ **aus**, **nach**, **mit**, **bei**, **gegenüber** and **zu** can also be used as separable verb prefixes.

---

For further explanation of grammatical terms, please see pages viii-xii.

# Test yourself

**135  Complete the following sentences with the relevant preposition.**

**a**  Er wohnt schon ......................... drei Wochen bei uns.

**b**  Du solltest dich ihm ......................... etwas besser benehmen.

**c**  Wir wollen ......................... Schottland reisen.

**d**  Wo kommt sie her? – Sie kommt ......................... England.

**e**  ......................... uns ist heute Abend eine Party.

**f**  Er ist ......................... seiner Freundin gezogen.

**g**  Er ist ein sehr guter Freund ......................... mir.

**h**  Sie ist ......................... ihren Eltern im Kino.

**i**  Nach dem Laufen bin ich immer ganz ......................... Atem.

**j**  Hast du das Geschenk ......................... deiner Tante bekommen?

**136  Translate the following sentences into German.**

**a**  I've been living here for six months. ....................................................................

**b**  I sometimes go to Berlin by train.

.........................................................................................................

**c**  She lives opposite you. ....................................................................

**d**  Shall we meet at Peter's house?

.........................................................................................................

**e**  She is drinking out of a glass. ....................................................................

**f**  Gisela comes from Hamburg. ....................................................................

**g**  Do you know anything about his friends?

.........................................................................................................

**h**  Susanne is a friend of Erika's. ....................................................................

**i**  You should be polite towards him. ....................................................................

**j**  He came back after three hours. ....................................................................

# Test yourself

**137** **Fill the gap with *bei* or *zu*, combined with the definite article if appropriate. The first one has been done for you.**

**a** Sie ist ........*zum*........ Arzt gegangen.

**b** Sie ist ......................... Arzt.

**c** Er wohnt bei uns ......................... Hause.

**d** Sie ist ......................... ihrer Freundin.

**e** Kommst du bis ......................... Bahnhof mit?

**f** ......................... der Einreise muss man seinen Pass vorzeigen.

**g** Der Brief muss heute noch ......................... Post.

**h** Ich arbeite jetzt ......................... der Firma meines Vaters.

**i** Ich trage ......................... Autofahren immer eine Brille.

**j** Kommst du ......................... Hildes Party?

# Prepositions followed by the accusative case

➤ The most common prepositions taking the accusative case are: **durch**, **entlang**, **für**, **gegen**, **ohne**, **um**, **wider**

> *Tip*
> If you want an easy way to remember which prepositions take the accusative case, you could think of the word DOGWUF, which can stand for the prepositions **durch ohne gegen wider um für**.

- **durch**                                                      *through*
  **Sie guckte durch das Loch.**                She looked through the hole.
  **Durch Zufall trafen sie sich wieder.**     They met again, by chance.

- **entlang**                                                    *along*
  **Die Kinder kommen die Straße             The children are coming along the street.
   entlang.**

ℹ Note that **entlang** comes AFTER the noun in this meaning.

- **für**                                                        *for; to*
  **Ich habe es für dich getan.**               I did it for you.
  **Das ist für ihn sehr wichtig.**             That is very important to him.
  **Was für eins hat er?**                      What kind (of one) does he have?
  **Was für einen Wagen hat sie?**             What kind of car does she have?
  **Was für Äpfel sind das?**                  What kind of apples are they?

- **gegen**                                                      *against; around*
  **Stelle es gegen die Wand.**                 Put it against the wall.
  **Haben Sie etwas gegen                      Have you got something for hayfever?
   Heuschnupfen?**
  **Wir sind gegen vier angekommen.**          We arrived at around four o'clock.

- **ohne**                                                       *without*
  **Ohne sie gehts nicht.**                     It won't work without her.

- **um**                                                         *(a)round, round about; at (with time);
                                                                  by (with quantity)*
  **Der Bahnhof liegt um die Ecke.**            The station is round the corner.
  **Es fängt um neun Uhr an.**                  It begins at nine.
  **Es ist um zehn Euro billiger.**             It is cheaper by ten euros.

ℹ Note that **um** is used after certain verbs.

  **Sie baten um ein bisschen mehr Zeit.**      They asked for a bit more time.
  **Es handelt sich um dein Benehmen.**         It's a question of your behaviour.

⇨ *For more information on **Verbs followed by prepositions**, see page 198.*

- **wider**                                                      *contrary to, against*
  **Das geht mir wider die Natur.**             That's against my nature.

*Grammar Extra!*

Some of the above prepositions are also used as separable verb prefixes, that is the part at the beginning of a separable German verb.

| | |
|---|---|
| **durchmachen** | |
| **Sie hat viel durchgemacht in ihrem Leben entlanggehen** | She's been through a lot in her life. |
| **Wir gingen die Straße entlang.** | We went along the street. |

**um** and **wider** are also used as separable or inseparable verb prefixes (variable verb prefixes), depending on the verb and meaning.

| | | |
|---|---|---|
| **umarmen** | *inseparable* | to hug |
| **Er hat sie umarmt.** | | He gave her a hug. |
| | | |
| **umfallen** | *separable* | to fall over |
| **Sie ist umgefallen.** | | She fell over. |
| | | |
| **widersprechen** | *inseparable* | to go against |
| **Das hat meinen Wünschen widersprochen.** | | That went against my wishes. |
| | | |
| **(sich) widerspiegeln** | *separable* | to reflect |
| **Der Baum spiegelt sich im Wasser wider.** | | The tree is reflected in the water. |

⇨ *For more information on **Separable verbs** and **Inseparable verbs**, see page 150 and 149.*

---

### KEY POINTS

✔ **durch**, **entlang**, **für**, **gegen**, **ohne**, **um**, and **wider** are the most common prepositions used with the accusative case.

✔ Most of them have several different possible meanings, depending on the context they are used in.

✔ **durch**, **entlang** and **gegen** can also be used as separable verb prefixes.

✔ **um** and **wider** can also be used as variable verbal prefixes.

---

# Test yourself

**138** **Translate the following sentences into German.**

  **a** The film starts at around eight o'clock. .................................................

  **b** He went to the party without her. .................................................

  **c** We asked for a glass of water. .................................................

  **d** For you it's only a game. .................................................

  **e** Your feelings are very important to me.

    .................................................

  **f** He walked through the door. .................................................

  **g** This bottle is dearer by 50 cents. .................................................

  **h** What kind of car does your father drive?

    .................................................

  **i** I asked my boss for some more money.

    .................................................

  **j** We walked along the path. .................................................

**139** **Complete the following sentences with the relevant preposition.**

  **a** Dieses Argument ist ........................ mich nicht überzeugend.

  **b** Der Weg zur Post führt ........................ zwei Ecken.

  **c** ........................ einen Ball können wir nicht Fußball spielen.

  **d** Lass mich mal ........................ das Fernglas sehen.

  **e** Was ........................ Fleisch hast du mitgebracht?

  **f** Haben Sie ein Mittel ........................ Erkältung?

  **g** Bei der Diskussion ging es ........................ die Wirtschaftskrise.

  **h** Wir haben die ganze Nacht ........................ gefeiert.

  **i** Dieser Berg ist ........................ 500 Meter höher.

  **j** Er stellte die Leiter ........................ das Haus.

# Prepositions followed by the accusative or the dative case

➤ There are a number of prepositions which can be followed by the accusative or the dative case. You use:

- the accusative case when there is some movement towards a different place

- the dative case when a location is described rather than movement, or when there is movement within the same place

➤ The most common prepositions in this category are:
**an**, **auf**, **hinter**, **in**, **neben**, **über**, **unter**, **vor**, **zwischen**

➤ You use **an**:

- with the <u>accusative</u> case

  | | |
  |---|---|
  | **Die Lehrerin schrieb das Wort an die Tafel.** | The teacher wrote the word on the board. |
  | **Ich habe einen Brief an meine Mutter geschrieben.** | I wrote a letter to my mother. |
  | **Ich ziehe im Sommer an die Küste.** | In the summer I move to the coast. |

- with the <u>dative</u> case

  | | |
  |---|---|
  | **Das Wort stand an der Tafel.** | The word was written on the blackboard. |
  | **Wir treffen uns am Bahnhof.** | We're meeting at the station. |

  🗓 Note that **an** plus the definite article can be shortened to **am**.

  ⇨ For more information on **Shortened forms of prepositions**, see page 229.

➤ You use **auf**:

- with the <u>accusative</u> case

  | | |
  |---|---|
  | **Stell die Suppe bitte auf den Tisch.** | Put the soup on the table please. |
  | **Wir fahren morgen aufs Land.** | We're going to the country tomorrow. |
  | **Er warf einen Blick auf das Buch.** | He glanced at the book. |

  🗓 Note that **auf** plus the definite article can be shortened to **aufs**.

  ⇨ For more information on **Shortened forms of prepositions**, see page 229.

- with the <u>dative</u> case

  | | |
  |---|---|
  | **Die Suppe steht auf dem Tisch.** | The soup's on the table. |
  | **Auf dem Land ist die Luft besser.** | The air is better in the country. |

➤ You use **hinter**:

- with the <u>accusative</u> case

  | | |
  |---|---|
  | **Stell dich hinter deinen Bruder.** | Stand behind your brother. |

- with the <u>dative</u> case

  | | |
  |---|---|
  | **Sie saß hinter mir.** | She was sitting behind me. |

➤ You use **in**:

- with the accusative case

| | |
|---|---|
| **Sie ging ins Zimmer.** | She entered the room. |
| **Er wollte nicht in die Schule gehen.** | He didn't want to go to school. |

- with the dative case

| | |
|---|---|
| **Was hast du heute in der Schule gemacht?** | What did you do at school today? |
| **Im Zimmer warteten viele Leute auf ihn.** | A lot of people were waiting for him in the room. |

ℹ Note that **in** plus the definite article can be shortened to **im** or **ins**.

➪ *For more information on **Shortened forms of prepositions**, see page 229.*

➤ You use **neben**:

- with the accusative case

| | |
|---|---|
| **Stell dein Rad neben meines.** | Put your bike next to mine. |

- with the dative case

| | |
|---|---|
| **Dein Rad steht neben meinem.** | Your bike's next to mine. |

➤ You use **über**:

- with the accusative case

| | |
|---|---|
| **Zieh den Pullover über deinen Kopf!** | Pull the jumper over your head! |
| **Sie ging quer über das Feld.** | She went across the field. |
| **Flugzeuge dürfen nicht über dieses Gebiet fliegen.** | Planes are not allowed to fly over this area. |

- with the dative case

| | |
|---|---|
| **Die Lampe soll über dem Tisch hängen.** | The lamp should hang over the table. |

ℹ Note that when **über** means *about*, it is always followed by the accusative case, NOT the dative.

| | |
|---|---|
| **Wir haben viel über sie gesprochen.** | We talked about her a lot. |

➤ You use **unter**:

- with the accusative case

| | |
|---|---|
| **Sie stellte sich unter den Baum.** | She (came and) stood under the tree. |

- with the dative case

| | |
|---|---|
| **Sie lebte dort unter Freunden.** | She lived there among friends. |

➤ You use **vor**:

- with the accusative case

| | |
|---|---|
| **Stell den Stuhl vor das Fenster.** | Put the chair in front of the window. |

- with the <u>dative</u> case

  **Auf dem Foto stand sie <u>vor</u> <u>dem</u> Haus.**    In the photo she was standing in front of the house.

  **Ich war <u>vor</u> <u>ihm</u> da.**    I was there before him.

  **<u>Vor</u> <u>dem</u> Krankenhaus links abbiegen.**    Turn left at the hospital.

➤ You use **zwischen**:

- with the <u>accusative</u> case

  **Er legte es <u>zwischen</u> <u>die</u> beiden Teller.**    He put it between the two plates.

- with the <u>dative</u> case

  **Das Dorf liegt <u>zwischen</u> <u>den</u> Bergen.**    The village lies between the mountains.

➤ Each of these prepositions can also be used with verbs and are then called <u>prepositional objects</u>.

     **abhängen <u>von</u>** + *dative*      to depend on
     **Das hängt <u>von</u> dir ab.**      That depends on you.
     **schmecken <u>nach</u>** + *dative*      to taste of
     **Der Nachtisch schmeckt <u>nach</u> Zimt.**      The dessert tastes of cinnamon.

➤ When **auf** or **an** is used in this way, the case used depends on the verb – it's much easier to learn such examples together with the case which follows them.

     **sich verlassen <u>auf</u>** + *accusative*      to depend on
     **Ich verlasse mich <u>auf</u> dich.**      I'm depending on you.

     **bestehen <u>auf</u>** + *dative*      to insist on
     **Wir bestehen <u>auf</u> sofortiger Bezahlung.**      We insist on immediate payment.

     **glauben <u>an</u>** + *accusative*      to believe in
     **Sie glaubt <u>an</u> ihre Schwester.**      She believes in her sister.

     **leiden <u>an</u>** + *dative*      to suffer from
     **Er leidet <u>an</u> einer tödlichen Krankheit.**      He is suffering from a terminal illness.

     **sich freuen <u>auf</u>** + *accusative*      to look forward to
     **Ich freue mich <u>auf</u> die Sommerferien**.      I'm looking forward to the summer holidays.

     **warten <u>auf</u>** + *accusative*      to wait for
     **Er wartet jeden morgen <u>auf</u> den Bus.**      Every morning he waits for the bus.

⇨ *For more information on **Verbs with prepositional objects**, see page 198.*

## Grammar Extra!

Some of the above prepositions are also used as separable or inseparable verb prefixes.

| | | |
|---|---|---|
| **anrechnen** | *separable* | to charge for |
| **Das wird Ihnen später angerechnet.** | | You'll be charged for that later. |
| **auf**setzen | *separable* | to put on |
| **Er setzte sich die Mütze auf**. | | He put his cap on. |
| **überqueren** | *inseparable* | to cross |
| **Sie hat die Straße überquert**. | | She crossed the street. |

➪ *For more information on* **Separable verbs** *and* **Inseparable verbs**, *see page 150 and 149.*

---

**KEY POINTS**

✔ **an**, **auf**, **hinter**, **in**, **neben**, **über**, **unter**, **vor** and **zwischen** are the most common prepositions which can be followed by the accusative or dative case.

✔ Most of them have several different possible meanings, depending on the context they are used in.

✔ Each of them can also be prepositional objects of certain verbs.

✔ Many of them can also be used as verb prefixes.

# Test yourself

**140 Cross out the unlikely options.**

**a** Die Katze springt      auf das Sofa/auf den Tisch/in die Straße/vor das Auto

**b** Das Buch liegt      auf dem Tisch/unter den Tassen/in der Schublade/
auf dem Regal

**c** Wir gehen heute      ins Theater/aufs Dach/zum Strand/in den Himmel

**d** Mein Bruder ist      auf der Tür/im Bett/in der Flasche/in der Schule

**e** Er kommt      aus Wales/ins Zimmer/unter den Tisch/neben das Auto

**f** Der Mann steht      neben dem Auto/die Straße entlang/im Auto/vor der Schule

**g** Das Poster hängt      an der Wand/im Büro/am Stuhl/im Kinderzimmer

**h** Gestern sind wir      auf den Tisch gesprungen/ins Theater gegangen/
im Zoo gewesen/neben dem Auto eingeschlafen

**i** Ich wohne      in einer Großstadt/im Büro/neben meinem Haus/
auf dem Land

**j** Herr Langer arbeitet    in unserer Firma/neben der Straße/in einem Büro/in der Wüste

**141 Fill the gap with the most appropriate preposition.**

**a** Er stieg aus und stellte sich ......................... das Auto.

**b** Wir haben die ganze Zeit ......................... dich gesprochen.

**c** Es ist zu dunkel, stell die Lampe ......................... den Tisch.

**d** Die Straßenbahn hält direkt ......................... unserem Haus.

**e** Ich warte jeden Tag ......................... den Zug.

**f** Nächstes Jahr ziehen wir ......................... eine größere Stadt.

**g** Der Fußballspieler lief ......................... das Spielfeld.

**h** Der Löffel liegt rechts ......................... dem Teller.

**i** Du musst ......................... der nächsten Straße rechts abbiegen.

**j** Ich konnte nichts sehen, denn ein großer Mann stand ......................... mir.

# *Test yourself*

**142 Translate the following sentences into German.**

   **a** This soup tastes of lemon. ..................................................................

   **b** He put the knife beside the plate. ......................................................

   **c** We're meeting at the entrance. ...........................................................

   **d** I received an email from my sister.

     ..............................................................................................................

   **e** We're going to Cologne tomorrow. (use *fahren*)

     ..............................................................................................................

   **f** Stand in front of your mother. ............................................................

   **g** The students were waiting for the teacher.

     ..............................................................................................................

   **h** I was here before my sister. ................................................................

   **i** He likes to go to the cinema. ..............................................................

   **j** We should go home. It's already after midnight.

     ..............................................................................................................

# Prepositions followed by the genitive case

➤ The following are some of the more common prepositions which take the genitive case:
**außerhalb, infolge, innerhalb, statt, trotz, um … willen, während, wegen**

- **außerhalb**
  **Es liegt <u>außerhalb</u> der Stadt.**
  *outside*
  It's outside the town.

- **infolge**
  **<u>Infolge</u> des starken Regens kam
  es zu Überschwemmungen.**
  *as a result of*
  As a result of the heavy rain, there were
  floods.

- **innerhalb**
  **Ich schaffe das nicht <u>innerhalb</u>
  der gesetzten Frist.**
  *within, inside*
  I won't manage that within the deadline.

- **statt**
  **Sie kam <u>statt</u> ihres Bruders.**
  *instead of*
  She came instead of her brother.

- **trotz**
  **<u>Trotz</u> ihrer Krankheit ging sie
  jeden Tag spazieren.**
  *in spite of*
  In spite of her illness, she went for a walk
  every day.

- **um … willen**
  **Ich komme <u>um</u> deinet<u>willen</u>.**
  **Tun Sie das bitte <u>um</u> meiner
  Mutter <u>willen</u>.**
  *for … sake, because of …*
  I'm coming for your sake.
  Please do it, for my mother's sake.

- **während**
  **Was hast du <u>während</u> der Ferien
  gemacht?**
  *during*
  What did you do during the holidays?

- **wegen**
  **<u>Wegen</u> des schlechten Wetters
  wurde die Veranstaltung abgesagt.**
  *because of, on account of*
  The event was cancelled because of bad
  weather.

ⓘ Note that **statt**, **trotz**, **während** and **wegen** can also be followed by the dative case.

**Statt <u>dem</u> Abendessen musste
ich arbeiten.**
Instead of having dinner, I had to work.

**Trotz <u>allem</u> will ich weiterstudieren.**
In spite of everything, I want to continue
studying.

**Während <u>dem</u> Vortrag schlief er ein.**
He fell asleep during the lecture.

**Wegen <u>mir</u> musste sie früh nach
Hause.**
She had to go home early because of me.

---

*Grammar Extra!*
There are some other prepositions which take the genitive case.

- **beiderseits**  *on both sides of*
  **<u>Beiderseits</u> des Flusses
  gibt es ein Ufer.**
  On both sides of the river there is a
  river bank.

- diesseits
  **Diesseits der Grenze spricht man
  Polnisch und Deutsch.**

  *on this side of*
  On this side of the border Polish and
  German are spoken.

- ... halber
  **Vorsichtshalber nehme ich heute
  meinen Regenschirm mit.**
  **Sicherheitshalber verschließt
  er die Tür.**

  To be on the safe side I'm taking an
  umbrella today.
  For safety's sake he locks the door.

- hinsichtlich
  **Hinsichtlich Ihrer Beschwerde habe
  ich Ihren Brief an die zuständigen
  Behörden geschickt.**

  *with regard to*
  With regards to your complaint, I have
  passed on your letter to the relevant
  authorities.

- jenseits
  **Das Dorf liegt 2 km jenseits
  der Grenze.**

  *on the other side of*
  The village is 2km on the other side
  of the border.

---

## Grammar Extra!
Special forms of the possessive and relative pronouns are used with **wegen**.

- meinetwegen
  **Hat er sich meinetwegen
  so aufgeregt?**

  Did he get so upset on my account?

- deinetwegen
  **Ich ging nicht deinetwegen nach
  Hause.**

  I didn't go home because of you.

- seinetwegen
  **Ihr müsst seinetwegen nicht auf
  euren Urlaub verzichten.**

  You don't have to do without your
  holiday for his sake.

- ihretwegen
  **Wir sind ihretwegen früher
  gegangen.**

  We went earlier because of them
    *or* her.

- unsertwegen
  **Sie musste unsertwegen
  Strafe zahlen.**

  She had to pay a fine because of us.

- euretwegen
  **Euretwegen durfte er nicht
  mitspielen.**

  Because of you he wasn't allowed
  to play.

- Ihretwegen
  **Sollte es Ihretwegen Probleme
  geben, dann gehen wir alle nach
  Hause.**

  Should you cause any problems,
  then we'll all go home.

⇨ *For more information on **Possessive pronouns** and **Relative pronouns**, see pages 104
and 114.*

**KEY POINTS**

✔ **außerhalb**, **beiderseits**, **diesseits**, ... **halber**, **hinsichtlich**, **infolge**, **innerhalb**, **jenseits**, **statt**, **trotz**, **um** ... **willen**, **während** and **wegen** are the most common prepositions which take the genitive case.

✔ **statt**, **trotz**, **während** and **wegen** can also take the dative case.

✔ Special forms of possessive and relative pronouns are used with **wegen**.

# Test yourself

**143 Translate the following phrases into German.**

    **a** despite the bad weather .................................................................................................

    **b** as a result of the snowfalls .............................................................................................

    **c** in spite of my problems ...................................................................................................

    **d** outside the garden .........................................................................................................

    **e** for your family's sake .....................................................................................................

    **f** during the film ...............................................................................................................

    **g** because of the long holidays .........................................................................................

    **h** on this side of the Rhine ................................................................................................

    **i** instead of visiting his aunt ............................................................................................

    **j** inside the village ............................................................................................................

**144 Fill the gap with the appropriate preposition. The first one has been done for you.**

    **a** Ich durfte ........*statt*........ meines kranken Bruders in Urlaub fahren.

    **b** Mein Vater hat mich ......................... meiner guten Noten gelobt.

    **c** ......................... der Deutschstunde wurde mir schlecht.

    **d** Wie müssen diese Aufgabe ......................... einer Woche erledigen.

    **e** Unser Dorf liegt weit ......................... der Stadt.

    **f** ......................... ihrer Behinderung treibt sie gern Sport.

    **g** ......................... des Streiks kam der Verkehr zum Stillstand.

    **h** ......................... meiner Krankheit brauche ich nicht zur Schule zu gehen.

    **i** Wir sind ......................... der Ferien oft ins Kino gegangen.

    **j** ......................... meiner Eltern ging mein Onkel zum Treffen mit dem Schulleiter.

# Test yourself

**145** **Fill the gap with a form of -*wegen* relating to the pronoun given. The first one has been done for you.**

**a** Ich bin ...*deinetwegen*........... zu Hause geblieben. **[du]**

**b** Wir haben ......................................... einen Umweg gemacht. **[er]**

**c** Danke, dass ihr ......................................... gekommen seid. **[wir]**

**d** ......................................... hat es Schwierigkeiten gegeben. **[ihr]**

**e** Er hat sich ......................................... mit Frau Schmidt gestritten. **[ich]**

**f** Wir sollten uns ......................................... keine Sorgen machen. **[sie]**

**g** Wir haben uns ......................................... bei der Schulleitung beschwert. **[du]**

**h** Sie können nicht verlangen, dass wir ......................................... unsere Pläne ändern. **[Sie]**

**i** ......................................... habe ich meinen Urlaub abgebrochen. **[er]**

**j** Bitte machen Sie sich ......................................... keine Umstände. **[ich]**

## Shortened forms of prepositions

➤ After many German prepositions, a shortened or <u>contracted</u> form of the definite article can be merged with the preposition to make one word.

| | | |
|---|---|---|
| **auf + das** | → | **aufs** |
| **bei + dem** | → | **beim** |
| **zu + der** | → | **zur** |

⇨ *For more information on the **Definite article**, see page 28.*

➤ This can be done with all of the following prepositions:

| Preposition | + das | + den | + dem | + der |
|---|---|---|---|---|
| an | ans | | am | |
| auf | aufs | | | |
| bei | | | beim | |
| durch | durchs | | | |
| für | fürs | | | |
| hinter | hinters | hintern | hinterm | |
| in | ins | | im | |
| über | übers | übern | überm | |
| um | ums | | | |
| unter | unters | untern | unterm | |
| vor | vors | | vorm | |
| von | | | vom | |
| zu | | | zum | zur |

| | |
|---|---|
| **Er ging <u>ans</u> Fenster.** | He went to the window. |
| **Wir waren gestern <u>am</u> Meer.** | We were at the seaside yesterday. |
| **Er ist <u>beim</u> Friseur.** | He's at the hairdresser's. |
| **Wir gehen heute Abend <u>ins</u> Kino.** | We're going to the cinema tonight. |
| **Im Sommer lese ich gern <u>im</u> Garten.** | In the summer I like reading in the garden. |
| **Es ging immer <u>ums</u> Thema Geld.** | It was always about the subject of money. |
| **Der Hund lief <u>unters</u> Auto.** | The dog ran under the car. |
| **Der Ball rollte <u>untern</u> Tisch.** | The ball rolled under the table. |
| **Die Katze lag <u>unterm</u> Schreibtisch.** | The cat lay under the desk. |
| **Er erzählte <u>vom</u> Urlaub.** | He talked about his holiday. |
| **Sie fährt <u>zum</u> Bahnhof.** | She drives to the station. |
| **Er geht <u>zur</u> Schule.** | He goes to school. |

➤ The following shortened forms are normally only used in informal, spoken German:

- **aufs**
  **Wir fahren morgen <u>aufs</u> Land.** — We're going to the country tomorrow.

- **durchs**
  **Sie flog <u>durchs</u> Abitur.** — She failed her A-levels.

- **fürs**
  **Das ist <u>fürs</u> neue Haus.** — That's for the new house.

- hinters, hintern, hinterm
  **Er lief <u>hinters</u> Auto.**                He ran behind the car.
  **Stell es <u>hintern</u> Tisch.**            Put it behind the table.
  **Es liegt <u>hinterm</u> Sofa.**             It's behind the couch.

- übers, übern, überm
  **Sie legten ein Brett <u>übers</u> Loch.**        They put a board over the hole.
  **Man muss das <u>übern</u> Kopf ziehen.**     You have to pull it over your head.
  **<u>Überm</u> Tisch hängt eine Lampe.**        There's a lamp hanging over the table.

- unters, untern, unterm
  **Die Katze ging <u>unters</u> Bett.**            The cat went under the bed.
  **Der Ball rollte <u>untern</u> Tisch.**         The ball rolled under the table.
  **Der Hund liegt <u>unterm</u> Tisch.**          The dog is lying under the table.

- vors, vorm
  **Stell den Stuhl <u>vors</u> Fenster.**          Put the chair in front of the window.
  **Er stand <u>vorm</u> Spiegel.**                 He stood in front of the mirror.

*ⓘ* Note that if you want to stress the article in a sentence, shortened forms are <u>NOT</u> used.

**In <u>dem</u> Anzug kann ich mich**        I can't go out in *that* suit!
  **nicht sehen lassen!**

➤ Shortened forms of prepositions can also be used:

- with personal pronouns representing inanimate objects, that is objects
  which are not living things
  **Sie war <u>damit</u> zufrieden.**               She was satisfied with that.
  **Er hat es <u>darauf</u> angelegt, dass**        He was determined to get the best grade.
  **er die beste Note kriegen würde.**

⇨ *For more information on **Personal pronouns**, see page 89.*

---

**KEY POINTS**
✔ It is often possible to combine the definite article and a preposition to
  create a shortened form.
✔ Some of these shortened forms should only be used in spoken German.

---

**146 Cross out the unlikely or impossible options.**

| | | |
|---|---|---|
| **a** | ... Schrank | überm/unterm/hintern/zur |
| **b** | ... Haus | aufs/untern/vors/hinterm |
| **c** | ... Zimmer | aufs/ins/durchs/ums |
| **d** | ... Zaun | vorm/übern/ans/zum |
| **e** | ... Bett | aufs/durchs/ans/vors |
| **f** | ... Park | unterm/am/zum/vorm |
| **g** | ... Auto | übern/zum/hinterm/im |
| **h** | ... Fenster | ums/durchs/überm/unters |
| **i** | ... Radio | aufs/im/durchs/ums |
| **j** | ... Berg | zum/untern/hinterm/am |

**147 Translate the following sentences into German using the shortened form of the definite article with the appropriate preposition. The first one has been done for you.**

**a** The cat crawled under the bed. *Die Katze kroch unters Bett.*

**b** We went to the station. ...........................................................................................

**c** We found the book behind the sofa.

...............................................................................................................................

**d** The dog was sleeping under the chair.

...............................................................................................................................

**e** The bird flew over the house. ...............................................................................

**f** We have to go to school. ......................................................................................

**g** He was standing in front of the table.

...............................................................................................................................

**h** Put the book on the shelf. ....................................................................................

**i** The children are in the house. ...............................................................................

**j** She has gone to the baker's. .................................................................................

# Test yourself

**148** **Replace the highlighted words with the correct shortened form of preposition and object. The first one has been done for you.**

**a** Sie legte das Buch **auf den Tisch**. _darauf_ ..................................................................

**b** Hast du **an das Geschenk** gedacht? ................................................................................

**c** Er schob den Koffer **unter das Bett**. ................................................................................

**d** Sie regte sich **über seine Bemerkung** auf. ...................................................................

**e** Er stellte sich **vor das Haus**. .............................................................................................

**f** Die Teller sind **im Schrank**. ...............................................................................................

**g** Können Sie sich **zu diesem Problem** äußern? ..............................................................

**h** **Um diese Frage** geht es doch gar nicht. .........................................................................

**i** **Nach der Wahl** wurde sie Bundeskanzlerin. ................................................................

**j** Das Dorf liegt **hinter dem Wald**. .....................................................................................

# Conjunctions

## What is a conjunction?

A **conjunction** is a linking word such as *and, but, if* and *because*, that links two words or phrases of a similar type, for example, *Diane <u>and</u> I have been friends for years.* Conjunctions also link two clauses, for example, *I left <u>because</u> I was bored.* In German there are two types of conjunctions, called **coordinating conjunctions** and **subordinating conjunctions**.

## Coordinating conjunctions

➤ **aber**, **denn**, **oder**, **sondern** and **und** are the most important coordinating conjunctions.

- **aber**
  **Wir wollten ins Kino, <u>aber</u> wir hatten kein Geld.**

  *but*
  We wanted to go to the cinema, <u>but</u> we had no money.

  ⓘ Note that you can't use **aber** after a negative to mean *not ... but ...*: you must use **sondern**.

- **aber**
  **Ich wollte nach Hause, er <u>aber</u> wollte nicht mit.**

  *however*
  I wanted to go home; however, he wouldn't come.

  ⓘ Note that when **aber** means 'however', it comes between the subject and verb in the clause.

- **denn**
  **Wir wollten heute fahren, <u>denn</u> montags ist weniger Verkehr.**

  *because, since*
  We wanted to travel today because there is less traffic on Mondays.

- **oder**
  **Sie hatte noch nie Whisky <u>oder</u> Schnaps getrunken.**
  **Willst du eins <u>oder</u> hast du vielleicht keinen Hunger?**

  *or*
  She had never drunk whisky or schnapps.

  Do you want one or aren't you hungry?

- **sondern**
  **Es kostet nicht zwanzig, <u>sondern</u> fünfzig Euro.**

  *but*
  It doesn't cost twenty euros, but fifty.

- **und**
  **Susi <u>und</u> Oliver**
  **Er ging in die Stadt <u>und</u> kaufte sich ein neues Hemd.**

  *and*
  Susi and Oliver
  He went into town and bought himself a new shirt.

➤ If you use a coordinating conjunction, you do not put the verb at the end of the clause beginning with the conjunction.

| | |
|---|---|
| **Wir wollten ins Theater, <u>aber wir</u> <u>hatten</u> kein Geld.** | We wanted to go to the theatre but we had no money. |

**wir** = subject
**hatten** = verb

## Coordinating conjunctions with two parts

➤ German, like English, also has conjunctions which have more than one part. Here are the most common ones.

- **sowohl ... als (auch)** *both ... and*

  The verb is plural, whether the individual subjects are singular or plural.

  | | |
  |---|---|
  | <u>**Sowohl**</u> **sein Vater** <u>**als auch**</u> **seine Mutter haben sich darüber gefreut.** | Both his father and mother were pleased about it. |
  | <u>**Sowohl**</u> **unser Lehrkörper** <u>**als auch**</u> **unsere Schüler haben teilgenommen.** | Both our staff and pupils took part. |

- **weder ... noch** *neither ... nor*

  With this conjunction, the verb is plural unless both subjects are singular, as shown below.

  | | |
  |---|---|
  | <u>**Weder**</u> **die Lehrer** <u>**noch**</u> **die Schüler haben recht.** | Neither the teachers nor the pupils are right. |
  | <u>**Weder**</u> **du** <u>**noch**</u> **ich würde es schaffen.** | Neither you nor I would be able to do it. |

  When **weder ... noch** is used to link clauses, the subject and verb are swapped round in BOTH clauses.

  | | |
  |---|---|
  | <u>**Weder**</u> **mag ich ihn,** <u>**noch**</u> **respektiere ich ihn.** | I neither like nor respect him. |

- **nicht nur ... sondern auch** *not only ... but also*

  The verb agrees in number with the subject nearest to it.

  | | |
  |---|---|
  | <u>**Nicht nur**</u> **sie,** <u>**sondern auch**</u> **ich habe es gehört.** | They weren't the only ones to hear it – I heard it too. |

  When **nicht nur ... sondern auch** is used to link clauses, the subject and verb are only swapped round in the first clause, not the second, BUT if **nicht nur** does not begin the clause, word order is normal.

  | | |
  |---|---|
  | <u>**Nicht nur**</u> **ist sie geschickt,** <u>**sondern auch**</u> **intelligent.** | She is not only skilful but also intelligent. |
  | OR | |
  | **Sie ist** <u>**nicht nur**</u> **geschickt,** <u>**sondern auch**</u> **intelligent.** | |

● **entweder ... oder** *either ... or*

The verb agrees in number with the subject nearest to it. When **entweder ... oder** is used to link clauses, the subject and verb are only swapped round in the first clause, not the second.

| | |
|---|---|
| **<u>Entweder</u> du <u>oder</u> Karla muss es getan haben.** | It must have been either you or Karla. |
| **<u>Entweder</u> komme ich vorbei, <u>oder</u> ich rufe dich an.** | I'll either drop in or I'll give you a ring. |

---

**KEY POINTS**

✔ A conjunction is a word that links two words or clauses of a similar type, or two parts of a sentence.

✔ **Aber**, **denn**, **oder**, **sondern** and **und** are the most important coordinating conjunctions.

✔ Single-word coordinating conjunctions do not change the order of the subject and the verb in the clause.

# Test yourself

**149** **Translate the following sentences into German, using a coordinating conjunction.**

**a** She went to the bank and paid in 100 euros.

......................................................................................................................

**b** We wanted to go out but it was already late.

......................................................................................................................

**c** Petra and Susanne were at the party. ...............................................................

**d** Both you and I like pop music. .......................................................................

**e** Neither he nor she saw it. ..............................................................................

**f** He neither came nor phoned.

......................................................................................................................

**g** They are not just ugly but also stupid.

......................................................................................................................

**h** He doesn't owe me 300 euros but 500.

......................................................................................................................

**i** Both your and my school have 600 pupils.

......................................................................................................................

**j** They went to a restaurant because they were hungry.

......................................................................................................................

**150** **Complete these sentences by inserting the missing element of the two-part conjunction. The first one has been done for you.**

**a** In den letzten Tagen war das Wetter ........*weder*........ warm noch kalt.

**b** Entweder jetzt ......................... nie!

**c** ......................... Köln als auch Aachen haben einen Dom.

**d** ......................... er noch ich wollte noch bleiben.

**e** Ich will ......................... dich noch sonst jemanden sehen.

**f** Ich mag nicht nur Rotwein, ......................... Weißwein.

**g** Wir sollten ......................... nach Rom oder nach Paris reisen.

**h** Sowohl meine Mutter ......................... mein Vater sind über 50 Jahre alt.

**i** Sie schaute weder links ......................... rechts, als sie über die Straße ging.

# Test yourself

**151** **Match the two columns.**

| | | |
|---|---|---|
| **a** | nicht nur ich | oder gar nicht |
| **b** | weder Oliver | als auch Petra |
| **c** | entweder gleich | oder ich |
| **d** | sowohl Oliver | sondern auch er |
| **e** | entweder du | noch Petra |

# Subordinating conjunctions

➤ The subordinate clause is always separated from the main clause by a comma. It is called a subordinate clause because it cannot stand on its own without the other clause in the sentence and is linked to this by a subordinating conjunction.

| | |
|---|---|
| **Sie ist zu Fuß gekommen, <u>weil</u> der Bus zu teuer <u>ist</u>.** | She came on foot because the bus is too dear. |
| MAIN CLAUSE | = **Sie ist zu Fuß gekommen** |
| SUBORDINATE CLAUSE | = **weil der Bus zu teuer ist** |

[i] Note that the verb comes at the end of the subordinate clause.

➤ **als**, **da**, **damit**, **dass**, **ob**, **obwohl**, **während**, **wenn**, **weil**, **um ... zu**, and **ohne ... zu** are some of the most important subordinating conjunctions.

- **als** 
  **Es regnete, <u>als</u> ich in Glasgow ankam.**

  *when* 
  It was raining when I arrived in Glasgow.

- **da** 
  **<u>Da</u> du nicht kommen willst, gehe ich allein.**

  *as, since* 
  Since you don't want to come, I'll go on my own.

- **damit** 
  **Ich sage dir das, <u>damit</u> du es weißt.**

  *so (that)* 
  I'm telling you so that you know.

- **dass** 
  **Ich weiß, <u>dass</u> du besser in Mathe bist als ich.**

  *that* 
  I know (that) you're better at maths than me.

- **ob** 
  **Sie fragt, <u>ob</u> du auch kommst.**

  *if, whether* 
  She wants to know if you're coming too.

- **obwohl** 
  **Sie blieb lange auf, <u>obwohl</u> sie müde war.**

  *although* 
  She stayed up late although she was tired.

- **während** 
  **Sie sah fern, <u>während</u> sie ihre Hausaufgaben machte.**

  *while* 
  She was watching TV while she was doing her homework.

- **wenn** 
  **<u>Wenn</u> ich nach Hause komme, dusche ich erst mal.** 
  **<u>Wenn</u> er anruft, sag mir Bescheid.**

  *when, whenever, if* 
  When I get home, the first thing I'm going to do is have a shower. 
  If he calls, tell me.

> *Tip* 
> If translating *when* in a sentence which describes a single, completed action in the past, you use **als**, NOT **wenn**. You use **wenn** for single, momentary actions in the present or future.

- **weil**                                                                *because*
  **Morgen komme ich nicht, <u>weil</u> ich**        I'm not coming tomorrow because I don't
    **keine Zeit habe.**                                   have the time.

- **um ... zu**                                                         *in order to ...*
  **<u>Um</u> früh auf<u>zu</u>stehen, musste sie**      In order to get up early, she had to set
    **den Wecker stellen.**                              the alarm.

   ⓘ Note that **zu** is inserted between a separable verb and its prefix.

   ⇨ *For more information on **Separable verbs**, see page 150.*

- **ohne ... zu**  *without ...*
  **Er verließ das Haus, <u>ohne</u> ein Wort**         He left the house without saying a word.
    **<u>zu</u> sagen.**

   ⓘ Note that **um ... zu** and **ohne ... zu** are always used with infinitive constructions.

   ⓘ Note that with the subordinating conjunctions **als**, **da**, **damit**, **dass**, **ob**, **obwohl**,
   **während**, **wenn**, **weil**, **um ... zu**, and **ohne ... zu**, the subordinate clause can come
   <u>BEFORE</u> the main clause, as seen in the example with **da**. When this happens, the verb
   and subject of the main clause swap places.

   ⇨ *For more information on the **Infinitive**, see page 181.*

➤ In tenses which only have one verb part, such as the present and imperfect, the verb comes
  last in the subordinate clause.
    **<u>Wenn</u> er mich <u>sah</u>, lief er davon.**          Whenever he saw me, he ran away.

➤ In tenses which have two verb parts, such as the perfect tense, it is the form of **haben**, **sein**
  or **werden** which comes last in the subordinate clause, after the past participle.
    **Sie will nicht ausgehen, <u>weil</u> sie**          She doesn't want to go out because she
      **noch nichts <u>gegessen hat</u>.**                       hasn't eaten anything yet.

   ⇨ *For more information on the **Perfect** and **Imperfect tenses**, see pages 153 and 160.*

➤ Any modal verb, for example **mögen** (meaning *to like*) and **können** (meaning *can, to be*
  *able to*), used in a subordinate clause is placed last in the clause.
    **Sie wusste nicht, <u>ob</u> sie kommen**          She didn't know if she could come.
      **konnte.**

   ⇨ *For more information on **Modal verbs**, see page 184.*

## KEY POINTS

✔ Subordinating conjunctions link the main clause and subordinating clause in a sentence.

✔ After subordinating conjunctions, verbs go to the end of the clause.

✔ **Als**, **da**, **damit**, **dass**, **ob**, **obwohl**, **während**, **wenn**, **weil**, **um ... zu**, and **ohne ... zu** are some of the most important subordinating conjunctions.

✔ The subordinate clause can come before the main clause. When this happens, the verb and subject of the main clause swap places.

✔ In tenses which only have one verb part, the verb comes last in the subordinate clause. In tenses which have two verb parts, **haben**, **sein** or **werden** comes last in the subordinate clause, after the past participle.

# Test yourself

**152  Fill the gap by inserting *als*, *weil* or *wenn* as appropriate.**

**a**  Ich bin gekommen, ......................... ich dich sprechen will.

**b**  ......................... Sie möchten, kann ich das Geschenk einpacken.

**c**  ......................... ich ankam, putzte er gerade sein Auto.

**d**  Mir wird schlecht, ......................... ich nur daran denke.

**e**  Er war wütend, ......................... er so lange warten musste.

**f**  ......................... er sie sah, war er sofort verliebt.

**g**  Ich kann heute nicht kommen, ......................... ich für meine Mutter einkaufen muss.

**h**  Es wäre schön, ......................... du meine Frage beantworten würdest.

**i**  Das Auto ist so billig, ......................... es schon sehr alt ist.

**j**  Es wäre am besten, ......................... wir jetzt gehen.

**153  Fill the gap by inserting *ob*, *obwohl* or *während* as appropriate.**

**a**  ......................... sie krank war, blieb ihre Arbeit liegen.

**b**  Ich konnte schon gut rechnen, ......................... ich erst vier Jahre alt war.

**c**  Ich weiß nicht, ......................... ich dir glauben kann.

**d**  Man darf nicht aussteigen, ......................... der Zug fährt.

**e**  Wir stritten darüber, ......................... wir in den Zoo gehen sollten.

**f**  Er ging aus dem Haus, ......................... er Gäste erwartete.

**g**  Kannst du sehen, ......................... das dort das Schloss ist?

**h**  Er maß die Zeit, ......................... ich lief.

**i**  Wir gingen zur Schule, ......................... wir krank waren.

**j**  Ich bin im Zweifel, ......................... ich das tun soll.

**154  Match the two columns.**

**a  Ich weiß,**              obwohl ich mich langweile.

**b  Ich weiß nicht,**         dass wir es schaffen können.

**c  Ich kann nicht kommen,**  ob das eine gute Idee ist.

**d  Ich beeile mich,**        weil ich beschäftigt bin.

**e  Ich bleibe,**            damit ich nicht zu spät komme.

# Word Order

➤ Here is a ready-reference guide to the key points of German word order.

## Main clauses

➤ In a main clause the subject comes first and is followed by the verb, as in English.

**Seine Mutter** (subject) **trinkt** (verb) **Whisky.**　　　His mother (subject) drinks (verb) whisky.

➤ In tenses with more than one verb element, such as the perfect tense and the passive, **haben**, **sein** or **werden** comes after the subject, and the past participle or infinitive goes to the end of the clause.

**Sie <u>hat</u> mir nichts <u>gesagt</u>.**　　　She told me nothing.
**Er <u>ist</u> spät <u>angekommen</u>.**　　　He arrived late.
**Es <u>wurde</u> für ihn <u>gekauft</u>.**　　　It was bought for him.

➤ A direct object usually follows an indirect object, except where the direct object is a personal pronoun.

**Ich gab dem Mann** (indirect object) **das Geld** (direct object).　　　I gave the man the money.

**Ich gab ihm** (indirect object) **das Geld** (direct object).　　　I gave him the money.
BUT
**Ich gab es** (direct object) **ihm** (indirect object).　　　I gave it to him.

> *ⓘ* Note that the indirect object can also be placed last for emphasis, providing it is NOT a pronoun.
> **Er gab das Geld seiner Schwester.**　　　He gave the money to his sister.

⇨ For more information on **Direct** and **Indirect objects**, see pages 11 and 14.

⇨ For more information on **Using direct** and **Indirect object pronouns**, see pages 94 and 98.

➤ As a general rule, adverbs are placed next to the words to which they refer.

- Adverbs of <u>time</u> often come first in the clause, but this is not fixed.
  **<u>Gestern</u> gingen wir ins Theater.**　　　We went to the theatre yesterday
  OR
  **Wir gingen <u>gestern</u> ins Theater.**.

- Adverbs of <u>place</u> can also come first in the clause when you want to emphasize something.
  **<u>Dort</u> haben sie Fußball gespielt.**　　　That's where they played football.

- Adverbs of <u>manner</u> comment on verbs and so are likely to come immediately after the verb they refer to.
  **Sie spielen <u>gut</u> Fußball.**　　　They play football well.

- Where there is more than one adverb, a useful rule of thumb is:
  'TIME, MANNER, PLACE'

  **Wir haben <u>gestern gut hierhin</u>**          We found our way here all right yesterday.
  **gefunden.**
  **gestern** = adverb of time
  **gut** = adverb of manner
  **hierhin** = adverb of place

- If there is a pronoun object (a word like *her, it, me* or *them*) in the clause, it comes before
  all adverbs.

  **Sie haben <u>es</u> gestern sehr billig**          They bought it very cheaply yesterday.
  **gekauft.**

➤ The normal word order in a main clause is subject followed by verb. The subject can be
  replaced as the first element by any of the words and phrases below. In such cases, the verb
  is the second element in the clause.

  - an adverb
    **<u>Gestern</u> sind wir ins Theater**          We went to the theatre yesterday.
    **gegangen.**

  - a direct or indirect object
    **<u>Seinen Freunden</u> wollte er es nicht**          He wouldn't show it to his friends.
    **zeigen.**

  - an infinitive phrase
    **<u>Ihren Freunden zu helfen</u>, hat sie**          She didn't try to help her friends.
    **nicht versucht.**

  - another noun or pronoun
    **<u>Deine Schwester</u> war es.**          It was your sister.
    **<u>Sie</u> war es.**          It was her.

  - a past participle
    **<u>Geraucht</u> hatte er nie.**          He had never, ever smoked.

  - a phrase with a preposition
    **<u>In diesem Haus</u> bin ich auf die Welt**          I was born in this house.
    **gekommen.**

  - a clause which acts as the object of the verb
    **<u>Was mit ihm los war</u>, haben wir nie**          We never found out what was wrong
    **herausgefunden.**           with him.

  - a subordinate clause
    **<u>Nachdem ich ihn gesehen hatte</u>,**          I went home after seeing him.
    **ging ich nach Hause.**

## Subordinate clauses

➤ A subordinate clause may be introduced by a relative pronoun (a word such as **der**, **die** or **dessen**) or a subordinating conjunction (a word such as **da**, **als** or **ob**).

| | |
|---|---|
| **Die Kinder, <u>die</u> wir gesehen haben** … | The children whom we saw … |
| **<u>Da</u> sie nicht schwimmen wollte, ist sie nicht mitgekommen.** | As she didn't want to swim, she didn't come. |

➤ The subject follows the conjunction or relative pronoun.

| | |
|---|---|
| **Ich weiß nicht, <u>ob er</u> kommt.** | I don't know if he's coming. |

➤ The main verb ALMOST ALWAYS goes to the end of a subordinate clause.

| | |
|---|---|
| **<u>Als</u> ich nach Hause <u>kam</u>, war ich ganz müde.** | When I came home I was really tired. |

---

*Grammar Extra!*
The exceptions to this are:

- A clause which normally begins with **wenn**, but from which it can be left out.

| | |
|---|---|
| **<u>Findest</u> du mein Handy, so ruf mich bitte an.** | If you find my mobile, please give me a call. |

  INSTEAD OF
  **<u>Wenn</u> du mein Handy findest, ruf mich bitte an.**

- Indirect speech without the conjunction **dass** (meaning *that*).

| | |
|---|---|
| **Sie meint, sie <u>werde</u> es innerhalb einer Stunde schaffen.** | She thinks (that) she will manage it inside an hour. |

  INSTEAD OF
  **Sie meint, <u>dass</u> sie es innerhalb einer Stunde schaffen wird.**

---

➤ The rules applying to the order of articles, nouns, adjectives, adverbs, direct and indirect objects are the same in subordinate clauses as in main clauses, EXCEPT that all these words are placed between the subject of the clause and the relevant verb part.

| | |
|---|---|
| MAIN CLAUSE: | |
| **Sie ist <u>gestern mit ihrer Mutter in die Stadt</u> gefahren.** | She went into town with her mother yesterday. |
| SUBORDINATE CLAUSE: | |
| **<u>Da</u> sie <u>gestern mit ihrer Mutter in die Stadt</u> gefahren ist…** | Since she went into town with her mother yesterday… |

> **Tip**
> The rule 'time, manner, place' applies equally to subordinate clauses,
> EXCEPT that the verb goes to the end.

➤ Word order in the imperative, in direct and indirect speech and in verbs with separable
  prefixes is covered in the relevant chapters:

⇨ *For more information on the **Imperative**, see page 143.*

⇨ *For more information on **Direct** and **Indirect speech**, see page 175.*

⇨ *For more information on **Verbs with separable prefixes**, see page 150.*

# Negatives

---

### What is a negative?
A **negative** question or statement is one which contains a word such as *not*, *never* or *nothing* and is used to say that something is not happening, is not true or is absent.

---

## Using negatives

➤ In English we use words like *not*, *no*, *nothing* and *never* to show a negative.
  I'm <u>not</u> very pleased.
  Dan <u>never</u> rang me.
  Nothing <u>ever</u> happens here!
  There's <u>no</u> milk left.

➤ In German, if you want to make something negative, you generally add **nicht** (meaning *not*) or **nie** (meaning *never*) next to the phrase or word referred to.

  | | |
  |---|---|
  | **Ich will <u>nicht</u> mitgehen.** | I <u>don't</u> want to come. |
  | **Sie fährt <u>nie</u> mit ans Meer.** | She <u>never</u> comes with us to the seaside. |

➤ Here is a list of the other common German negatives:

  - nein      *no*
    **<u>Nein</u>, ich habe keine Zeit.**      No, I don't have any time.

  - nichts      *nothing*
    **Sie hat <u>nichts</u> damit zu tun.**      She has nothing to do with it.

  - nicht mehr      *not ... any more, no longer*
    **Ich rauche <u>nicht mehr</u>.**      I don't smoke any more/I no longer smoke.
    **Sie geht <u>nicht mehr</u> hin.**      She doesn't go any more.

  *ⓘ* Note that **nicht** and **mehr** always appear next to each other.

  kein      *none*
  **<u>Keiner</u> meiner Freunde wollte kommen.**      None of my friends wanted to come.
  **Wo ist die Milch? – Es ist <u>keine</u> mehr da.**      Where is the milk? – There is none left.

---

  *Tip*
  **Nicht** applies to verbs. Remember that when you want to make a negative statement about a noun, you must use **kein**. If you want to say *I don't drink milk any more*, you would say **Ich trinke <u>keine</u> Milch <u>mehr</u>**.

---

⇨ *For more information on the **Indefinite article in negative sentences** and on **Indefinite pronouns**, see pages 44 and 108.*

- niemand                      *nobody* or *no one*
  **Es war <u>niemand</u> im Büro.**      There was nobody in the office.

⇨ *For more information on **Indefinite pronouns**, see page 108.*

- nirgendwo or nirgends         *nowhere, not ... anywhere*
  **<u>Nirgends</u> sonst gibt es so schöne**   Nowhere else will you find such beautiful
     **Blumen.**                        flowers.
  **Hier gibts <u>nirgendwo</u> ein**       There isn't a swimming pool anywhere here.
     **Schwimmbad.**

- weder noch                  *neither of two things*
  **Karotten oder Erbsen? –**       Carrots or peas? – Neither, thanks.
     **<u>Weder noch</u>, danke.**

- weder ... noch              *neither ... nor*
  **<u>Weder</u> Sabina <u>noch</u> Oliver kommen**   Neither Sabina nor Oliver are coming to
     **zur Party.**                     the party.

⇨ *For more information on **Coordinating conjunctions with two parts**, see page 234.*

- ... auch nicht              *neither have I, nor does he, nor are we* etc
  **Ich mag ihn nicht. – Ich <u>auch</u> <u>nicht</u>!**   I don't like him. – Neither do I!
  **Er war noch nie in Spanien. –**    He's never been to Spain. – Neither has she!
     **Sie <u>auch</u> <u>nicht</u>!**

## Word order with negatives

➤ In a sentence with only one verb part, such as the present tense, **nicht** and **nie** usually
come directly after the verb. However, in direct questions, the negative word comes after
the subject.

   **Du arbeitest <u>nicht</u>.**          You're not working.
   BUT
   **Arbeitest du <u>nicht</u>?**         Aren't you working?

➤ In a sentence with two verb parts, such as the perfect tense and the passive, **haben**, **sein** or
**werden** come after the subject and the negative word usually comes directly before the
past participle or infinitive. The position of the negative doesn't change in direct questions.

   **Sie haben es <u>nicht</u> gemacht.**    You haven't done it.
   **Haben Sie es <u>nicht</u> gemacht?**   Haven't you done it?

➤ You can change the emphasis in a sentence by moving the position of the negative. For
example, **nie** can be placed at the start of the sentence. The subject and verb then swap
positions.

   **<u>Nie</u> waren sie glücklicher gewesen.**   They had <u>never</u> been happier.
   **<u>Nie</u> im Leben hatte er so etwas**    <u>Never</u> in his life had he seen such a thing.
   **gesehen.**

➤ **nicht** comes at the end of a negative imperative, except if the verb is separable, in which case it comes before the separable prefix.

| | |
|---|---|
| **Iss das <u>nicht</u>!** | Don't eat that! |
| **Setzen Sie sich <u>nicht</u>!** | Don't sit down! |
| BUT | |
| **Geh <u>nicht</u> weg!** | Don't go away! |

➤ **nicht** + the indefinite article **ein** is usually replaced by forms of **kein**.

| | |
|---|---|
| **Gibt es <u>keine</u> Plätzchen?** | Aren't there any biscuits? |
| **<u>Kein</u> einziger Student hatte die Arbeit gemacht.** | Not a single student had done the work. |

➪ *For more information on the* **Indefinite article**, *see page 43.*

➤ To contradict a negative statement, **doch** is used instead of **ja**, to mean *yes*.

| | |
|---|---|
| **Du kommst nicht mit. – <u>Doch</u>, ich komme mit.** | You're not coming. – Yes, I am. |
| **Das ist nicht wahr. – <u>Doch</u>!** | That isn't true! – Yes, it is! |

➤ **nicht ... sondern** (meaning *not ... but*) is used to correct a wrong idea or false impression.

| | |
|---|---|
| **<u>Nicht</u> Susi, <u>sondern</u> ihr Bruder war es.** | It wasn't Susi, it was her brother. |

---

**KEY POINTS**

✔ A statement is usually made negative by adding **nicht** (meaning *not*) or **nie** (meaning *never*).

✔ The most common German negatives are: **nicht**, **nein**, **nie**, **nichts**, **nicht mehr**, **kein**, **niemand**, **nirgends** or **nirgendwo**, **weder noch**, **weder ... noch** and **... auch nicht**.

✔ **Nicht** comes at the end of a negative imperative, except if the verb is separable, in which case it comes before the separable prefix.

✔ **Nicht** + the indefinite article **ein** is usually replaced by forms of **kein**.

✔ To contradict a negative statement, **doch** is used instead of **ja**, to mean *yes*.

✔ **Nicht ... sondern** (meaning *not ... but*) is used to correct a wrong idea or false impression.

---

# Test yourself

**155 Replace the highlighted words with negatives as appropriate. The first one has been done for you.**

**a** Meine Augen **sind blau**. *sind nicht blau* ..................

**b** Ich **habe Angst**. ..................

**c** Ich **mag Erbsen**. ..................

**d** Er **kommt mit**. ..................

**e** Sonntags gehen wir **immer** einkaufen. ..................

**f** Ich war **schon einmal** in einem Schloss. ..................

**g** Hier ist **irgendwo** ein Postamt. ..................

**h** Wir haben **etwas** gegessen. ..................

**i** Möchten Sie Nachtisch oder Kaffee? – **Beides,** danke. ..................

**j** Ich habe ihn **schon immer** gemocht. ..................

**156 Translate the following sentences into German.**

**a** I have never been to Germany. ..................

**b** There was nobody in the room. ..................

**c** I can't find him anywhere. ..................

**d** That cannot be true. ..................

**e** She never pays attention at school. ..................

**f** I don't like him either. ..................

**g** Neither Brigitte nor her brother were at the party.

..................

**h** We should never forget it. ..................

**i** Nobody remembers it any more ..................

**j** I never want to see you again. ..................

# Questions

## What is a question?

A **question** is a sentence which is used to ask someone about something and which in English normally has the verb in front of the subject. Question words such as *why*, *where*, *who*, *which* or *how* are also used to ask a question.

## How to ask a question in German

### The basic rules

➤ There are three ways of asking direct questions in German:

- by changing round the order of words in a sentence

- by adding **nicht**, **nicht wahr**, **oder** or **doch** (meaning *isn't it*) to a sentence

- by using a question word

### Asking a question by changing word order

➤ Many questions are formed in German by simply changing the normal word order of a sentence. You swap round the subject and verb, and add a question mark.

| | |
|---|---|
| **Magst** *(verb)* **du** *(subject)* **ihn?** | Do you like him? |
| **Gehst** *(verb)* **du** *(subject)* **ins Kino?** | Do you go to the cinema? OR |
| | Are you going to the cinema? |

➤ In tenses with more than one verb, such as the perfect tense and the passive, **haben**, **sein** or **werden** come <u>BEFORE</u> the subject, and the past participle or infinitive goes to the end of the clause.

| | |
|---|---|
| <u>**Haben**</u> Sie es <u>gesehen</u>? | Did you see it? |

### Asking a question by adding nicht, nicht wahr, oder or doch

➤ A statement can be made into a question by adding **nicht**, **nicht wahr**, **oder** or **doch**, in the same way as *isn't it*, *won't you* etc is added in English. You'd normally expect the answer to such questions to be a simple *yes* or *no*.

| | |
|---|---|
| **Das stimmt, <u>nicht wahr</u>?** | That's true, isn't it? |
| **Das Essen ist fertig, <u>nicht</u>?** | The food's ready, isn't it? |
| **Sie machen das, <u>oder</u>?** | They'll do it, won't they? |
| **Das schaffst du <u>doch</u>?** | You'll manage, won't you? |

➤ When a question is put in the negative, **doch** can be used to answer it more positively than **ja**.

| | |
|---|---|
| **Glaubst du mir nicht? – Doch!** | Don't you believe me? – Yes, I do! |

For further explanation of grammatical terms, please see pages viii-xii.

# Asking a question by using a question word

➤ A question word is a word like *when* or *how* that is used to ask for information. In German, these words are a mixture of interrogative adverbs, pronouns and adjectives. Listed below are the most common question words:

| | | |
|---|---|---|
| **wie?** (*how?*) | **wo?** (*where?*) | **wem?** (*whom?*) |
| **was?** (*what?*) | **welcher?** (*which?*) | **wessen?** (*whose?*) |
| **wann?** (*when?*) | **wer?** (*who?*) | **warum?** (*why?*) |

ⓘ Note that **wer** means *who*, NOT *where*.

➤ When questions are formed with interrogative adverbs like **wann**, **wo**, **wie** and **warum**, normal word order changes and the subject and verb swap places.

| | |
|---|---|
| <u>**Wann**</u> **ist er gekommen?** | When did he come? |
| <u>**Wo**</u> **willst du hin?** | Where are you off to? |
| <u>**Wie**</u> **haben Sie das gemacht?** | How did you do that? |
| <u>**Warum**</u> **ist sie so spät aufgestanden?** | Why did she get up so late? |

> *Tip*
> Remember to use **woher** and **wohin** when direction is involved.
>
> | | |
> |---|---|
> | <u>**Woher**</u> **kommst du?** | Where do you come from? |
> | <u>**Wohin**</u> **fahren Sie?** | Where are you going? |

➤ When questions are formed with interrogative pronouns and adjectives, word order is normal if the interrogative pronoun or adjective is the subject of the verb at the beginning of the clause.

| | |
|---|---|
| <u>**Wer**</u> (*subject*) **hat** (*verb*) **das gemacht?** | Who did that? |

➤ If the interrogative pronoun or adjective is NOT the subject of the verb at the beginning of the clause, the subject and verb swap places.

| | |
|---|---|
| <u>**Wem**</u> **hast** (*verb*) **du** (*subject*) **es geschenkt?** | Who did you give it to? |

⇨ *For more information on* **Interrogative pronouns**, *see page 119.*

ⓘ Note that in indirect questions, that is questions following verbs of *asking* and *wondering*, the verb comes at the end of the question.

| | |
|---|---|
| <u>**Sie fragte, ob du mitkommen wolltest.**</u> | She asked if you wanted to come. |

> ### KEY POINTS
> ✔ There are three basic ways of asking direct questions in German: changing the word order; adding **nicht**, **nicht wahr**, **oder** or **doch**; and using a question word.
> ✔ When a question is put in the negative, **doch** can be used to answer it more positively than **ja**.
> ✔ The most common question words are the interrogative adverbs **wann**, **wo**, **wie** and **warum**, the interrogative pronouns **was**, **wer**, **wem** and **wessen**, and the interrogative adjective **welcher**.

**157** **Transform these statements into questions by changing the word order. The first one has been done for you.**

**a** Das Haus ist sauber. *Ist das Haus sauber?* .................................................................

**b** Das stimmt nicht. ....................................................................................................

**c** Er ist heute angekommen. ......................................................................................

**d** Ihr seid spät aufgestanden. ...................................................................................

**e** Sie hat großen Hunger. ...........................................................................................

**f** Zac Efron neuer Film ist gut. ..................................................................................

**g** Du bist zu spät gekommen. ....................................................................................

**h** Du glaubst mir. ........................................................................................................

**i** Wir schaffen das noch. ...........................................................................................

**j** Der Stuhl steht neben dem Tisch. ..........................................................................

**158** **Fill the gap with the appropriate question word. The first one has been done for you.**

**a** ........*Woher*........ seid ihr gekommen?

**b** ........................ fahren Sie?

**c** ........................ bist du gestern nicht gekommen?

**d** ........................ Pullover ist das?

**e** ........................ gibst du ihm die Schuld?

**f** ........................ ist der Mörder?

**g** ........................ gehört die Armbanduhr?

**h** ........................ hast du da gesagt?

**i** ........................ Buch sollen wir morgen mitbringen?

**j** ........................ können Sie das behaupten?

# Test yourself

**159 Form questions using the elements below.**

**a** du/nicht/warum/gekommen/bist ........................................................

**b** wir/sollen/machen/morgen/was ........................................................

**c** ins/wollen/gehen/Kino/wir ........................................................

**d** Mann/gesehen/du/welchen/hast ........................................................

**e** gemacht/du/das/hast/wie ........................................................

**f** stimmt/nicht/doch/das/wahr ........................................................

**g** du/Hausaufgaben/hast/gemacht/deine

........................................................

**h** du/keinen/warum/Appetit/hast ........................................................

**i** kommt/morgen/sie/besuchen/uns ........................................................

**j** Fernseher/das/neuer/unser/ist ........................................................

# Numbers

| | |
|---|---|
| 0 | **null** |
| 1 | **eins** |
| 2 | **zwei** |
| 3 | **drei** |
| 4 | **vier** |
| 5 | **fünf** |
| 6 | **sechs** |
| 7 | **sieben** |
| 8 | **acht** |
| 9 | **neun** |
| 10 | **zehn** |
| 11 | **elf** |
| 12 | **zwölf** |
| 13 | **dreizehn** |
| 14 | **vierzehn** |
| 15 | **fünfzehn** |
| 16 | **sechzehn** |
| 17 | **siebzehn** |
| 18 | **achtzehn** |
| 19 | **neunzehn** |
| 20 | **zwanzig** |
| 21 | **einundzwanzig** |
| 22 | **zweiundzwanzig** |
| 30 | **dreißig** |
| 40 | **vierzig** |
| 50 | **fünfzig** |
| 60 | **sechzig** |
| 70 | **siebzig** |
| 80 | **achtzig** |
| 90 | **neunzig** |
| a hundred | **hundert** |
| one hundred | **einhundert** |
| 101 | **hunderteins** |
| 102 | **hundertzwei** |
| 121 | **hunderteinundzwanzig** |
| 200 | **zweihundert** |
| a thousand | **tausend** |
| one thousand | **eintausend** |
| 1001 | **tausendeins** |
| 2000 | **zweitausend** |
| 100,000 | **hunderttausend** |
| 1,000,000 | **eine Million** |

ⓘ Note that **zwo** often replaces **zwei** in speech, to distinguish it clearly from **drei**.

---

*Tip*
In German, spaces or full stops are used with large numbers where English uses a comma. Decimals are written with a comma instead of a full stop.

| | |
|---|---|
| 1,000,000 | **1.000.000** *or* **1 000 000** |
| 7.5 *(seven point five)* | 7,5 **(sieben Komma fünf)** |

---

For further explanation of grammatical terms, please see pages viii-xii.

| | | |
|---|---|---|
| 1st | 1. | **der erste** |
| 2nd | 2. | **der zweite** |
| 3rd | 3. | **der dritte** |
| 4th | 4. | **der vierte** |
| 5th | 5. | **der fünfte** |
| 6th | 6. | **der sechste** |
| 7th | 7. | **der siebte** |
| 8th | 8. | **der achte** |
| 9th | 9. | **der neunte** |
| 10th | 10. | **der zehnte** |
| 11th | 11. | **der elfte** |
| 12th | 12. | **der zwölfte** |
| 13th | 13. | **der dreizehnte** |
| 14th | 14. | **der vierzehnte** |
| 15th | 15. | **der fünfzehnte** |
| 16th | 16. | **der sechzehnte** |
| 17th | 17. | **der siebzehnte** |
| 18th | 18. | **der achtzehnte** |
| 19th | 19. | **der neunzehnte** |
| 20th | 20. | **der zwanzigste** |
| 21st | 21. | **der einundzwanzigste** |
| 22nd | 22. | **der zweiundzwanzigste** |
| 30th | 30. | **der dreißigste** |
| 40th | 40. | **der vierzigste** |
| 50th | 50. | **der fünfzigste** |
| 60th | 60. | **der sechzigste** |
| 70th | 70. | **der siebzigste** |
| 80th | 80. | **der achtzigste** |
| 90th | 90. | **der neunzigste** |
| 100th | 100. | **der hundertste** |
| 101st | 101. | **der hunderterste** |
| 102nd | 102. | **der hundertzweite** |
| 121st | 121. | **der hunderteinundzwanzigste** |
| 200th | 200. | **der zweihundertste** |
| 1000th | 1000. | **der tausendste** |
| 1001st | 1001. | **der tausenderste** |
| 2000th | 2000. | **der zweitausendste** |
| 100,000th | 100 000. | **der hunderttausendste** |
| 1,000,000th | 1 000 000. | **der millionste** |

---

*Tip*

When these numbers are used as nouns, they are written with a capital letter.

**Sie ist die Zehnte.**　　　　She's the tenth.

---

| | | |
|---|---|---|
| half | ½ | **halb, die Hälfte** |
| third | ⅓ | **das Drittel** |
| two thirds | ⅔ | **zwei Drittel** |
| quarter | ¼ | **das Viertel** |
| three quarters | ¾ | **drei Viertel** |
| one and a half | 1½ | **anderthalb, eineinhalb** |
| two and a half | 2½ | **zweieinhalb** |

| BEISPIELE | EXAMPLES |
|---|---|
| **Sie hat zwei Autos.** | She has two cars. |
| **Er ist zwanzig Jahre alt.** | He is twenty years old. |
| **Sie wohnt im dritten Stock.** | She lives on the third floor. |
| **Er hat am 31. August Geburtstag.** | His birthday is on the 31st of August. |
| **Ich brauche anderthalb Stunden,** | I need an hour and a half or |
| **um nach Hause zu kommen.** | one and a half hours to get home. |
| **Sie aß zwei Drittel von dem Kuchen.** | She ate two thirds of the cake. |

*ⓘ* Note that ordinal numbers (**erste**, **zweite**, and so on) are declined according to the number, case and gender of the noun.

| | |
|---|---|
| **Ich habe gerade mein erstes** | I've just bought my first car. |
| **Auto gekauft.** | |
| **Sie kam zum zweiten Mal mit** | She arrived late for the second time. |
| **Verspätung an.** | |

## DIE ZEIT / THE TIME

| DIE ZEIT | THE TIME |
|---|---|
| **Wie spät ist es?** *or* | What time is it? |
| **Wie viel Uhr ist es?** | |
| **Es ist ...** | It's ... |
| **Mitternacht** *or* **null Uhr** *or* | midnight *or* twelve o'clock |
| **vierundzwanzig Uhr** *or* **zwölf Uhr** | |
| **zehn (Minuten) nach zwölf** *or* | ten (minutes) past twelve |
| **null Uhr zehn** | |
| **Viertel nach zwölf** *or* | quarter past twelve |
| **null Uhr fünfzehn** | |
| **halb eins** *or* **null Uhr dreißig** | half past twelve |
| **zwanzig (Minuten) vor eins** *or* | twenty (minutes) to one |
| **null Uhr vierzig** | |
| **Viertel vor eins** *or* **drei viertel eins** *or* | quarter to one |
| **null Uhr fünfundvierzig** | |
| **ein Uhr** | one o'clock |
| **zehn (Minuten) nach eins** *or* | ten (minutes) past one |
| **ein Uhr zehn** | |
| **Viertel nach eins** *or* **ein Uhr fünfzehn** | quarter past one |
| **halb zwei** *or* **ein Uhr dreißig** | half past one |
| **zwanzig (Minuten) vor zwei** *or* | twenty (minutes) to two |
| **ein Uhr vierzig** | |
| **Viertel vor zwei** *or* **drei viertel zwei** *or* | quarter to two |
| **ein Uhr fünfundvierzig** | |
| **zehn (Minuten) vor zwei** *or* | ten (minutes) to two |
| **ein Uhr fünfzig** | |
| **zwölf Uhr** | twelve o'clock (midday) |
| **halb eins** *or* **zwölf Uhr dreißig** | half past twelve |
| **ein Uhr** *or* **dreizehn Uhr** | one o'clock |
| **halb fünf** *or* **sechzehn Uhr dreißig** | half past four |
| **zehn Uhr** *or* **zweiundzwanzig Uhr** *or* | ten o'clock |
| **zwoundzwanzig Uhr** | |
| **Um wie viel Uhr?** | At what time? |

| | |
|---|---|
| **Wann?** | **When?** |
| **morgen um halb drei** | tomorrow at half past two |
| **um drei Uhr (nachmittags)** | at three (pm) |
| **kurz vor zehn Uhr** | just before ten o'clock |
| **gegen vier Uhr (nachmittags)** | around four o'clock (in the afternoon) |
| **erst um halb neun** | not until half past-eight |
| **ab neun Uhr** | from nine o'clock onwards |
| **morgen früh** | tomorrow morning |
| **morgen Abend** | tomorrow evening |

| | |
|---|---|
| DAS DATUM | THE DATE |
| WOCHENTAGE | DAYS OF THE WEEK |
| **Montag** | Monday |
| **Dienstag** | Tuesday |
| **Mittwoch** | Wednesday |
| **Donnerstag** | Thursday |
| **Freitag** | Friday |
| **Samstag** | Saturday |
| **Sonntag** | Sunday |

| | |
|---|---|
| Wann? | When? |
| **Montag** | (on) Monday |
| **montags** | (on) Mondays |
| **jeden Montag** | every Monday |
| **letzten Dienstag** | last Tuesday |
| **nächsten Freitag** | next Friday |
| **Samstag in einer Woche** or | a week on Saturday |
| **in acht Tagen** | |
| **Samstag in zwei Wochen** | two weeks on Saturday |

| | |
|---|---|
| MONATE | MONTHS |
| **Januar** | January |
| **Februar** | February |
| **März** | March |
| **April** | April |
| **Mai** | May |
| **Juni** | June |
| **Juli** | July |
| **August** | August |
| **September** | September |
| **Oktober** | October |
| **November** | November |
| **Dezember** | December |

| | |
|---|---|
| Wann? | When? |
| **im Dezember** | in December |
| **im April** | in April |
| **nächsten Januar** | next January |
| **letzten August** | last August |
| **Anfang/Ende September** | at the beginning/end of September |

| | |
|---|---|
| **Der Wievielte is heute?** | What's the date today? |
| **Welches Datum haben wir heute?** | |
| **Heute ist …** | It's … |
| der zwanzigste März | the twentieth of March |
| der Zwanzigste | the twentieth |
| | |
| **Heute haben wir …** | It's … |
| den zwanzigsten März | the twentieth of March |
| den Zwanzigsten | the twentieth |
| | |
| **Am Wievielten findet es statt?** | When does it take place? |
| am ersten April … | … on the first of April |
| am Ersten … | … on the first |
| (am) Montag, den ersten April *or* | on Monday, the first of April *or* |
| Montag, den 1. April | April 1ˢᵗ |

**JAHRESZEITEN**      **SEASONS**

| | |
|---|---|
| **im Winter** | in winter |
| **im Sommer** | in summer |
| **im Herbst** | in autumn |
| **im Frühling** | in spring |

**NÜTZLICHE VOKABELN**      **USEFUL VOCABULARY**

| | |
|---|---|
| **Wann?** | **When?** |
| heute | today |
| heute Morgen | this morning |
| heute Nachmittag | this afternoon |
| heute Abend | this evening |
| (im Jahr(e)) 2015 | in 2015 |

| | |
|---|---|
| **Wie oft?** | **How often?** |
| jeden Tag | every day |
| alle zwei Tage | every other day |
| einmal in der Woche/pro Woche | once a week |
| zweimal pro Woche | twice a week |
| einmal im Monat/pro Monat | once a month |

| | |
|---|---|
| **Wann ist das passiert?** | **When did it happen?** |
| am Morgen/Vormittag | in the morning |
| morgens/vormittags | in the mornings |
| am Abend | in the evening |
| abends | in the evenings |
| gestern | yesterday |
| gestern Abend | yesterday evening |
| vorgestern | the day before yesterday |
| vor einer Woche | a week ago |
| vor zwei Wochen | two weeks ago |
| letztes Jahr | last year |

---

For further explanation of grammatical terms, please see pages viii-xii.

| | |
|---|---|
| **Wann passiert das?** | **When is it going to happen?** |
| **morgen** | tomorrow |
| **morgen früh** | tomorrow morning |
| **übermorgen** | the day after tomorrow |
| **in zwei Tagen** | in two days |
| **in einer Woche** | in a week |
| **in vierzehn Tagen/zwei Wochen** | in two weeks |
| **nächsten Monat** | next month |
| **nächstes Jahr** | next year |

*i* Note that to talk about the year in which something happens, you don't use **in** in German.

| | |
|---|---|
| **Das findet 2016 statt.** | That's taking place in 2016. |
| **Sie wurde 1990 geboren.** | She was born in 1990. |
| **Ich ging 2001 für ein Jahr nach Deutschland.** | I went to Germany for a year in 2001. |

# Some Common Difficulties

## General problems

➤ You can't always translate German into English and English into German word for word. While occasionally it is possible to do this, often it is not. For example:

- Sentences which contain a verb and preposition in English might <u>NOT</u> contain a preposition in German.

  **jemanden/etwas ansehen**                to look <u>at</u> somebody/something
  **jemandem/etwas zuhören**                to listen <u>to</u> somebody/something

- However, many sentences which contain a verb and preposition in German <u>DO</u> contain a preposition in English.

  **sich interessiern <u>für</u>**                to be interested <u>in</u>
  **denken <u>über</u>**                to think <u>about</u>

➤ Remember that German prepositions are of two types:

- Some are only ever used with one case, such as **gegen** (accusative), **bei** (dative) and **außerhalb** (genitive). For all of these it is useful to learn the preposition and its case by heart.

- The second type are used either with the accusative or the dative, according to whether movement from one place to another is involved or not. The translation of the same preposition from the last group can change according to the case being used.

  **Sie schrieb einen Brief <u>an ihren</u>**                She wrote a letter <u>to</u> her brother.
  **Bruder.**
  **Wir treffen uns <u>am</u> Bahnhof.**                We're meeting <u>at</u> the station.

  ⇨ *For more information on **Prepositions**, see page 210.*

➤ A word which is plural in English may not be in German.

  **eine Brille**                glasses, spectacles
  **eine Schere**                scissors
  **eine Hose**                trousers

  🛈 Note that they are only used in the plural in German to mean more than one pair, for example, **zwei Hosen** = two pairs of trousers.

➤ In English, you use 's to show who or what something belongs to; in German you generally either use the genitive case or **von** + the dative case.

  **das Auto meiner Schwester**                my sister's car
  OR
  **das Auto von meiner Schwester**

  ⇨ *For more information on the **Genitive case**, see page 12.*

➤ German punctuation differs from English in several ways.

- Decimal places are always shown by a comma, NOT a full stop.
  **3,4 (drei Komma vier)** 3.4 (three point four)

- Large numbers are separated by means of a space or a full stop, NOT a comma.
  **20 000** 20,000 (twenty thousand)
  OR: **20.000 (zwanzigtausend)**

- Subordinate clauses are always separated from the rest of the sentence by a comma.
  **Er bleibt gesund, obwohl er zu viel** He stays healthy, even though he drinks
  **trinkt.** too much.

➭ For more information on **Subordinate clauses**, see page 244.

- When two main clauses are linked by **und** (meaning *and*) or **oder** (meaning *or*), no comma is required.
  **Wir gehen ins Kino oder wir bleiben** We'll go to the cinema or stay at home.
  **zu Hause.**

## Specific problems

### Nouns with capital letters

➤ Unlike English, <u>ALL</u> German nouns start with a capital letter, not just proper names.
  **der Tisch** the table
  **die Politikerin** the politician
  **die Königin** the Queen

  ⓘ Note that this also applies to verbs being used as nouns.

  **Sie hat ihr <u>Können</u> bewiesen.** She has proved her ability.

### Three forms of you

➤ In English we have only <u>one</u> way of saying *you*. In German, there are <u>three</u> words: **du**, **ihr** and **Sie**. You use:

- the familiar **du** if talking to one person <u>you know well</u>, such as a friend, someone younger than you or a relative
  **Kommst <u>du</u> mit ins Kino?** Are you coming to the cinema?

- the familiar **ihr** if talking to more than one person <u>you know well</u>.
  **Also, was wollt <u>ihr</u> heute Abend** So, what do you want to do tonight?
  **machen?**

- the formal or polite **Sie** if talking to one or more people <u>you do not know so well</u>, such as your teacher, your boss or a stranger
  **Was haben <u>Sie</u> gemacht?** What did you do?

## -ing

➤ Although English sometimes uses parts of the verb *to be* to form the present tense of other verbs (for example, *I am listening*, *she's talking*), German **NEVER** uses the verb **sein** in this way. Instead, it uses the normal present tense of the verb.

| | |
|---|---|
| **Ich spiele Tennis.** | I play tennis. |
| | OR |
| | I am playing tennis. |

## To be

➤ The verb *to be* is generally translated by **sein**.

| | |
|---|---|
| **Es ist spät.** | It's late. |
| **Das ist nicht möglich.** | That's not possible. |

➤ When you are talking about the physical position of something you can use **liegen**. You may also come across **sich befinden** in more formal contexts.

| | |
|---|---|
| **Wo liegt/befindet sich der Bahnhof?** | Where's the station? |

➤ In certain set phrases which describe how you are feeling or a state you are in, the verb **haben** is used.

| | |
|---|---|
| **Hunger haben** | to be hungry |
| **Durst haben** | to be thirsty |
| **Angst haben** | to be afraid |
| **unrecht haben** | to be wrong |
| **recht haben** | to be right |

⟦*i*⟧ Note that to say *I am hot* or *I am cold* etc, you use a personal pronoun in the dative case followed by **sein**.

| | |
|---|---|
| **Mir ist heiß.** | I am hot. |
| NOT | |
| **Ich bin heiß.** | |
| | |
| **Ihr is kalt.** | She is cold. |
| NOT | |
| **Sie ist kalt.** | |

➤ When talking about your health, use the following forms of the verb **gehen**.

| | |
|---|---|
| **Wie geht es dir/Ihnen?** | How are you? |
| **Es geht mir gut** | |
| OR | |
| **Mir geht es gut.** | I'm fine. |

## It

➤ There are three ways of saying *it* in German: **er**, **sie** and **es**. These correspond to the three different genders, masculine, feminine and neuter.

| | |
|---|---|
| **Wo ist der Wagen? – Er steht da drüben.** | Where is the car? – <u>It</u>'s over there. |
| **Ich finde meine Uhr nicht. Hast du sie gesehen?** | I can't find my watch. Have you seen <u>it</u>? |
| **Was hältst du von meinem Haus? – Es ist ganz schön.** | What do you think of my house? – it's really nice. |

⇨ *For more information on **Gender**, see page 2.*

## Date and time

➤ When talking about a particular day or date, use the preposition **an** + the dative case in the following constructions:

| | |
|---|---|
| **Ich fahre am Montag nach Hause.** | I'm going home <u>on Monday</u>. |
| **Sie wurde am Dienstag, den 1. April aus dem Krankenhaus entlassen.** | She was discharged from hospital <u>on Tuesday, the 1st of April</u>. |
| **Meine Nichte hat am 6. September Geburtstag.** | My niece's birthday is <u>on the 6th of September</u>. |

➤ When stating the time of a particular event, use the preposition **um** + the accusative case in the following construction.

| | |
|---|---|
| **Ich bin um 9 Uhr aufgestanden.** | I got up <u>at 9 o'clock</u>. |
| **Der Zug ist um 22.30 Uhr abgefahren**. | The train left <u>at 10.30 hours</u>. |

⇨ *For more information on **Prepositions**, see page 210.*

## There is, there are

➤ Both *there is* and *there are* are translated by **es gibt**.

| | |
|---|---|
| **Hier gibt es ein schönes Freibad.** | <u>There's</u> a lovely open-air pool here. |
| **In Stuttgart gibt es viele Parks.** | <u>There are</u> lots of parks in Stuttgart. |

## The imperfect of modal verbs

➤ Modal verbs never have an umlaut in the imperfect tense.

| | | |
|---|---|---|
| **können** | (*can, to be able to*) | **konnte** |
| **müssen** | (*must, to have to*) | **musste** |
| **mögen** | (*to like*) | **mochte** |
| **dürfen** | (*to be allowed to*) | **durfte** |
| **sollen** | (*to ought to*) | **sollte** |
| **wollen** | (*to want*) | **wollte** |

⇨ *For more information on **Modal verbs**, see page 184.*

## Er/sie/es parts of strong verbs in the imperfect

➤ You do <u>NOT</u> add a –t to the **er/sie/es** parts of the imperfect tense of strong verbs.

**er/sie/es ging**                          he/she/it went
NOT
**er/sie/es gingt**

**er/sie/es sang**                          he/she/it sang
NOT
**er/sie/es sangt**

⇨ *For more information on the **Imperfect tense**, see page 160.*

## Inseparable verbs in the perfect tense

➤ Inseparable verbs have no **ge-** added to beginning of the past participle in the perfect tense.

**Das habe ich schon <u>bezahlt</u>.**          I've already paid for that.
**Er hat sich endlich <u>entschlossen</u>.**     He's finally decided.

⇨ *For more information on **Inseparable verbs**, see page 149.*

## Can, to be able to

➤ If you want to say *could*, meaning *was able to*, you use **konnte**, the imperfect form of **können**, you do <u>NOT</u> use the conditional form **könnte**.

**Sie <u>konnte</u> nicht kommen.**             She couldn't make it.
**Er <u>konnte</u> das einfach nicht.**          He just wasn't able to do it.

# Alphabet

➤ The German alphabet is pronounced differently from the way it is pronounced in English. Use the list below to help you sound out the letters.

| | | | |
|---|---|---|---|
| **A, a** | [aː] | (ah) | |
| **Ä, ä** | [ɛː] | (eh) | |
| **B, b** | [beː] | (bay) | |
| **C, c** | [tseː] | (tsay) | |
| **D, d** | [deː] | (day) | |
| **E, e** | [eː] | (ay) | |
| **F, f** | [ɛf] | (ef) | |
| **G, g** | [geː] | (gay) | |
| **H, h** | [haː] | (hah) | |
| **I, i** | [iː] | (ee) | |
| **J, j** | [jɔt] | (yot) | |
| **K, k** | [kaː] | (kah) | |
| **L, l** | [ɛl] | (el) | |
| **M, m** | [ɛm] | (em) | |
| **N, n** | [ɛn] | (en) | |
| **O, o** | [oː] | (oh) | |
| **Ö, ö** | [ø] | (ö) | like ö in 'ökonomisch' |
| **P, p** | [peː] | (pay) | |
| **Q, q** | [kuː] | (koo) | |
| **R, r** | [ɛr] | (air) | |
| **S, s** | [ɛs] | (es) | |
| **T, t** | [teː] | (tay) | |
| **U, u** | [uː] | (oo) | |
| **Ü, ü** | [ʏː] | (ü) | like ü in 'über' |
| **V, v** | [fau] | (fow) | |
| **W, w** | [veː] | (vay) | |
| **X, x** | [iks] | (ix) | |
| **Y, y** | [ʏpsilɔn] | (üpsilon) | like 'ü' in 'über' |
| **Z, z** | [tsɛt] | (tset) | |

# solutions

# Solutions

**1**
a die Ministerin
b eine Königin
c eine Studentin
d die Schülerin
e eine Deutsche
f die Schauspielerin
g eine Angestellte
h eine Ärztin
i eine Löwin
j die Besitzerin

**2**
a der Sonnabend **ein Wochentag**
b das Mädchen **eine weibliche Person**
c die Stadt **ein größerer Ort**
d der Frühling **eine Jahreszeit**
e das Pfund **ein Gewicht**

**3**
a das
b die
c die
d der
e die
f das
g der
h die
i die
j der

**4**
a der Gummiball
b die Handtasche
c der Blumentopf
d der Wandschrank
e die Kaffeetasse
f das Kartenhaus
g die Papiertüte
h das Titelbild
i der Lastwagen
j die Telefonzelle

**5**
a das
b dem
c des
d dem
e Das
f der
g des
h die
i der
j die

**6**
a einen
b eines
c ein
d eine
e einem
f ein

**7**
a accusative/genitive/dative
b nominative/accusative
c genitive/dative
d genitive/dative
e nominative/accusative/genitive
f genitive/dative
g nominative/accusative/dative
h genitive/dative
i nominative/genitive/dative
j nominative/accusative

**8**
a Ich gab das Buch meiner Schwester.
b Die Schwester des Mannes heißt Martina.
c Er stand neben dem Auto.
d Wir gingen über die Brücke.
e Markus setzte sich auf das Sofa.
f Wir flogen hoch über dem Meer.
g Er konnte ohne einen Stock gehen.
h Ich möchte ein Bier.
i Las Vegas wurde in einer Wüste gebaut.
j Ihr Sohn hat einen deutschen Pass.

**9**
a Freunde
b Wespen
c Hotels
d Zahlen
e Geschenke
f Meter
g Monate
h Jahreszeiten
i Jahre
j Karten

**10**
a 1
b 2
c 1
d 2
e 2
f 1
g 1
h 1
i 2
j 1

g einen
h einem
i ein
j einen

**11**
a Mäuse
b Bücher
c Dächer
d Frösche
e Gläser
f Häfen
g Köche
h Küsse
i Träume
j Wörter

**12**
a das Haus und das Dach
b der Schüler und der Lehrer
c die Schülerin und die Lehrerin
d der Monat und das Jahr
e die Deutsche und der Engländer
f das Buch und die Seite
g der Computer und die Maus
h das Telefon und der Hörer
i die Oper und der Sänger
j das Fenster und der Rahmen

**13**
a das
b der
c die
d das
e das
f die
g die
h das
i die
j das

**14**
a der
b des
c der
d der
e der
f des
g des
h der
i der
j des

**15**
a die
b Der
c dem
d Die
e Die
f der
g der
h Das
i Der
j dem

**16**
a ins
b ums
c übers
d Hinterm
e im
f zum
g am
h zur
i am
j aufs

**17**
a Alle Eltern lieben ihre Kinder.
b Dieses Kind ist sehr klug.
c Einige Vasen sind rund.
d Ich habe beide Filme gesehen.
e Es gibt manche, die keine Briefe schreiben.
f Welches Buch liest du?
g Diese Frau kommt aus Irland.
h Das ganze Haus war leer.
i Er weiß alles.
j Dies ist meine Schwester.

**18**
a beide
b beiden
c Beides
d beider
e beiden
f beide
g beiden
h Beide
i beide
j beider

**19**
a einige **Mütter**
b mancher **Mann**
c welches **Haus**
d dieselbe **Frau**
e allen **Kindern**

**20**
a ein
b eine
c ein
d eine
e ein
f eine
g eine
h ein
i eine
j eine

**21**
a Das ist eine Tatsache.
b Ich habe ein Auto gekauft.
c Ich habe ein neues Auto.
d Er ist ein alter Mann.

e Sie ist eine Freundin von mir.
f Vor dem Haus ist ein Baum.
g Hast du ein Smartphone?
h Wir müssen einen Arzt fragen.
i Hast du eine Freundin?
j Sie ist ein sehr schönes Mädchen.

**22**
a kein
b keine
c keinen
d kein
e keine
f keiner
g keine
h Kein
i Keines
j keine

**23**
a Männer/Haus
b —
c Telefon/Blumen
d Mannes/Telefon
e Kerze/Decken
f Lampe
g Bücherei
h Hamster/Katze
i Kinder/Filme
j Brille/Auto/Papier

**24**
a Wie geht es deinem Bruder?
b Welche Farbe hat sein Auto?
c Sie wohnt bei ihren Eltern.
d Rita ist meine Verlobte.
e Wir sollten unsere Rechnung bezahlen.
f Das ist nicht unser Tisch.
g Eva und Karin, habt ihr eure Hausaufgaben gemacht?
h Ich möchte meine Kinder nicht verlieren.
i Wo ist dein grüner Anorak?
j Sie sagten ihm ihre Namen.

**25**
a meinem
b euer
c Ihren
d unserer
e deine
f seiner

g unserem
h Ihrer
i eure
j deinen

**26**
a deutscher
b deutsches
c deutsche
d deutsches
e deutscher
f deutsche
g deutsche
h deutsches
i deutscher
j deutsches

**27**
a ein altes Buch
b die neue Schule
c ein englischer Junge
d ein großer Baum
e eine lange Geschichte
f die weiße Katze
g ein schwerer Stein
h ein gutes Bild
i das kluge Mädchen
j eine schlechte Idee

**28**
a Ich sehe ein **schönes Auto.**
b Er ist ein **großer Mann.**
c Ich trinke ein **Glas Wein.**
d Ich kaufe eine **neue Gitarre.**
e Sie bestellt eine **würzige Suppe.**

**29**
a alter
b lange
c guter
d junge
e gesunde
f schönen
g reiche
h dickes
i armen
j guten

**30**
a Ich sah zwei kleine Jungen.
b Sie sind auf einer langen Reise.
c Ich habe guten Käse gekauft.
d Die junge Frau wohnt nebenan.
e Ich helfe meiner Nachbarin beim Einkaufen.
f Das ist ein schönes Bild!

# Solutions

**g** Wie fliegen in einem großen Flugzeug.

**h** Ich ging in ein großes Geschäft.

**i** Hast du den großen Mann gesehen?

**j** Wir trinken einen französischen Wein.

**31**
**a** schönes
**b** glückliche
**c** freie
**d** herrliche
**e** kalorienreiches
**f** bunte
**g** lange
**h** frische
**i** kaltes
**j** süßen

**32**
**a** hohe
**b** englischer
**c** schönes/guter
**d** großer/schöne
**e** reichen
**f** attraktive
**g** rechte/lange/kurze
**h** neues
**i** reichen/schönen/jungen
**j** hoch/alter

**33**
**a** ihm
**b** uns
**c** Ihnen
**d** mir
**e** dem Park
**f** ihnen
**g** euch
**h** mir
**i** dir
**j** diesem Mann

**34**
**a** eine verschlossene **Tür**
**b** ein lachender **Clown**
**c** eine verlorene **Geldbörse**
**d** eine gut ausgebildete **Studentin**
**e** ein gut gesalzenes **Essen**

**35**
**a** Bekannte
**b** Angestellter
**c** Gute
**d** Tote
**e** Erste
**f** Verletzten
**g** Dreijährige
**h** Verwandten
**i** Verlobter
**j** Unbekannten

**36**
**a** eine **schwierige** Prüfung
**b** ein **wichtiges** Fußballspiel
**c** ein **schwerer** Stein
**d** eine **spannende** Geschichte
**e** ein **entscheidender** Gedanke

**37**
**a** Engländer
**b** Schweizerin
**c** Stuttgarter
**d** Italiener
**e** Hamburgerin
**f** Amerikaner
**g** Deutsche
**h** Japaner
**i** Berlinerin
**j** Leipziger

**38**
**a** Frankfurter **Würstchen**
**b** Kölner **Dom**
**c** Schweizer **Käse**
**d** Münchner **Oktoberfest**
**e** Wiener **Schnitzel**

**39**
**a** Mein Bruder ist jünger als ich.
**b** Er ist mein jüngerer Bruder.
**c** Ich bin kleiner als meine Schwester.
**d** Ich bin genauso alt wie du.
**e** Meine Jacke ist teurer als deine.
**f** Es war leichter für mich.
**g** Ich bin stärker als du.
**h** Dein Haus ist größer als meins.
**i** Diese Frage ist viel leichter.
**j** Du bist nicht so alt wie ich.

**40**
**a** kleiner
**b** älter
**c** dunkler
**d** schärfer
**e** teurer
**f** glücklicher
**g** wärmer
**h** dünner
**i** härter
**j** kälter

**41**
**a** als
**b** wie
**c** wie
**d** als

**e** als
**f** als
**g** wie
**h** als
**i** als
**j** wie

**42**
**a** der höchste Berg
**b** das teuerste Auto
**c** die kleinste Stadt
**d** das größte Geschäft
**e** das süßeste Getränk
**f** der intelligenteste Junge
**g** die schlechteste Zeitung
**h** die interessanteste Frage
**i** der jüngste Schüler
**j** die neuesten Nachrichten

**43**
**a** das jüngste
**b** den meisten
**c** der höchsten
**d** die schlechteste
**e** der stärkste
**f** den kleinsten
**g** das größte
**h** der erfolgreichste
**i** die herrlichste
**j** die schnellste

**44**
**a** hoch **höher; höchste**
**b** gut **besser; beste**
**c** viel **mehr; meiste**
**d** nah **näher; nächste**
**e** gern **lieber; liebste**

**45**
**a** erstaunlicherweise
**b** beispielsweise
**c** schrittweise
**d** klugerweise
**e** glücklicherweise
**f** zeitweise
**g** literweise
**h** netterweise
**i** verständlicherweise
**j** möglicherweise

**46**
**a** Mein Zimmer ist unten.
**b** Wir haben das Spiel leider verloren.
**c** Bitte mache es sofort.
**d** Es ist fast drei Uhr.
**e** Ich gehe morgen einkaufen.
**f** Ich war auch da.
**g** Ich glaube wirklich nicht, dass das eine gute Idee ist.
**h** Habe ich dich richtig verstanden?

# Solutions

**i** Bitte mache schnell deine Hausaufgaben.
**j** Leider konnte ich nicht hören, was er sagte.

**47**
**a** hin
**b** her
**c** her
**d** hin
**e** hin
**f** her
**g** hin
**h** her
**i** hin
**j** hin

**48**
**a** lauter
**b** öfter
**c** schneller
**d** mehr
**e** weniger
**f** wärmer
**g** besser
**h** länger
**i** höher
**j** dunkler

**49**
**a** Sie hat teuer eingekauft. **Sie hat viel bezahlen müssen.**
**b** Sie ist sehr fit. **Sie treibt viel Sport.**
**c** Sie isst zu viel. **Sie liebt gutes Essen.**
**d** Sie geht abends in die Kneipe. **Sie trinkt gerne Bier.**
**e** Sie ist arm. **Sie hat wenig Geld.**

**50**
**a** am fleißigsten
**b** am liebsten
**c** am schnellsten
**d** am seltensten
**e** am lautesten
**f** am besten
**g** am ehesten
**h** am meisten
**i** am schlechtesten
**j** am wenigsten

**51**
**a** Ich habe es billig gekauft.
**b** Sollen wir heute ins Kino gehen?
**c** Du hast dich gestern gut benommen.
**d** Sie verdient viel Geld.
**e** Es hat ziemlich lange gedauert.

**f** Es ist nicht genug Milch im Kühlschrank.
**g** Sie kauft zu viele Schuhe.
**h** In Schottland regnet es viel.
**i** Hier gibt es nicht viel zu sehen.
**j** Sie haben gestern Fußball gespielt.

**52**
**a** Wir haben gestern billig eingekauft.
**b** Wir wollen heute Fußball spielen.
**c** Wir haben alle gut gegessen.
**d** Warum bist du dorthin gegangen?
**e** Ich möchte gern nach Hause gehen.
**f** Wer von euch verdient am meisten?
**g** Er kam langsam auf mich zu.
**h** Musst du dich so schlecht benehmen?
**i** Sie schwimmt schneller als ihre Schwester.
**j** Er kommt meistens zu spät.

**53**
**a** am höchsten/leider
**b** langsamer/dorthin
**c** gestern/schnell
**d** bald
**e** gestern
**f** schneller/äußerst
**g** schrittweise
**h** heute/fast
**i** spätestens
**j** am höchsten

**54**
**a** Das ist aber billig!
**b** Komm doch mal her!
**c** Das ist es ja gerade.
**d** Ich habe dich schon verstanden.
**e** Das ist wirklich ärgerlich.
**f** Was war denn da los?
**g** Das kann schon gut sein.
**h** Ich weiß es ja auch nicht.
**i** Hören Sie mir doch mal zu!
**j** Lass ihn doch reden!

**55**
**a** Du hast ihn nicht gesehen? – Doch! **Yes, I did.**
**b** Du bist mir nicht böse? – Doch! **Yes, I am.**

**c** Du magst kein Kaugummi? – Doch! **Yes, I do.**
**d** Du hast nicht abgenommen? – Doch! **Yes, I have.**
**e** Du warst nicht in der Schule? – Doch! **Yes, I was.**

**56**
**a** Er spricht Deutsch.
**b** Sie isst viel.
**c** Hat er Schwestern?
**d** Wir haben eine Katze.
**e** Ich kann nicht schwimmen.
**f** Sie hat schwarze Haare.
**g** Wie alt ist sie?
**h** Ich wohne in Birmingham.
**i** Wie sagt man das?
**j** Sie sind verheiratet.

**57**
**a** der Zug **er**
**b** das Buch **es**
**c** meine Klassenkameraden **sie**
**d** mein Vater und ich **wir**
**e** Max und du **ihr**

**58**
**a** es
**b** Er
**c** sie
**d** es
**e** sie
**f** sie
**g** Er
**h** sie
**i** Sie
**j** sie

**59**
**a** den Direktor
**b** das Publikum
**c** meine Katze/mein Buch
**d** die Lehrer/den Lehrer
**e** meine Katze
**f** euch und sie
**g** meine Mutter/meinen Bruder
**h** alle Menschen/die Leute
**i** meinen Hund
**j** das Publikum/meine Eltern

**60**
**a** sie
**b** sie
**c** ihn
**d** es
**e** ihn
**f** sie

# Solutions

**g** sie
**h** uns
**i** sie
**j** es

**61**
**a** Kannst du sie sehen?
**b** Magst du diesen Lehrer? – Nein, ich hasse ihn.
**c** Ich mag diese CD. – Warum kaufst du sie nicht?
**d** Ich konnte ihn sehen, aber ich konnte ihn nicht hören.
**e** Kennst du dieses Buch? – Ja, ich habe es gelesen.
**f** Wo ist Paul? – Ich habe ihn nicht gesehen.
**g** Möchtest du diesen Apfel? – Nein, ich möchte ihn nicht.
**h** Hast du Petra und Ruth gesehen? – Nein, ich habe sie nicht gesehen.
**i** Warum besuchst du uns nicht?
**j** Ich habe sie im Park getroffen.

**62**
**a** Gib ihm eine Banane.
**b** Gib uns die Schlüssel.
**c** Bring mir einen Stuhl.
**d** Sag mir die Wahrheit.
**e** Gib ihr das Geschenk.
**f** Sie hat mir nicht geantwortet.
**g** Er hat es uns nicht gegeben.
**h** Sie gab mir eine Flasche Wein.
**i** Ich schicke ihr jede Woche Geld.
**j** Kannst du mir sagen, warum du das gemacht hast?

**63**
**a** Martina schrieb ihrer Schwester einen Brief. **Sie schrieb ihr einen Brief.**
**b** Sophie schrieb Peter und mir eine Karte. **Sie schrieb uns eine Karte.**
**c** Marius schickte seiner Mutter ein Paket. **Er schickte ihr ein Paket.**
**d** Gisela schrieb ihrem Chef einen Brief. **Sie schrieb ihm einen Brief.**

**e** Peter schickte Frank und Lina ein Paket. **Er schickte ihnen ein Paket.**

**64**
**a** ihnen
**b** ihm
**c** mir
**d** mir
**e** ihr
**f** ihm
**g** ihnen
**h** Ihnen
**i** ihnen
**j** dir

**65**
**a** Es ist für sie.
**b** Sie kamen ohne ihn.
**c** Ich ging mit ihm.
**d** Das ist zwischen dir und mir.
**e** Alle außer mir haben es gesehen.
**f** Das Flugzeug fliegt über uns.
**g** Hast du von ihm gehört?
**h** Ich habe es für sie gemacht.
**i** Die Vase ist auf dem Tisch.
**j** Wir fliegen nach Köln.

**66**
**a** daran
**b** darüber
**c** darunter
**d** daneben
**e** daraus
**f** dazwischen
**g** darauf
**h** darüber
**i** darin
**j** danach

**67**
**a** Gib es ihr nicht. **Don't give it to her.**
**b** Zeige sie mir. **Show them to me.**
**c** Sag ihm das nicht. **Don't tell him that.**
**d** Kauf es für sie. **Buy it for her.**
**e** Sag mir warum. **Tell me why.**

**68**
**a** Dieses Auto ist meins.
**b** Ist dieses Fahrrad deins?
**c** Diese Bleistifte sind ihre.
**d** Sind diese Bücher deine oder meine?

**e** Paul und Leo, diese Stühle sind eure.
**f** Dieses Haus ist unsres.
**g** Diese Kleider sind ihre.
**h** Dieses Zimmer ist seins.
**i** Das Haus ist eures.
**j** Diese zwei Zeitungen sind meine.

**69**
**a** seine
**b** ihre
**c** meins
**d** unserer
**e** ihre
**f** seins
**g** meine
**h** ihre
**i** meine
**j** eure

**70**
**a** unsere
**b** deins
**c** deiner
**d** seiner
**e** eurer
**f** seins
**g** Ihrer
**h** ihres
**i** eure
**j** meiner

**71**
**a** jemandem
**b** niemanden
**c** niemandem
**d** jemand
**e** niemanden
**f** niemand
**g** jemanden
**h** jemandem
**i** niemand
**j** jemanden

**72**
**a** Das Telefon ist kaputt. **Keiner kann anrufen.**
**b** Ich lebe allein. **Niemand wohnt bei mir.**
**c** Er ist arm. **Er hat kein Geld.**
**d** Ich habe die Hausaufgaben allein gemacht. **Keiner hat mir geholfen.**
**e** Er weiß Bescheid. **Er hat jemanden gefragt.**

**73**
**a** jemanden/einen
**b** niemanden
**c** keiner/jemandem
**d** keiner/einer
**e** keiner

**f** keins/keinen
**g** keinem/keiner
**h** einem
**i** einem
**j** jemandem/einer

**74**
**a** mir
**b** sich
**c** uns
**d** mich
**e** mich
**f** euch
**g** sich
**h** dich
**i** sich
**j** dich

**75**
**a** Wir redeten miteinander.
**b** Sie sind sich am Montag begegnet.
**c** Wir haben uns sehr darüber gefreut.
**d** Sie kannten sich schon.
**e** Ich habe mich gebadet.
**f** Ich frage mich, ob es eine gute Idee ist.
**g** Erinnerst du dich an meinen Bruder?
**h** Wir müssen uns beeilen.
**i** Soll ich mir eine Tasse Tee holen?
**j** Interessierst du dich für Autos?

**76**
**a** Ich bemühe **mich**
**b** Er rasiert **sich**
**c** Du setzt **dich**
**d** Ich erlaube es **mir**
**e** Du wünschst **dir**

**77**
**a** die Frau, die ich gestern gesehen habe
**b** der Mann, dessen Auto rot ist
**c** die Familie, die hier wohnt
**d** das Auto, das ich kaufen will
**e** meine Brüder, von denen einer Arzt ist
**f** der Mann, den ich liebe
**g** der Freund, dem ich schreibe
**h** die Kinder, die auf der Straße spielen
**i** das Kleid, das am meisten kostet
**j** die Freunde, die wir besucht haben

**78**
**a** der Stuhl **auf dem ich sitze**
**b** das Kind **von dem ich sprach**
**c** der Freund **auf den ich vertraue**
**d** die Probleme **über die ich nachdenke**
**e** die Krankheit **an der sie leidet**

**79**
**a** dem
**b** deren
**c** die
**d** dessen
**e** der
**f** das
**g** denen
**h** den
**i** denen
**j** dessen

**80**
**a** alles, was er gesagt hat
**b** nichts, was sie gesehen hat
**c** das, was sie jetzt macht
**d** alles, was er gelesen hat
**e** vieles, was er denkt
**f** wenig, was er macht
**g** das, was wirklich wichtig ist
**h** vieles, was du gesagt hast
**i** alles, was wir gekauft haben
**j** nichts, das wir gesagt haben

**81**
**a** Wem
**b** wen
**c** wer
**d** wem
**e** wessen
**f** Wen
**g** was
**h** Wer
**i** wem
**j** was

**82**
**a** Wessen Fahrrad ist das?
**b** Wen hast du eingeladen?
**c** Was ist das?
**d** Wer hat dir das gesagt?
**e** Mit wem bist du gekommen?
**f** Wem gehört dieses Buch?
**g** Was kosten diese Äpfel?
**h** Von wem hast du dieses Auto gekauft?

**i** Wie viele möchten Sie?
**j** Wessen Haus hast du besucht?

**83**
**a** Sie spielen Fußball.
**b** Er arbeitet in einer Fabrik.
**c** Wir machen unsere Hausaufgaben.
**d** Sie liebt dich.
**e** Wir lernen viel.
**f** Es regnet draußen.
**g** Wir malen ein Bild.
**h** Ich danke dir für deine Hilfe.
**i** Sie sucht ihre Schlüssel.
**j** Er sammelt Briefmarken.

**84**
**a** er **zeichnet**
**b** Sie **zeichnen**
**c** ich **zeichne**
**d** ihr **zeichnet**
**e** du **zeichnest**

**85**
**a** pflücken
**b** handelt
**c** hängen
**d** repariert
**e** jobbt
**f** Hört
**g** rollt
**h** bügelt
**i** benutzen
**j** räumst

**86**
**a** gehen
**b** helft
**c** fahre
**d** bitte
**e** riecht
**f** singt
**g** waschen
**h** rate
**i** zwingt
**j** komme

**87**
**a** Mein Bruder hilft ihr bei den Hausaufgaben.
**b** Mein Vater fährt mich zur Schule.
**c** Wir wachsen sehr schnell.
**d** Du reitest auf einem Pferd.
**e** Siehst du den Vogel auf dem Baum?
**f** Zum Frühstück esse ich immer Brötchen.
**g** Sie bieten uns 2000 Euros für das Auto.

# Solutions

**h** Am Sonntag fahren wir in Urlaub.
**i** Hilfst du mir?
**j** Geben Sie uns etwas mehr Zeit?

**88**
**a** fährst
**b** sieht
**c** darf
**d** schläft
**e** läuft
**f** hält
**g** sieht
**h** muss
**i** trägt
**j** Triffst

**89**
**a** brennt
**b** bringt
**c** wende
**d** rennt
**e** nenne
**f** senden
**g** brennt
**h** Kennen
**i** weiß
**j** denkst

**90**
**a** Wir rufen die Feuerwehr. **Das Haus brennt.**
**b** Ich muss mich beeilen. **Ich renne zur Schule.**
**c** Ich habe ihn noch nie gesehen. **Ich kenne ihn nicht.**
**d** Er fragt mich, wer ich bin. **Ich nenne ihm meinen Namen.**
**e** Ich bin meiner Freundin dankbar. **Ich bringe ihr ein Geschenk.**

**91**
**a** mich
**b** mir
**c** mir
**d** mich
**e** mir
**f** mich
**g** mich
**h** mich
**i** mir
**j** mir

**92**
**a** Du musst dich beeilen.
**b** Ich freue mich auf die Sommerferien.
**c** Wir sehen uns sein neues Auto an.

**d** Mein Vater rasiert sich immer vor dem Frühstück.
**e** Ich irre mich nie.
**f** Was wünschtst du dir zum Geburtstag?
**g** Wir nähern uns dem Schloss.
**h** Ich erlaube mir ein Eis.
**i** Ich traue mich nicht, von der Mauer zu springen.
**j** Wir sehen uns im Dorf um.

**93**
**a** Er wäscht sich die Hände.
**b** Ich leiste mir einen neuen Computer.
**c** Was bildet er sich ein?
**d** Ich erinnere mich an gar nichts.
**e** Du regst dich immer so auf.
**f** Ich freue mich auf meinen Geburtstag.
**g** Ich wünsche mir ein neues Fahrrad.
**h** Wir setzen uns auf die Bank.
**i** Wir erlauben uns eine kleine Pause.
**j** Ich nähere mich der Stadt.

**94**
**a** Gib mir das!
**b** Gib sie mir!
**c** Sag das nicht!
**d** Geh weg!
**e** Hol mir einen Kaffee!
**f** Hör mir zu!
**g** Sprich mit mir!
**h** Öffne die Tür!
**i** Lass mich in Ruhe!
**j** Lies das Buch!

**95**
**a** Geben Sie
**b** Laufen Sie
**c** Seien Sie
**d** Lassen Sie
**e** Machen Sie
**f** Nehmen Sie sich
**g** Sagen Sie
**h** Hören Sie
**i** Waschen Sie sich
**j** Kommen Sie

**96**
**a** dem Bild
**b** den Hund
**c** das Buch
**d** etwas Geduld

**e** die Wand
**f** günstig/langsam
**g** den Ball/das Kind
**h** in den Baum
**i** etwas Geduld/ein Buch
**j** sie fest

**97**
**a** Gehen wir nach Hause! **Es ist schon spät.**
**b** Hab ein bisschen Geduld! **Sie kommt bestimmt gleich.**
**c** Sei still! **Du redest zu viel.**
**d** Mach ihm einen Tee! **Er hat Durst.**
**e** Warte auf uns! **Du gehst zu schnell.**

**98**
**a** passen
**b** geben
**c** riechen
**d** sprechen
**e** kehren/lernen
**f** lernen/geben
**g** kehren
**h** sprechen
**i** lesen
**j** lachen

**99**
**a** Der Bus kommt heute spät an.
**b** Wann kehrt er zu uns zurück?
**c** Diese Farben passen nicht zusammen.
**d** Ich legf das Buch hier hin.
**e** Er steht morgens immer sehr früh auf.
**f** Warum gibst du ihr immer nach?
**g** Hältst du mir diesen Platz frei?
**h** Ich gehe heute Abend mit Brigitte aus.
**i** Mit 1000 Euro kommen wir nicht aus.
**j** Schau mir bitte nicht zu.

**100**
**a** Wirs sind gestern zu Hause geblieben.
**b** Ich habe meine Schlüssel verloren.
**c** Sabine hat zwei Paar Schuhe gekauft.
**d** Er hat mir seine Telefonnummer gegeben.

# Solutions

**e** Ich habe sie heute schon zweimal getroffen.

**f** Ich habe letzte Nacht schlecht geschlafen.

**g** Sie sind gestern ins Theater gegangen.

**h** Ich habe den Film schon gesehen.

**i** Wer hat dir das gesagt?

**j** Habt ihr eure Hausaufgaben gemacht?

**101 a** gefahren
**b** gelungen
**c** mitgebracht
**d** verloren
**e** gerufen
**f** gestorben
**g** geschlafen
**h** ausgestiegen
**i** gekauft
**j** gewesen

**102 a** Hast
**b** bin
**c** ist
**d** haben
**e** Hast
**f** bin
**g** ist
**h** Sind
**i** haben
**j** hat

**103 a** Wir gingen die Straße entlang.
**b** Sie wussten nicht, wer er war.
**c** Sie war hübscher als ihre Schwester.
**d** Fünf Freunde von uns kamen zum Mittagessen.
**e** Wir sahen uns sehr oft.
**f** Sie sagten, sie wollten ins Kino gehen.
**g** Als ich ein Kind war, hatten wir ein Haus auf dem Land.
**h** Sie verlor immer ihre Schlüssel.
**i** Die Kinder liebten ihre Mutter.
**j** Als es zu regnen begann, gingen wir in ein Café.

**104 a** riefen
**b** wussten

**c** sah
**d** verkauften
**e** dachte
**f** brauchten
**g** verbrachten
**h** fing
**i** war
**j** kannte

**105 a** Sie war verheiratet. **Ihr Mann hieß Günter.**
**b** Sie lebte auf dem Land. **Ihre Eltern hatten einen Bauernhof.**
**c** Sie war Kellnerin. **Sie arbeitete in einem Hotel.**
**d** Sie war Vegetarierin. **Sie aß kein Fleisch.**
**e** Sie liebte teure Kleider. **Sie ging oft in die Stadt einkaufen.**

**106 a** Ich stehe morgen früh auf.
**b** Ich komme um 10 Uhr an.
**c** Du musst vorsichtig sein.
**d** Andrea kann dir helfen.
**e** Im August fahren wir nach Italien.
**f** Morgen nach dem Frühstück gehe ich schwimmen.
**g** Ich fahre mit dem Zug nach Hause.
**h** Sie ruft dich am Wochenende an.
**i** Bist du nächste Woche in Berlin?
**j** Morgen gehen wir ins Museum.

**107 a** wird
**b** werde
**c** wirst
**d** wird
**e** werden
**f** wirst
**g** wird
**h** werdet
**i** wird
**j** werden

**108 a** Morgen gewinnen wir im Lotto. **Wir werden reich sein.**
**b** Ich habe mich verschlafen. **Ich werde**

zu spät zur Schule kommen.
**c** Wir lieben uns sehr. **Wir werden heiraten.**
**d** Wir haben kein Geld, um zu verreisen. **Wir werden in den Ferien zu Hause bleiben.**
**e** Ich will studieren. **Ich werde zur Universität gehen.**

**109 a** würde
**b** Würdet
**c** würden
**d** würde
**e** würden
**f** würde
**g** Würdest
**h** würde
**i** würde
**j** Würden

**110 a** Wie viel würdest du für das Auto bezahlen?
**b** Würdest du bitte aufhören zu reden?
**c** Was würde sein Vater sagen?
**d** Den Kindern würde es hier gefallen.
**e** Ich würde es kaufen, aber ich habe kein Geld.
**f** Würdest du so etwas jemals machen?
**g** Wenn ich eine Kamera hätte, würde ich Fotos machen.
**h** Was würdest du tun?
**i** Ich habe ihm gesagt, dass ich es tun würde.
**j** Ich würde ihm helfen, wenn ich Zeit hätte.

**111 a** gegangen
**b** gegessen
**c** gefragt
**d** gefahren
**e** nachgedacht
**f** gegeben
**g** gerechnet
**h** geflogen
**i** gemacht
**j** gebracht

**112 a** Er hatte den Film immer noch nicht gesehen.
**b** Sie waren noch nie in Irland gewesen.

# Solutions

**c** Wir hatten uns bereits entschlossen, das Haus zu verkaufen.
**d** Sie hatte noch nie dort gearbeitet.
**e** Er hatte viel getrunken.
**f** Sie hatte ihn schon danach gefragt.
**g** Ich hatte es sofort bemerkt.
**h** Er hatte sie oft im Supermarkt gesehen.
**i** Das hatte ich nicht erwartet.
**j** Ich hatte ihn schon lange nicht mehr gesehen.

**113 a** Er sagte, er spreche Französisch.
**b** Sie sagte, sie komme morgen.
**c** Sie sagte, er habe keine Manieren.
**d** Er erklärte, er sei eigentlich aus Kanada.
**e** Er sagte, er haben viel Geld.
**f** Sie sagten, sie seien weit gereist.
**g** Er meinte, er trage keine Schuld daran.
**h** Sie sagte, sie wisse es nicht.
**i** Er erklärte, er werde das nicht tun.
**j** Sie meinte, sie sei allwissend.

**114 a** du **gebest**
**b** er **gäbe**
**c** Sie **gäben**
**d** wir **geben**
**e** ihr **gebet**

**115 a** Ich sah ihn die Straße entlanggehen.
**b** Ich hörte sie reden.
**c** Siehst du sie kommen?
**d** Bitte nicht rauchen!
**e** Gehen wir einkaufen!
**f** Ich habe keine Zeit, meine Hausaufgaben zu machen.
**g** Bitte bleiben Sie sitzen!
**h** Er kann gut laufen.
**i** Wirst du ihn morgen besuchen?
**j** Sein Englisch ist leicht zu verstehen.

**116 a** zu
**b** -
**c** -
**d** zu
**e** -
**f** -
**g** -
**h** zu
**i** -
**j** zu

**117 a** Ich darf keinen Alkohol trinken.
**b** Sie soll sehr schön sein.
**c** Sie will einmal Ärztin werden.
**d** Möchtest du etwas essen?
**e** Du brauchst ihn nicht fragen.
**f** Wir können das Spiel nicht gewinnen.
**g** Ich muss um 6 Uhr zu Hause sein.
**h** Ich darf mit in die Ausstellung kommen.
**i** Das kann ich mir vorstellen.
**j** Da kann man nur staunen.

**118 a** Er wollte gerade gehen.
**b** Zuerst solltest du das Licht anmachen.
**c** Möchtest du eine Tasse Tee?
**d** Magst du Pfefferminztee?
**e** Musst du immer zu spät kommen?
**f** Er will immer recht haben.
**g** Er soll ein guter Schauspieler sein.
**h** Könnten wir sie morgen besuchen?
**i** Darfst du abends ausgehen?
**j** Es muss wahr sein.

**119 a** soll
**b** Kannst/Sollst
**c** kann/will
**d** sollst/musst
**e** Kannst/Musst
**f** will
**g** Sollst
**h** Will/Mag
**i** mag/muss
**j** Soll/Will

**120 a** Es schneit. **Wir können einen Schneemann bauen.**
**b** Es regnet. **Wir werden nass.**
**c** Es donnert. **Gleich kommt der Blitz.**
**d** Es ist warm. **Zieh deinen Mantel aus.**
**e** Es friert. **Es ist 3 Grad unter null.**

**121 a** Es ist mir egal, ob du reich oder arm bist.
**b** Es macht mir nichts aus, wenn wir um 6 Uhr essen.
**c** Es tur mir leid, dass Sie warten mussten.
**d** Es stimmt, dass ich erst 16 bin.
**e** Es wird nicht nötig sein, sie morgen zu besuchen.
**f** Es hat keinen Zweck, das weiter zu diskutieren.
**g** Es hängt davon ab, ob er Zeit hat oder nicht.
**h** Es ist mir egal, ob wir zwei Stunden zu spät ankommen.
**i** Es freut mich, dich zu sehen.
**j** Es ist schade, dass das Wetter so schlecht ist.

**122 a** Sie haben mich beleidigt. **Es tut mir leid.**
**b** Wir haben das Spiel verloren. **Das ist schade.**
**c** Ich will mit Regine ins Kino gehen. **Das geht nicht.**
**d** Du gehst zur Tür? **Es hat geklingelt.**
**e** Er ist dir immer noch böse. **Das ist mir egal.**

**123 a** sind
**b** gibt
**c** ist
**d** gibt
**e** gibt
**f** gibt
**g** ist
**h** sind
**i** ist
**j** Gibt

# Solutions

**124**
a Es ist kein Bier da. **Dann müssen wir eben Wasser trinken.**
b Es sind viele Dosen im Automaten. **Ich habe kein Kleingeld.**
c Es ist jemand an der Tür. **Ich habe nichts gehört.**
d Es gibt kein Wasser in der Wüste. **Vielleicht müssen wir verdursten.**
e Es gibt nichts zu trinken. **Ich habe aber Durst.**

**125**
a Er versteht es, **die Leute zu betrügen.**
b Ich habe es satt, **jeden Tag zur Schule zu gehen.**
c Sie wagt es nicht, **mir zu widersprechen.**
d Ich bereue es, **dass ich ihn geheiratet habe.**
e Sie erträgt es nicht, **dass er sie ständig beleidigt.**

**126**
a Sie hatte es nicht leicht, die Familie zusammenzuhalten.
b Ich habe es nicht nötig, mir deine Argumente anzuhören.
c Er versteht es, Leute zu überreden.
d Er lehnt es ab, mit uns zu Mittag zu essen.
e Ich ertrage es nicht, dass er mich verlässt.
f Man hört es ihm an, dass er aus Bayern ist.
g Seine Mutter verbietet es ihm, seine Freundin zu besuchen.
h Ich bereue es nicht, dass ich ihnen das Geld gegeben habe.
i Sie wagte es nicht, ihm die Wahrheit zu sagen.
j Er versteht es, Computer zu programmieren.

**127**
a Kannst du dich um meine Katze kümmern, wenn ich im Urlaub bin?
b Er interessiert sich für ihre CD-Sammlung.
c Sie unterhielten sich über Politik.
d Die Arbeiter kämpfen um ihre Rechte.
e Ich weiß nicht, ob ich mich auf dich verlassen kann.
f Ich denke immer an meine Schwester.
g Ich bat sie um etwas mehr Zeit.
h Ich kann mich nicht daran gewöhnen, in einer Großstadt zu leben.
i Ich warte immer noch auf eine Antwort.
j Ich freue mich auf meinen Geburtstag.

**128**
a sehne
b versteht
c gestorben
d träume
e schmeckt
f verabschiedet
g besteht
h hängt
i beschäftigen
j leidet

**129**
a Ich kümmere mich **um sie**
b Ich sehne mich **nach ihr**
c Ich interessiere mich **für sie**
d Ich träume **von ihr**
e Ich ärgere mich **über sie**

**130**
a Sie zeigte mir ihre Hausaufgaben.
b Er brachte mir ein Bier.
c Leider konnte ich es ihm nicht beweisen.
d Sie kaufte mir das Handy zum Geburtstag.
e Sie erzählte mir alles über ihren Mann.
f Sandra schrieb ihm eine Karte aus dem Urlaub.
g Sie gab ihm einen Scheck.
h Sie bot mir ein Glas Apfelsaft an.
i Er schenkte mir ein Fahrrad zu Weihnachten.
j Die Wanderer zeigten uns den Weg.

**131**
a Wem gehört dieser Computer?
b Traust du ihm wirklich?
c Hat dir das Mittagessen geschmeckt?
d Ich kann dir nicht helfen.
e Er ist mir in einer Kneipe begegnet.
f Zu viel Sonne schadet der Haut.
g Dieses Geld gehört mir nicht.
h Ich möchte dir für deine Hilfe danken.
i Schmeckt dir die Suppe?
j Ich bin beim Einkaufen meinem Kollegen begegnet.

**132**
a gesehen
b geschrieben
c verhaftet
d uraufgeführt
e ausgelost
f geehrt
g ernannt
h verurteilt
i nachgewiesen
j umgebracht

**133**
a Die Veranstaltung wurde von Demonstranten gestört.
b Sein Kredit wurde von der Bank gekündigt.
c Ihm wurde mitgeteilt, dass er gehen musste.
d Der Koffer wurde von den Zöllnern sehr genau untersucht.
e Das Stück wurde von der Theaterleitung abgesetzt.
f Die Eröffnungszeremonie wurde von allen Sendern ausgestrahlt.
g Ihm wurden von der Behörde finanzielle Unregelmäßigkeiten vorgeworfen.
h Die Regierung wurde von der Opposition zum Rücktritt gezwungen.
i Die Besucherzahl wurde auf 20.000 geschätzt.
j Gestern wurde ihr vom Vermieter die Wohnung gekündigt.

# Solutions

**134** 
a Der Krieg wurde 1918 beendet.
b Die Frage wurde einvernehmlich geklärt.
c Den Schülern wurde ein Lob erteilt.
d Das Buch wurde allgemein gelobt.
e Das Gesetz wurde vom Parlament einstimmig verabschiedet.
f Auf der Party wurde viel getanzt.
g Das Geld wurde gleichmäßig verteilt.
h Der Vorschlag wurde zustimmend aufgenommen.
i Drei Minister wurden vom Kanzler entlassen.
j Der Beginn der Veranstaltung wurde auf drei Uhr festgesetzt.

**135**
a seit
b gegenüber
c nach
d aus
e Bei
f zu
g von
h mit
i außer
j von

**136**
a Ich wohne seit sechs Monaten hier.
b Ich fahre manchmal mit dem Zug nach Berlin.
c Sie wohnt dir gegenüber.
d Sollen wir uns bei Peter treffen?
e Sie trinkt aus einem Glas.
f Gisela kommt aus Hamburg.
g Weißt du etwas von seinen Freunden?
h Susanne ist eine Freundin von Erika.
i Du solltest ihm gegenüber höflich sein.
j Nach drei Stunden kam er zurück.

**137**
a zum
b beim

c zu
d bei
e zum
f Bei
g zur
h bei
i beim
j zu

**138**
a Der Film fängt gegen acht Uhr an.
b Er ging ohne sie zur Party.
c Wir baten um ein Glas Wasser.
d Für dich ist es nur ein Spiel.
e Deine Gefühle sind für mich sehr wichtig.
f Er ging durch die Tür.
g Diese Flasche ist um 50 Cent teurer.
h Was für ein Auto fährt dein Vater?
i Ich bat meinen Chef um etwas mehr Geld.
j Wir gingen den Weg entlang.

**139**
a für
b um
c Ohne
d durch
e für
f gegen
g um
h durch
i um
j gegen

**140**
a in die Straße
b unter den Tassen
c aufs Dach/in den Himmel
d auf der Tür/in der Flasche
e unter den Tisch/neben das Auto
f die Straße entlang/im Auto
g am Stuhl
h auf den Tisch gesprungen/neben dem Auto eingeschlafen
i im Büro/neben meinem Haus
j neben der Straße/in der Wüste

**141**
a neben
b über
c auf
d vor
e auf
f in
g auf
h neben
i an
j vor

**142**
a Diese Suppe schmeckt nach Zitrone.
b Er legte das Messer neben den Teller.
c Wir treffen uns am Eingang.
d Ich habe eine E-Mail von meiner Schwester bekommen.
e Wir fahren morgen nach Köln.
f Stell dich vor deine Mutter.
g Die Schüler warteten auf den Lehrer.
h Ich war vor meiner Schwester hier.
i Er geht gerne ins Kino.
j Wir sollten nach Hause gehen. Es ist schon nach Mitternacht.

**143**
a trotz des schlechten Wetters
b infolge der Schneefälle
c trotz meiner Probleme
d außerhalb des Gartens
e um deiner Familie willen
f während des Films
g wegen der langen Ferien
h diesseits des Rheins
i statt seine Tante zu besuchen
j innerhalb des Dorfs

**144**
a statt
b wegen
c Während
d innerhalb
e außerhalb
f Trotz
g Infolge
h Wegen
i während
j Statt

# Solutions

**145**
a deinetwegen
b seinetwegen
c unsertwegen
d Euretwegen
e meinetwegen
f ihretwegen
g deinetwegen
h Ihretwegen
i Seinetwegen
j meinetwegen

**146**
a zur
b untern
c aufs/ums
d ans
e durchs
f unterm
g übern
h ums
i durchs/ums
j untern

**147**
a Die Katze kroch unters Bett.
b Wir gingen zum Bahnhof.
c Wir fanden das Buch hinterm Sofa.
d Der Hund schlief unterm Stuhl.
e Der Vogel flog übers Haus.
f Wir müssen zur Schule gehen.
g Er stand vorm Tisch.
h Stell das Buch aufs Regal.
i Die Kinder sind im Haus.
j Sie ist zur Bäckerei gegangen.

**148**
a darauf
b daran
c darunter
d darüber
e davor
f darin
g dazu
h Darum
i Danach
j dahinter

**149**
a Sie ging zur Bank und zahlte 100 Euro ein.
b Wir wollten ausgehen, aber es war schon spät.
c Petra und Susanne waren auf der Party.
d Sowohl du als auch ich

mögen Popmusik.
e Weder er noch sie hat es gesehen.
f Er ist weder gekommen, noch hat er angerufen.
g Sie sind nicht nur hässlich, sondern auch dumm.
h Er schuldet mir nicht 300 Euro, sondern 500.
i Sowohl deine als auch meine Schule haben 600 Schüler.
j Sie gingen in ein Restaurant, denn sie hatten Hunger.

**150**
a weder
b oder
c Sowohl
d weder
e weder
f sondern auch
g entweder
h als auch
i noch
j sondern auch

**151**
a nicht nur ich **sondern auch er**
b weder Oliver **noch Petra**
c entweder gleich **oder gar nicht**
d sowohl Oliver **als auch Petra**
e entweder du **oder ich**

**152**
a weil
b Wenn
c Als
d wenn
e weil
f Als
g weil
h wenn
i weil
j wenn

**153**
a Während
b obwohl
c ob
d während
e ob
f obwohl
g ob
h während
i obwohl
j ob

**154**
a Ich weiß, **dass wir es schaffen können.**
b Ich weiß nicht, **ob das eine gute Idee ist.**
c Ich kann nicht kommen, **weil ich beschäftigt bin.**
d Ich beeile mich, **damit ich nicht zu spät komme.**
e Ich bleibe, **obwohl ich mich langweile.**

**155**
a sind nicht blau
b habe keine Angst
c mag keine Erbsen
d kommt nicht mit
e nie
f noch nie
g nirgendwo
h nichts
i Weder noch
j noch nie

**156**
a Ich war noch nie in Deutschland.
b Es war niemand im Zimmer.
c Ich kann ihn nirgends finden.
d Das kann nicht wahr sein.
e Sie passt in der Schule nie auf.
f Ich mag ihn auch nicht.
g Weder Brigitte noch ihr Bruder war auf der Party.
h Das sollten wir nie vergessen.
i Niemand erinnert sich mehr daran.
j Ich will dich nie wiedersehen.

**157**
a Ist das Haus sauber?
b Stimmt das nicht?
c Ist er heute angekommen?
d Seid ihr spät aufgestanden?
e Hat sie großen Hunger?
f Ist Zac Efrons neuer Film gut?
g Bist du zu spät gekommen?
h Glaubst du mir?
i Schaffen wir das noch?
j Steht der Stuhl neben dem Tisch?

# Solutions

**158**
a Woher
b Wohin
c Warum
d Wessen
e Warum
f Wer
g Wem
h Was
i Welches
j Wie

**159**
a Warum bist du nicht gekommen?
b Was sollen wir morgen machen?
c Wollen wir ins Kino gehen?
d Welchen Mann hast du gesehen?
e Wie hast du das gemacht?
f Das stimmt doch, nicht wahr?
g Hast du deine Hausaufgaben gemacht?
h Warum hast du keinen Appetit?
i Kommt sie uns morgen besuchen?
j Ist das unser neuer Fernseher?

# index

# Index

# VERB TABLES

## Introduction

This section is designed to help you find all the verb forms you need in German.

From pages 2-7 you will find a list of 97 regular and irregular verbs with a summary of their main forms, followed on pages 8-18 by some very common regular and irregular verbs shown in full, with example phrases.

# German verb forms

| | INFINITIVE | PRESENT | PERFECT | IMPERFECT | FUTURE | PRESENT SUBJUNCTIVE |
|---|---|---|---|---|---|---|
| 1 | **annehmen** verb with a spelling change | ich nehme an du **nimmst** an er/sie/es **nimmt** an wir nehmen an | ich habe **angenommen** du **nahmst** an | ich **nahm** an du nehmest an er/sie/es **nahm** an wir **nahmen** an | ich werde annehmen | ich nehme an |
| 2 | **arbeiten** | ich arbeite | ich habe gearbeitet | ich arbeitete | ich werde arbeiten | ich arbeite |
| 3 | **atmen** | ich atme | ich habe geatmet | ich atmete | ich werde atmen | ich atme |
| 4 | **ausreichen** | ich reiche aus du reichst aus | ich habe ausgereicht | ich reichte aus | ich werde ausreichen | ich reiche aus du reichest aus |
| 5 | **beginnen** verb with a spelling change | ich beginne | ich habe **begonnen** | ich **begann** du **begannst** wir **begannen** | ich werde beginnen | ich beginne du beginnest |
| 6 | **beißen** verb with a spelling change | ich beiße du beißt | ich habe **gebissen** | ich **biss** du **bissest** er/sie/es **biss** wir **bissen** ihr **bisst** sie/Sie **bissen** | ich werde beißen | ich beiße du beißest |
| 7 | **bestellen** | ich bestelle du bestellst | ich habe **bestellt** | ich bestellte | ich werde bestellen | ich bestelle du bestellest |
| 8 | **bieten** verb with a spelling change | ich biete | ich habe **geboten** | ich **bot** du **bot(e)st** wir **boten** | ich werde bieten | ich biete |
| 9 | **bitten** verb with a spelling change | ich bitte | ich habe **gebeten** du **bat(e)st** wir **baten** | ich **bat** | ich werde bitten | ich bitte |
| 10 | **bleiben** verb with a spelling change | ich bleibe du bleibst | ich bin **geblieben** du **bliebst** wir **blieben** | ich **blieb** | ich werde bleiben | ich bleibe du bleibest |
| 11 | **brechen** verb with a spelling change | ich breche du brichst er/sie/es bricht wir brechen | ich habe/bin **gebrochen** | ich **brach** du **brachst** er/sie/es **brach** wir **brachen** | ich werde brechen | ich breche du brechest |
| 12 | **brennen** verb with a spelling change | ich brenne du brennst | ich habe gebrannt | ich brannte du branntest wir brannten | ich werde brennen | ich brenne du brennest |
| 13 | **bringen** verb with a spelling change | ich bringe du bringst | ich habe **gebracht** | ich **brachte** du **brachtest** wir **brachten** | ich werde bringen | ich bringe du bringest |
| 14 | **denken** verb with a spelling change | ich denke du denkst | ich habe **gedacht** | ich **dachte** du **dachtest** wir **dachten** | ich werde denken | ich denke du denkest |
| 15 | **durchsetzen** | ich setze durch du setzt durch | ich habe durchgesetzt | ich setzte durch | ich werde durchsetzen | ich setze durch du setzest durch |

| INFINITIVE | PRESENT | PERFECT | IMPERFECT | FUTURE | PRESENT SUBJUNCTIVE |
|---|---|---|---|---|---|
| **16 dürfen** verb with a spelling change | ich **darf** du **darfst** er/sie/es **darf** wir dürfen ihr dürft sie/Sie dürfen | ich habe ged**u**rft/ **dürfen** | ich durfte du durftest er/sie/es durfte | ich werde dürfen | ich dürfe du dürfest wir durften ihr durftet sie/Sie durften |
| **17 empfehlen** verb with a spelling change | ich empfehle du empf**ie**hlst er/sie/es empf**ie**hlt wir empfehlen | ich habe **empfohlen** | ich **empfahl** du **empfahlst** er/sie/es **empfahl** wir **empfahlen** | ich werde empfehlen | ich empfehle du empfehlest |
| **18 entdecken** | ich entdecke | ich habe **entdeckt** | ich entdeckte | ich werde entdecken | ich entdecke |
| **19 erzählen** | ich erzähle du erzählst | ich habe **erzählt** | ich erzählte | ich werde erzählen | ich erzähle du erzählest |
| **20 essen** | see full verb table page 8 | | | | |
| **21 fahren** | see full verb table page 9 | | | | |
| **22 fallen** verb with a spelling change | ich falle du f**ä**llst er/sie/es f**ä**llt wir fallen | ich bin **gefallen** | ich **fiel** du **fielst** er/sie/es **fiel** wir **fielen** | ich werde fallen | ich falle du fallest |
| **23 fangen** verb with a spelling change | ich fange du f**ä**ngst er/sie/es f**ä**ngt wir fangen | ich habe **gefangen** | ich **fing** du **fingst** er/sie/es **fing** wir **fingen** | ich werde fangen | ich fange du fangest |
| **24 finden** verb with a spelling change | ich finde du findest | ich habe **gefunden** | ich **fand** du **fand(e)st** wir **fanden** | ich werde finden | ich finde |
| **25 fliegen** verb with a spelling change | ich fliege du fliegst | ich habe/ bin **geflogen** | ich **flog** du **flogst** wir **flogen** | ich werde fliegen | ich fliege du fliegest |
| **26 fliehen** verb with a spelling change | ich fliehe du fliehst | ich bin/ habe **geflohen** | ich **floh** du **flohst** wir **flohen** | ich werde fliehen | ich fliehe du fliehest |
| **27 fließen** verb with a spelling change | ich fließe du fließt | ich bin **geflossen** | ich **floss** du **flossest** wir **flossen** | ich werde fließen | ich fließe du fließest |
| **28 geben** verb with a spelling change | ich gebe du g**i**bst er/sie/es g**i**bt wir geben | ich habe **gegeben** | ich **gab** du **gabst** er/sie/es **gab** wir **gaben** | ich werde geben | ich gebe du gebest |
| **29 gehen** | see full verb table page 10 | | | | |
| **30 gewinnen** verb with a spelling change | ich gewinne du gewinnst | ich habe **gewonnen** | ich **gewann** du **gewannst** wir **gewannen** | ich werde gewinnen | ich gewinne du gewinnest |
| **31 grüßen** | ich grüße du grüßt | ich habe gegrüßt | ich grüßte | ich werde grüßen | ich grüße du grüßest |
| **32 haben** | see full verb table page 11 | | | | |
| **33 halten** verb with a spelling change | ich halte du h**ä**ltst er/sie/es h**ä**lt wir halten | ich habe **gehalten** | ich **hielt** du **hielt(e)st** er/sie/es **hielt** wir **hielten** | ich werde halten | ich halte du haltest |

| INFINITIVE | PRESENT | PERFECT | IMPERFECT | FUTURE | PRESENT SUBJUNCTIVE |
|---|---|---|---|---|---|
| 34 **handeln** | ich handle<br>du handelst | ich habe gehandelt | ich handelte | ich werde handeln | ich handle<br>du handlest |
| 35 **hängen**<br>verb with a<br>spelling change | ich hänge<br>du hängst | ich habe **gehangen** | ich **hing**<br>du **hingst**<br>wir **hingen** | ich werde hängen | ich hänge<br>du hängest |
| 36 **heizen** | ich heize<br>du heizt | ich habe geheizt | ich heizte | ich werde heizen | ich heize<br>du heizest |
| 37 **helfen**<br>verb with a<br>spelling change | ich helfe<br>du **hilfst**<br>er/sie/es **hilft**<br>wir helfen | ich habe **geholfen** | ich **half**<br>du **halfst**<br>er/sie/es **half**<br>wir **halfen** | ich werde helfen | ich helfe<br>du helfest |
| 38 **holen** | ich hole<br>du holst | ich habe geholt | ich holte | ich werde holten | ich hole<br>du holest |
| 39 **kennen**<br>verb with a<br>spelling change | ich kenne<br>du kennst | ich habe **gek**annt | ich **k**annte<br>du **k**anntest<br>wir **k**annten | ich werde kennen | ich kenne<br>du kennest |
| 40 **kommen** | see full verb table page 12 | | | | |
| 41 **können** | see full verb table page 13 | | | | |
| 42 **lassen**<br>verb with a<br>spelling change | ich lasse<br>du **lässt**<br>er/sie/es **lässt**<br>wir lassen | ich habe **gelassen** | ich **ließ**<br>du **ließest**<br>er/sie/es **ließ**<br>wir **ließen** | ich werde lassen | ich lasse<br>du lassest |
| 43 **laufen**<br>verb with a<br>spelling change | ich laufe<br>du **läufst**<br>er/sie/es **läuft**<br>wir laufen | ich bin **gelaufen** | ich **lief**<br>du **liefst**<br>er/sie/es **lief**<br>wir **liefen** | ich werde laufen | ich laufe<br>du laufest |
| 44 **leiden**<br>verb with a<br>spelling change | ich leide | ich habe **gelitten** | ich **litt**<br>du **litt(e)st**<br>wir **litten** | ich werde leiden | ich leide |
| 45 **lesen**<br>verb with a<br>spelling change | ich lese<br>du **liest**<br>er/sie/es **liest**<br>wir lesen | ich habe **gelesen** | ich **las**<br>du **lasest**<br>er/sie/es **las**<br>wir **lasen** | ich werde lesen | ich lese<br>du lesest |
| 46 **liegen**<br>verb with a<br>spelling change | ich liege<br>du liegst | ich habe **gelegen** | ich **lag**<br>du **lagst**<br>wir **lagen** | ich werde legen | ich liege<br>du liegest |
| 47 **lügen**<br>verb with a<br>spelling change | ich lüge<br>du lügst | ich habe **gelogen** | ich **log**<br>du **logst**<br>wir **logen** | ich werde lügen | ich lüge<br>du lügest |
| 48 **machen** | see full verb table page 14 | | | | |
| 49 **misstrauen** | ich misstraue<br>du misstraust | ich habe **misstraut** | ich misstraute | ich werde misstrauen | ich misstraue<br>du misstrauest |
| 50 **mögen**<br>verb with a<br>spelling change | ich **mag**<br>du **mag**st<br>er/sie/es **mag**<br>wir mögen<br>ihr mögt<br>sie/Sie mögen | ich habe **gemocht/<br>mögen** | ich **mochte**<br>du **mochtest**<br>er/sie/es **mochte**<br>wir **mochten**<br>ihr **mochtet**<br>sie/Sie **mochten** | ich werde mögen | ich möge<br>du mögest |
| 51 **müssen** | see full verb table page 15 | | | | |

| INFINITIVE | PRESENT | PERFECT | IMPERFECT | FUTURE | PRESENT SUBJUNCTIVE |
|---|---|---|---|---|---|
| **52 nehmen**<br>verb with a<br>spelling change | ich nehme<br>du **nimmst**<br>er/sie/es **nimmt**<br>wir nehmen | ich habe<br>**genommen** | ich **nahm**<br>du **nahmst**<br>er/sie/es **nahm**<br>wir **nahmen** | ich werde<br>nehmen | ich nehme<br>du nehmest |
| **53 rechnen** | ich rechne | ich habe<br>gerechnet | ich rechnete | ich werde<br>rechnen | ich rechne |
| **54 reden** | ich rede | ich habe geredet | ich redete | ich werde redden | ich rede |
| **55 rennen**<br>verb with a<br>spelling change | ich renne<br>du rennst | ich bin ger**a**nnt | ich r**a**nnte<br>du r**a**nntest<br>wir r**a**nnten | ich werde rennen | ich renne<br>du rennest |
| **56 rufen**<br>verb with a<br>spelling change | ich rufe<br>du rufst | ich habe<br>**gerufen** | ich **rief**<br>du **riefst**<br>wir **riefen** | ich werde rufen | ich rufe<br>du rufest |
| **57 scheinen**<br>verb with a<br>spelling change | ich scheine<br>du scheinst | ich habe<br>**geschienen** | ich **schien**<br>du **schienst**<br>wir **schienen** | ich werde<br>scheinen | ich scheine<br>du scheinest |
| **58 schlafen**<br>verb with a<br>spelling change | ich schlafe<br>du schl**ä**fst<br>er/sie/es schl**ä**ft<br>wir schlafen | ich habe<br>**geschlafen** | ich **schlief**<br>du **schliefst**<br>er/sie/es **schlief**<br>wir **schliefen** | ich werde<br>schlafen | ich schlafe<br>du schlafest |
| **59 schlagen**<br>verb with a<br>spelling change | ich schlage<br>du schl**ä**gst<br>er/sie/es schl**ä**gt<br>wir schlagen | ich habe<br>**geschlagen** | ich **schlug**<br>du **schlugst**<br>er/sie/es **schlug**<br>wir **schlugen** | ich werde<br>schlagen | ich schlage<br>du schlagest |
| **60 schneiden**<br>verb with a<br>spelling change | ich schneide | ich habe<br>**geschnitten** | ich **schnitt**<br>du **schnittst**<br>wir **schnitten** | ich werde<br>schneiden | ich schneide |
| **61 schreiben**<br>verb with a<br>spelling change | ich schreibe<br>du schreibst | ich habe<br>**geschrieben** | ich **schrieb**<br>du **schriebst**<br>wir **schrieben** | ich werde<br>schreiben | ich schreibe<br>du schreibest |
| **62 schreien**<br>verb with a<br>spelling change | ich schreie<br>du schreist | ich habe<br>**geschrien** | ich **schrie**<br>du **schriest**<br>wir **schrien** | ich werde<br>schreien | ich schreie<br>du schreiest |
| **63 schwimmen**<br>verb with a<br>spelling change | ich schwimme<br>du schwimmst | ich bin **gesch-<br>wommen** | ich **schwamm**<br>du **schwammst**<br>wir **schwammen** | ich werde<br>schwimmen | ich schwimme<br>du schwimmest |
| **64 sehen**<br>verb with a<br>spelling change | ich sehe<br>du s**ie**hst<br>er/sie/es s**ie**ht<br>wir sehen | ich habe<br>**gesehen** | ich **sah**<br>du **sahst**<br>er/sie/es **sah**<br>wir **sahen** | ich werde sehen | ich sehe<br>du sehest |
| **65 sein** | see full verb table page 16 | | | | |
| **66 singen**<br>verb with a<br>spelling change | ich singe<br>du singst | ich habe<br>**gesungen** | ich **sang**<br>du **sangst**<br>wir **sangen** | ich werde singen | ich singe<br>du singest |
| **67 sinken**<br>verb with a<br>spelling change | ich sinke<br>du sinkst | ich bin<br>**gesunken** | ich **sank**<br>du **sankst**<br>wir **sanken** | ich werde sinken | ich sinke<br>du sinkest |
| **68 sitzen**<br>verb with a<br>spelling change | ich sitze<br>du sitzt | ich habe<br>**gesessen** | ich **saß**<br>du **saßest**<br>wir **saßen** | ich werde sitzen | ich sitze<br>du sitzest |

| INFINITIVE | PRESENT | PERFECT | IMPERFECT | FUTURE | PRESENT SUBJUNCTIVE |
|---|---|---|---|---|---|
| 69 **sollen** | ich soll<br>du sollst | ich habe<br>gesollt/**sollen** | ich sollte | ich werde sollen | ich solle<br>du sollest |
| 70 **sprechen**<br>verb with a<br>spelling change | ich spreche<br>du sprichst<br>er/sie/es spricht<br>wir sprechen | ich habe<br>**gesprochen** | ich **sprach**<br>du **sprachst**<br>er/sie/es **sprach**<br>wir **sprachen** | ich werde<br>sprechen | ich spreche<br>du sprechest |
| 71 **springen**<br>verb with a<br>spelling change | ich springe<br>du springst | ich bin<br>**gesprungen** | ich **sprang**<br>du **sprangst**<br>wir **sprangen** | ich werde<br>springen | ich springe<br>du springest |
| 72 **stehen**<br>verb with a<br>spelling change | ich stehe<br>du stehst | ich habe<br>**gestanden** | ich **stand**<br>du **stand(e)st**<br>wir **standen** | ich werde stehen | ich stehe<br>du stehest |
| 73 **stehle**<br>verb with a<br>spelling change | ich stehle<br>du stiehlst<br>er/sie/es stiehlt<br>wir stehlen | ich habe<br>**gestohlen** | ich **stahl**<br>du **stahlst**<br>er/sie/es **stahl**<br>wir **stahlen** | ich werde stehlen | ich stehle<br>du stehlest |
| 74 **steigen**<br>verb with a<br>spelling change | ich steige<br>du steigst | ich bin<br>**gestiegen** | ich **stieg**<br>du **stiegst**<br>wir **stiegen** | ich werde steigen | ich steige<br>du steigest |
| 75 **sterben**<br>verb with a<br>spelling change | ich sterbe<br>du stirbst<br>er/sie/es stirbt<br>wir sterben | ich bin<br>**gestorben** | ich **starb**<br>du **starbst**<br>er/sie/es **starb**<br>wir **starben** | ich werde sterben | ich sterbe<br>du sterbest |
| 76 **studieren** | ich studiere<br>du studierst | ich habe<br>**studiert** | ich studierte | ich werde<br>studieren | ich studiere<br>du studierest |
| 77 **tragen**<br>verb with a<br>spelling change | ich trage<br>du trägst<br>er/sie/es trägt<br>wir tragen | ich habe<br>**getragen** | ich **trug**<br>du **trugst**<br>er/sie/es **trug**<br>wir **trugen** | ich werde tragen | ich trage<br>du tragest |
| 78 **treffen**<br>verb with a<br>spelling change | ich treffe<br>du triffst<br>er/sie/es trifft<br>wir treffen | ich habe<br>**getroffen** | ich **traf**<br>du **trafst**<br>er/sie/es **traf**<br>wir **trafen** | ich werde treffen | ich treffe<br>du treffest |
| 79 **treten**<br>verb with a<br>spelling change | ich trete<br>du **trittst**<br>er/sie/es **tritt**<br>wir treten | ich habe/<br>bin **getreten** | ich **trat**<br>du **trat(e)st**<br>er/sie/es **trat**<br>wir **traten** | ich werde treten | ich trete<br>du tretest |
| 80 **trinken**<br>verb with a<br>spelling change | ich trinke<br>du trinkst | ich habe<br>**getrunken** | ich **trank**<br>du **trankst**<br>wir **tranken** | ich werde trinken | ich trinke<br>du trinkest |
| 81 **tun**<br>verb with a<br>spelling change | ich tue<br>du tust<br>er/sie/es tut<br>wir tun<br>ihr tut<br>sie/Sie tun | ich habe **getan** | ich **tat**<br>du **tat(e)st**<br>er/sie/es **tat**<br>wir **taten**<br>ihr **tatet**<br>sie/Sie **taten** | ich werde tun | ich tue<br>du tuest |
| 82 **sich<br>überlegen** | ich überlege mir<br>du überlegst dir | ich habe mir<br>**überlegt** | ich überlegte mir | ich werde mir<br>überlegen | ich überlege mir<br>du überlegest dir |

| INFINITIVE | PRESENT | PERFECT | IMPERFECT | FUTURE | PRESENT SUBJUNCTIVE |
|---|---|---|---|---|---|
| 83 **vergessen** verb with a spelling change | ich vergesse du vergisst er/sie/es vergisst wir vergessen | ich habe **vergessen** | ich **vergaß** du **vergaßest** er/sie/es **vergaß** wir **vergaßen** | ich werde vergessen | ich vergesse du vergessest |
| 84 **verlangen** | ich verlange du verlangst | ich habe **verlangt** | ich verlangte | ich werde verlangen | ich verlange du verlangest |
| 85 **verlieren** verb with a spelling change | ich verliere du verlierst | ich habe **verloren** | ich **verlor** du **verlorst** wir **verloren** | ich werde verlieren | ich verliere du verlierest |
| 86 **verschwin-den** verb with a spelling change | ich verschwinde | ich bin **ver-schwunden** | ich **verschwand** du **ver-schwand(e)st** wir **ver-schwanden** | ich werde verschwinden | ich verschwinde |
| 87 **wachsen** verb with a spelling change | ich wachse du **wächst** er/sie/es **wächst** wir wachsen | ich bin **gewachsen** | ich **wuchs** du **wuchsest** er/sie/es **wuchs** wir **wuchsen** | ich werde wachsen | ich wachse du wachsest |
| 88 **wandern** | ich wand(e)re du wanderst | ich bin gewandert | ich wanderte | ich werde wandern | ich wand(e)re du wandrest |
| 89 **waschen** verb with a spelling change | ich wasche du **wäschst** er/sie/es **wäscht** wir waschen | ich habe **gewaschen** | ich **wusch** du **wuschest** er/sie/es **wusch** wir **wuschen** | ich werde waschen | ich wasche du waschest |
| 90 **werben** verb with a spelling change | ich werbe du **wirbst** er/sie/es **wirbt** wir werben | ich habe **geworben** | ich **warb** du **warbst** er/sie/es **warb** wir **wurben** | ich werde werben | ich werbe du werbest |
| 91 **werden** | see full verb table page 17 | | | | |
| 92 **werfen** verb with a spelling change | ich werfe du **wirfst** er/sie/es **wirft** wir werfen | ich habe **geworfen** | ich **warf** du **warfst** er/sie/es **warf** wir **warfen** | ich werde werfen | ich werfe du werfest |
| 93 **wissen** | see full verb table page 18 | | | | |
| 94 **wollen** verb with a spelling change | ich **will** du willst er/sie/es **will** wir wollen ihr wollt sie/Sie wollen | ich habe gewollt/**wollen** | ich wollte | ich werde werfen | ich wolle du wollest |
| 95 **zerstören** | ich zerstöre du zerstörst | ich habe zerstört | ich zerstörte | ich werde zerstören | ich zerstöre du zerstörest |
| 96 **ziehen** verb with a spelling change | ich ziehe du ziehst | ich bin/habe **gezogen** | ich **zog** du **zogst** wir **zogen** | ich werde ziehen | ich ziehe du ziehest |
| 97 **zwingen** verb with a spelling change | ich zwinge du zwingst | ich habe **gezwungen** | ich **zwang** du **zwangst** wir **zwangen** | ich werde zwingen | ich zwinge du zwingest |

# essen (to eat)

| **PRESENT** | | **PRESENT SUBJUNCTIVE** | |
|---|---|---|---|
| ich | **esse** | ich | **esse** |
| du | **isst** | du | **essest** |
| er/sie/es | **isst** | er/sie/es | **esse** |
| wir | **essen** | wir | **essen** |
| ihr | **esst** | ihr | **esset** |
| sie/Sie | **essen** | sie/Sie | **essen** |

| **PERFECT** | | **IMPERFECT** | |
|---|---|---|---|
| ich | **habe gegessen** | ich | **aß** |
| du | **hast gegessen** | du | **aßest** |
| er/sie/es | **hat gegessen** | er/sie/es | **aß** |
| wir | **haben gegessen** | wir | **aßen** |
| ihr | **habt gegessen** | ihr | **aßt** |
| sie/Sie | **haben gegessen** | sie/Sie | **aßen** |

| **FUTURE** | | **CONDITIONAL** | |
|---|---|---|---|
| ich | **werde essen** | ich | **würde essen** |
| du | **wirst essen** | du | **würdest essen** |
| er/sie/es | **wird essen** | er/sie/es | **würde essen** |
| wir | **werden essen** | wir | **würden essen** |
| ihr | **werdet essen** | ihr | **würdet essen** |
| sie/Sie | **werden essen** | sie/Sie | **würden essen** |

| **PAST PARTICIPLE** | **PRESENT PARTICIPLE** |
|---|---|
| **gegessen** | **essend** |

**IMPERATIVE**

**iss!/essen wir!/esst!/essen Sie!**

---

**EXAMPLE PHRASES**

Ich **esse** kein Fleisch. I don't eat meat.
Wir **haben** nichts **gegessen**. We haven't had anything to eat.
Ich möchte etwas **essen**. I'd like something to eat.

# fahren (to drive/to go)

| PRESENT | |
|---|---|
| ich | **fahre** |
| du | **fährst** |
| er/sie/es | **fährt** |
| wir | **fahren** |
| ihr | **fahrt** |
| sie/Sie | **fahren** |

| PRESENT SUBJUNCTIVE | |
|---|---|
| ich | **fahre** |
| du | **fahrest** |
| er/sie/es | **fahre** |
| wir | **fahren** |
| ihr | **fahret** |
| sie/Sie | **fahren** |

| PERFECT | |
|---|---|
| ich | **bin gefahren** |
| du | **bist gefahren** |
| er/sie/es | **ist gefahren** |
| wir | **sind gefahren** |
| ihr | **seid gefahren** |
| sie/Sie | **sind gefahren** |

| IMPERFECT | |
|---|---|
| ich | **fuhr** |
| du | **fuhrst** |
| er/sie/es | **fuhr** |
| wir | **fuhren** |
| ihr | **fuhrt** |
| sie/Sie | **fuhren** |

| FUTURE | |
|---|---|
| ich | **werde fahren** |
| du | **wirst fahren** |
| er/sie/es | **wird fahren** |
| wir | **werden fahren** |
| ihr | **werdet fahren** |
| sie/Sie | **werden fahren** |

| CONDITIONAL | |
|---|---|
| ich | **würde fahren** |
| du | **würdest fahren** |
| er/sie/es | **würde fahren** |
| wir | **würden fahren** |
| ihr | **würdet fahren** |
| sie/Sie | **würden fahren** |

**PAST PARTICIPLE**

gefahren

**PRESENT PARTICIPLE**

fahrend

**IMPERATIVE**

fahr(e)!/fahren wir!/fahrt!/fahren Sie!

## EXAMPLE PHRASES

Sie **fahren** mit dem Bus in die Schule. They go to school by bus.
Rechts **fahren**! Drive on the right!
Ich **bin** mit der Familie nach Spanien **gefahren**. I went to Spain with my family.
Sie **hat** das Auto **gefahren**. She drove the car.

**ich** = I **du** = you **er** = he/it **sie** = she/it **es** = it/he/she **wir** = we **ihr** = you **sie** = they **Sie** = you

# gehen (to go)

| | **PRESENT** | | **PRESENT SUBJUNCTIVE** |
|---|---|---|---|
| ich | **gehe** | ich | **gehe** |
| du | **gehst** | du | **gehest** |
| er/sie/es | **geht** | er/sie/es | **gehe** |
| wir | **gehen** | wir | **gehen** |
| ihr | **geht** | ihr | **gehet** |
| sie/Sie | **gehen** | sie/Sie | **gehen** |

| | **PERFECT** | | **IMPERFECT** |
|---|---|---|---|
| ich | **bin gegangen** | ich | **ging** |
| du | **bist gegangen** | du | **gingst** |
| er/sie/es | **ist gegangen** | er/sie/es | **ging** |
| wir | **sind gegangen** | wir | **gingen** |
| ihr | **seid gegangen** | ihr | **gingt** |
| sie/Sie | **sind gegangen** | sie/Sie | **gingen** |

| | **FUTURE** | | **CONDITIONAL** |
|---|---|---|---|
| ich | **werde gehen** | ich | **würde gehen** |
| du | **wirst gehen** | du | **würdest gehen** |
| er/sie/es | **wird gehen** | er/sie/es | **würde gehen** |
| wir | **werden gehen** | wir | **würden gehen** |
| ihr | **werdet gehen** | ihr | **würdet gehen** |
| sie/Sie | **werden gehen** | sie/Sie | **würden gehen** |

**PAST PARTICIPLE**

gegangen

**PRESENT PARTICIPLE**

gehend

**IMPERATIVE**

geh(e)!/gehen wir!/geht!/gehen Sie!

**EXAMPLE PHRASES**

Die Kinder **gingen** ins Haus. The children went into the house.
Wie **geht** es dir? How are you?
Wir **sind** gestern schwimmen **gegangen**. We went swimming yesterday.

**ch** = I **du** = you **er** = he/it **sie** = she/it **es** = it/he/she **wir** = we **ihr** = you **sie** = they **Sie** = you

# haben (to have)

### PRESENT

| | |
|---|---|
| ich | **habe** |
| du | **hast** |
| er/sie/es | **hat** |
| wir | **haben** |
| ihr | **habt** |
| sie/Sie | **haben** |

### PRESENT SUBJUNCTIVE

| | |
|---|---|
| ich | **habe** |
| du | **habest** |
| er/sie/es | **habe** |
| wir | **haben** |
| ihr | **habet** |
| sie/Sie | **haben** |

### PERFECT

| | |
|---|---|
| ich | **habe gehabt** |
| du | **hast gehabt** |
| er/sie/es | **hat gehabt** |
| wir | **haben gehabt** |
| ihr | **habt gehabt** |
| sie/Sie | **haben gehabt** |

### IMPERFECT

| | |
|---|---|
| ich | **hatte** |
| du | **hattest** |
| er/sie/es | **hatte** |
| wir | **hatten** |
| ihr | **hattet** |
| sie/Sie | **hatten** |

### FUTURE

| | |
|---|---|
| ich | **werde haben** |
| du | **wirst haben** |
| er/sie/es | **wird haben** |
| wir | **werden haben** |
| ihr | **werdet haben** |
| sie/Sie | **werden haben** |

### CONDITIONAL

| | |
|---|---|
| ich | **würde haben** |
| du | **würdest haben** |
| er/sie/es | **würde haben** |
| wir | **würden haben** |
| ihr | **würdet haben** |
| sie/Sie | **würden haben** |

### PAST PARTICIPLE

**gehabt**

### PRESENT PARTICIPLE

**habend**

### IMPERATIVE

**hab(e)!/haben wir!/habt!/haben Sie!**

---

### EXAMPLE PHRASES

**Hast** du eine Schwester? Have you got a sister?
Er **hatte** Hunger. He was hungry.
Sie **hat** heute Geburtstag. It's her birthday today.

---

ich = I du = you er = he/it sie = she/it es = it/he/she wir = we ihr = you sie = they Sie = you

# kommen (to come)

| | **PRESENT** | | **PRESENT SUBJUNCTIVE** |
|---|---|---|---|
| ich | komme | ich | komme |
| du | kommst | du | kommest |
| er/sie/es | kommt | er/sie/es | komme |
| wir | kommen | wir | kommen |
| ihr | kommt | ihr | kommet |
| sie/Sie | kommen | sie/Sie | kommen |

| | **PERFECT** | | **IMPERFECT** |
|---|---|---|---|
| ich | bin gekommen | ich | kam |
| du | bist gekommen | du | kamst |
| er/sie/es | ist gekommen | er/sie/es | kam |
| wir | sind gekommen | wir | kamen |
| ihr | seid gekommen | ihr | kamt |
| sie/Sie | sind gekommen | sie/Sie | kamen |

| | **FUTURE** | | **CONDITIONAL** |
|---|---|---|---|
| ich | werde kommen | ich | würde kommen |
| du | wirst kommen | du | würdest kommen |
| er/sie/es | wird kommen | er/sie/es | würde kommen |
| wir | werden kommen | wir | würden kommen |
| ihr | werdet kommen | ihr | würdet kommen |
| sie/Sie | werden kommen | sie/Sie | würden kommen |

**PAST PARTICIPLE**

gekommen

**PRESENT PARTICIPLE**

kommend

**IMPERATIVE**

komm(e)!/kommen wir!/kommt!/kommen Sie!

---

**EXAMPLE PHRASES**

Er **kam** die Straße entlang. He was coming along the street.
Ich **komme** zu deiner Party. I'm coming to your party.
Woher **kommst** du? Where do you come from?

# könnon (to be able to)

| | **PRESENT** | | **PRESENT SUBJUNCTIVE** |
|---|---|---|---|
| ich | **kann** | ich | **könne** |
| du | **kannst** | du | **könnest** |
| er/sie/es | **kann** | er/sie/es | **könne** |
| wir | **können** | wir | **können** |
| ihr | **könnt** | ihr | **könnet** |
| sie/Sie | **können** | sie/Sie | **können** |

| | **PERFECT** | | **IMPERFECT** |
|---|---|---|---|
| ich | **habe gekonnt/können** | ich | **konnte** |
| du | **hast gekonnt/können** | du | **konntest** |
| er/sie/es | **hat gekonnt/können** | er/sie/es | **konnte** |
| wir | **haben gekonnt/können** | wir | **konnten** |
| ihr | **habt gekonnt/können** | ihr | **konntet** |
| sie/Sie | **haben gekonnt/können** | sie/Sie | **konnten** |

| | **FUTURE** | | **CONDITIONAL** |
|---|---|---|---|
| ich | **werde können** | ich | **würde können** |
| du | **wirst können** | du | **würdest können** |
| er/sie/es | **wird können** | er/sie/es | **würde können** |
| wir | **werden können** | wir | **würden können** |
| ihr | **werdet können** | ihr | **würdet können** |
| sie/Sie | **werden können** | sie/Sie | **würden können** |

| **PAST PARTICIPLE** | **PRESENT PARTICIPLE** |
|---|---|
| **gekonnt/können\*** | **könnend** |

\*This form is used when combined with another infinitive.

---

### EXAMPLE PHRASES

Er **kann** gut schwimmen. He can swim well.
Sie **konnte** kein Wort Deutsch. She couldn't speak a word of German.
**Kann** ich gehen? Can I go?

**ich** = I **du** = you **er** = he/it **sie** = she/it **es** = it/he/she **wir** = we **ihr** = you **sie** = they **Sie** = you

# machen (to do *or* to make)

| | **PRESENT** | | **PRESENT SUBJUNCTIVE** |
|---|---|---|---|
| ich | **mache** | ich | **mache** |
| du | **machst** | du | **machest** |
| er/sie/es | **macht** | er/sie/es | **mache** |
| wir | **machen** | wir | **machen** |
| ihr | **macht** | ihr | **machet** |
| sie/Sie | **machen** | sie/Sie | **machen** |

| | **PERFECT** | | **IMPERFECT** |
|---|---|---|---|
| ich | **habe gemacht** | ich | **machte** |
| du | **hast gemacht** | du | **machtest** |
| er/sie/es | **hat gemacht** | er/sie/es | **machte** |
| wir | **haben gemacht** | wir | **machten** |
| ihr | **habt gemacht** | ihr | **machtet** |
| sie/Sie | **haben gemacht** | sie/Sie | **machten** |

| | **FUTURE** | | **CONDITIONAL** |
|---|---|---|---|
| ich | **werde machen** | ich | **würde machen** |
| du | **wirst machen** | du | **würdest machen** |
| er/sie/es | **wird machen** | er/sie/es | **würde machen** |
| wir | **werden machen** | wir | **würden machen** |
| ihr | **werdet machen** | ihr | **würdet machen** |
| sie/Sie | **werden machen** | sie/Sie | **würden machen** |

| **PAST PARTICIPLE** | **PRESENT PARTICIPLE** |
|---|---|
| **gemacht** | **machend** |

**IMPERATIVE**

**mach!/macht!/machen Sie!**

---

**EXAMPLE PHRASES**

Was **machst** du? What are you doing?
Ich **habe** die Betten **gemacht**. I made the beds.
Ich **werde** es morgen **machen**. I'll do it tomorrow.

# müssen (to have to)

### PRESENT

| | |
|---|---|
| ich | **muss** |
| du | **musst** |
| er/sie/es | **muss** |
| wir | **müssen** |
| ihr | **müsst** |
| sie/Sie | **müssen** |

### PRESENT SUBJUNCTIVE

| | |
|---|---|
| ich | **müsse** |
| du | **müssest** |
| er/sie/es | **müsse** |
| wir | **müssen** |
| ihr | **müsset** |
| sie/Sie | **müssen** |

### PERFECT

| | |
|---|---|
| ich | **habe gemusst/müssen** |
| du | **hast gemusst/müssen** |
| er/sie/es | **hat gemusst/müssen** |
| wir | **haben gemusst/müssen** |
| ihr | **habt gemusst/müssen** |
| sie/Sie | **haben gemusst/müssen** |

### IMPERFECT

| | |
|---|---|
| ich | **musste** |
| du | **musstest** |
| er/sie/es | **musste** |
| wir | **mussten** |
| ihr | **musstet** |
| sie/Sie | **mussten** |

### FUTURE

| | |
|---|---|
| ich | **werde müssen** |
| du | **wirst müssen** |
| er/sie/es | **wird müssen** |
| wir | **werden müssen** |
| ihr | **werdet müssen** |
| sie/Sie | **werden müssen** |

### CONDITIONAL

| | |
|---|---|
| ich | **würde müssen** |
| du | **würdest müssen** |
| er/sie/es | **würde müssen** |
| wir | **würden müssen** |
| ihr | **würdet müssen** |
| sie/Sie | **würden müssen** |

### PAST PARTICIPLE

**gemusst/müssen***

### PRESENT PARTICIPLE

**müssend**

*This form is used when combined with another infinitive.

### EXAMPLE PHRASES

Ich **muss** auf die Toilette. I must go to the loo.
Wir **müssen** jeden Abend unsere Hausaufgaben machen. We have to do our homework every night.
Sie **hat** abwaschen **müssen**. She had to wash up.

**ich** = I **du** = you **er** = he/it **sie** = she/it **es** = it/he/she **wir** = we **ihr** = you **sie** = they **Sie** = you

# sein (to be)

| | PRESENT | | PRESENT SUBJUNCTIVE |
|---|---|---|---|
| ich | **bin** | ich | **sei** |
| du | **bist** | du | **sei(e)st** |
| er/sie/es | **ist** | er/sie/es | **sei** |
| wir | **sind** | wir | **seien** |
| ihr | **seid** | ihr | **seiet** |
| sie/Sie | **sind** | sie/Sie | **seien** |

| | PERFECT | | IMPERFECT |
|---|---|---|---|
| ich | **bin gewesen** | ich | **war** |
| du | **bist gewesen** | du | **warst** |
| er/sie/es | **ist gewesen** | er/sie/es | **war** |
| wir | **sind gewesen** | wir | **waren** |
| ihr | **seid gewesen** | ihr | **wart** |
| sie/Sie | **sind gewesen** | sie/Sie | **waren** |

| | FUTURE | | CONDITIONAL |
|---|---|---|---|
| ich | **werde sein** | ich | **würde sein** |
| du | **wirst sein** | du | **würdest sein** |
| er/sie/es | **wird sein** | er/sie/es | **würde sein** |
| wir | **werden sein** | wir | **würden sein** |
| ihr | **werdet sein** | ihr | **würdet sein** |
| sie/Sie | **werden sein** | sie/Sie | **würden sein** |

| PAST PARTICIPLE | PRESENT PARTICIPLE |
|---|---|
| **gewesen** | **seiend** |

**IMPERATIVE**

**sei!/seien wir!/seid!/seien Sie!**

---

**EXAMPLE PHRASES**

Er **ist** zehn Jahre alt. He is ten years old.
Wir **waren** gestern im Theater. We were at the theatre yesterday.
Mir **war** kalt. I was cold.

= I **du** = you **er** = he/it **sie** = she/it **es** = it/he/she **wir** = we **ihr** = you **sie** = they **Sie** = you

# werden (to become)

| | **PRESENT** | | **PRESENT SUBJUNCTIVE** |
|---|---|---|---|
| ich | werde | ich | werde |
| du | wirst | du | werdest |
| er/sie/es | wird | er/sie/es | werde |
| wir | werden | wir | werden |
| ihr | werdet | ihr | werdet |
| sie/Sie | werden | sie/Sie | werden |

| | **PERFECT** | | **IMPERFECT** |
|---|---|---|---|
| ich | bin geworden | ich | wurde |
| du | bist geworden | du | wurdest |
| er/sie/es | ist geworden | er/sie/es | wurde |
| wir | sind geworden | wir | wurden |
| ihr | seid geworden | ihr | wurdet |
| sie/Sie | sind geworden | sie/Sie | wurden |

| | **FUTURE** | | **CONDITIONAL** |
|---|---|---|---|
| ich | werde werden | ich | würde werden |
| du | wirst werden | du | würdest werden |
| er/sie/es | wird werden | er/sie/es | würde werden |
| wir | werden werden | wir | würden werden |
| ihr | werdet werden | ihr | würdet werden |
| sie/Sie | werden werden | sie/Sie | würden werden |

**PAST PARTICIPLE**

geworden

**PRESENT PARTICIPLE**

werdend

**IMPERATIVE**

werde!/werden wir!/werdet!/werden Sie!

---

**EXAMPLE PHRASES**

Mir **wird** schlecht. I feel ill.
Ich will Lehrerin **werden**. I want to be a teacher.
Der Kuchen **ist** gut **geworden**. The cake turned out well.

---

**ich** = I **du** = you **er** = he/it **sie** = she/it **es** = it/he/she **wir** = we **ihr** = you **sie** = they **Sie** = \

# wissen (to know)

| | PRESENT | | PRESENT SUBJUNCTIVE |
|---|---|---|---|
| ich | **weiß** | ich | **wisse** |
| du | **weißt** | du | **wissest** |
| er/sie/es | **weiß** | er/sie/es | **wisse** |
| wir | **wissen** | wir | **wissen** |
| ihr | **wisst** | ihr | **wisset** |
| sie/Sie | **wissen** | sie/Sie | **wissen** |

| | PERFECT | | IMPERFECT |
|---|---|---|---|
| ich | **habe gewusst** | ich | **wusste** |
| du | **hast gewusst** | du | **wusstest** |
| er/sie/es | **hat gewusst** | er/sie/es | **wusste** |
| wir | **haben gewusst** | wir | **wussten** |
| ihr | **habt gewusst** | ihr | **wusstet** |
| sie/Sie | **haben gewusst** | sie/Sie | **wussten** |

| | FUTURE | | CONDITIONAL |
|---|---|---|---|
| ich | **werde wissen** | ich | **würde wissen** |
| du | **wirst wissen** | du | **würdest wissen** |
| er/sie/es | **wird wissen** | er/sie/es | **würde wissen** |
| wir | **werden wissen** | wir | **würden wissen** |
| ihr | **werdet wissen** | ihr | **würdet wissen** |
| sie/Sie | **werden wissen** | sie/Sie | **würden wissen** |

| PAST PARTICIPLE | PRESENT PARTICIPLE |
|---|---|
| **gewusst** | **wissend** |

**IMPERATIVE**

**wisse!/wissen wir!/wisset!/wissen Sie!**

---

**EXAMPLE PHRASES**

Ich **weiß** nicht. I don't know.
Er **hat** nichts davon **gewusst**. He didn't know anything about it.
e **wussten**, wo das Kino war. They knew where the cinema was.

= you **er** = he/it **sie** = she/it **es** = it/he/she **wir** = we **ihr** = you **sie** = they **Sie** = you